TODAY'S POETS

American and British Poetry Since the 1930's

TODAY'S POETS ❦

AMERICAN AND BRITISH POETRY SINCE THE 1930'S ❦ ❦ ❦ EDITED WITH AN INTRODUCTION BY *CHAD WALSH*

BELOIT COLLEGE

CHARLES SCRIBNER'S SONS
NEW YORK

ACKNOWLEDGMENTS

THE BELOIT POETRY JOURNAL. Gil Orlovitz, "The Rooster."

CARL BODE. "Sonnet: The Window," "Variation on a Theme by Dylan Thomas," "The Planet," "Nocturne."

JONATHAN CAPE LIMITED. Six poems from Derek Walcott, *In a Green Night: Poems 1948–1960*, 1962.

CHATTO & WINDUS LTD. Twelve poems from Richard Eberhart, *Collected Poems 1930–1960*, 1960. Sixteen poems from William Empson, *Collected Poems*, 1955.

UNIVERSITY OF CHICAGO PRESS. "On the Move," "The Silver Age," "The Inherited Estate," "The Corridor," reprinted from *A Sense of Movement* by Thom Gunn by permission of The University of Chicago Press. Copyright, 1957, by the University of Chicago Press. "Innocence," "Flying Above California," "My Sad Captains," reprinted from *My Sad Captains* by Thom Gunn by permission of the University of Chicago Press. Copyright, 1961, by the University of Chicago Press.

CUMMINGTON PRESS. "In Defense of Felons," "Carmina," "Street Scene," from Robert Mezey, *The Lovemaker*, 1961.

J. M. DENT & SONS LTD. Poems from Dylan Thomas, *Collected Poems*.

UNIVERSITY OF DETROIT PRESS. "Hospice of the Word," "A Canticle to the Christ in the Holy Eucharist," from Brother Antoninus, *The Crooked Lines of God*, 1959.

ANDRE DEUTSCH LIMITED. Poems from Roy Fuller, *Collected Poems 1936–1961*. Following poems by Laurie Lee: "Bombay Arrival," "The Edge of Day," "Sunken Evening," "Home from Abroad," "Town Owl," "Scot in the Desert," "Long Summer."

DOUBLEDAY & COMPANY, INC. "A Siege of Silence" copyright © 1958 by Brother Antoninus. From *The Hazards of Holiness* by Brother Antoninus. Reprinted by permission of Doubleday & Company, Inc. "What Birds Were There," copyright © 1962 by Brother Antoninus. From *The Hazards of Holiness* by Brother Antoninus. Reprinted by permission of Doubleday & Company, Inc. "In All These Acts," copyright © 1962 by Brother Antoninus. From *The Hazards of Holiness* by Brother Antoninus. Reprinted by permission of Doubleday & Company, Inc. "The Long War," "First Love," "Fields of Autumn," from *The Sun My Monument* by Laurie Lee. Copyright, 1944 by Laurie Lee. Reprinted by permission of Doubleday & Company, Inc. "The Cycle" by Theodore Roethke, copyright, 1941 by The Virginia Quarterly Review, The University of Virginia.

From *Words for the Wind* by Theodore Roethke. Reprinted by permission of Doubleday & Company, Inc. "A Field of Light," copyright 1948 by Tiger's Eye, "Praise to the End!" copyright 1950 by Theodore Roethke, "The Waking" copyright 1953 by Theodore Roethke, "I Knew a Woman" copyright 1954 by Theodore Roethke, all from the book, *Words for the Wind* by Theodore Roethke. Reprinted by permission of Doubleday & Company, Inc.

E. P. DUTTON & CO., INC. "Feast of Saint Andrew the Apostle," "Eastertide," "The City Considered as a Tulip Tree," "Who Calls the English Cold?" "Covent Garden Market," "Personal Letter to the Ephesians," "The Bad Children," "Requiem," "The Burial of Terror," "Head Next to Mine," from the book *The Man Behind You* by Carl Bode. Copyright, ©, 1959, by Carl Bode. Reprinted by permission of E. P. Dutton & Co., Inc. "The Lost Cities," "Alexandria," "Conon in Exile," "On First Looking into Loeb's Horace," "The Critics," "Song for Zarathustra," from the book *Collected Poems* by Lawrence Durrell. Copyright, ©, 1956, 1960 by Lawrence Durrell. Reprinted by permission of E. P. Dutton & Co., Inc.

RICHARD EBERHART. "The Spider," "Hark Back," "To Laughter, to Leering," "Am I My Neighbor's Keeper?"

FABER AND FABER LTD. George Barker, poems from *Collected Poems*. George Barker, "A Little Song in Assisi," from *The View from a Blind I*. Thom Gunn, "The Beach Head," from *Fighting Terms*; poems from *My Sad Captains*; poems from *The Sense of Movement*. Ted Hughes, poems from *Lupercal*.

FARRAR, STRAUS & COMPANY, INC. "Inauguration Day: January 1953," "Grandparents," "Memories of West Street and Lepke," reprinted from *Life Studies* by Robert Lowell, by permission of Farrar, Straus & Company, Inc. Copyright © 1956, 1959 by Robert Lowell.

THOM GUNN. "The Goddess."

HARCOURT, BRACE & WORLD, INC. Sixteen poems from *Collected Poems of William Empson*, copyright, 1949, by William Empson. Reprinted by permission of Harcourt, Brace & World, Inc. "The Holy Innocents," "Christmas in Black Rock," "The Quaker Graveyard in Nantucket," "Winter in Dunbarton," "Salem," "Children of Light," "Mr. Edwards and the Spider," "The Dead in Europe," from *Lord Weary's Castle*, copyright, 1944, 1946, by Robert Lowell. Reprinted by permission of Harcourt, Brace & World, Inc. "Falling Asleep Over the Aeneid," copyright, 1948, by Robert Lowell. Reprinted from his volume *The Mills of the Kavanaughs* by permission of Harcourt, Brace & World, Inc. "The Picador Bit," © 1962 by Bink Noll, "All My Pretty Ones? Did You Say All?" © 1960 by Bink Noll, "Air Tunnel, Monticello," © 1961 by Bink Noll, "Lunch on Omaha Beach," © 1962 by Bink Noll, "For Jane Kane, Whom We Knew in Our Young Marriages," © 1962 by Bink Noll, "Abraham's Madness," © 1960 by Bink Noll, "Afternoon for a Small Boy," © 1960 by Bink Noll, "The Rented Garden," © 1958 by Bink Noll, "Song in a Winter Night," © 1958 by Bink Noll, all reprinted from his volume *The Center of the Circle* by permission of Harcourt, Brace & World, Inc. "The Pardon," "Still, Citizen Sparrow," copyright, 1950, by Richard Wilbur. Reprinted from his volume *Ceremony and Other Poems* by permission of Harcourt, Brace & World, Inc. "Love Calls Us to the Things of this World," "A Voice from Under the Table," "Beasts," "A Baroque Wall-

ACKNOWLEDGMENTS

Fountain in the Villa Sciarra," from *Things of This World* © 1956, by Richard Wilbur. Reprinted by permission of Harcourt, Brace & World, Inc. "Advice to a Prophet," © 1959 by Richard Wilbur. Reprinted from his volume *Advice to a Prophet and Other Poems* by permission of Harcourt, Brace & World, Inc. First published in *The New Yorker*. "She," © 1958 by Richard Wilbur. Reprinted from his volume *Advice to a Prophet and Other Poems* by permission of Harcourt, Brace & World, Inc. "In the Smoking-Car," © 1960 by Richard Wilbur. Reprinted from his volume *Advice to a Prophet and Other Poems* by permission of Harcourt, Brace & World, Inc.

HARPER & ROW. "The Hawk in the Rain," "Secretary," "The Jaguar," "Childbirth," "Law in the Country of the Cats," from *The Hawk in the Rain* by Ted Hughes. Copyright © 1957 by Ted Hughes. Reprinted with the permission of Harper & Row, Publishers, Incorporated. "Mayday on Holderness," "Dick Straightup," "Lupercalia," from *Lupercal* by Ted Hughes. Copyright © 1960 by Ted Hughes. Reprinted with the permission of Harper & Row, Publishers, Incorporated.

RUPERT HART-DAVIS LIMITED. Poems by R. S. Thomas, from *Song at the Year's Turning: Poems 1942–1954*, 1955; *Poetry for Supper*, 1958; *Tares*, 1961.

WILLIAM HEINEMANN LTD. Ten poems from *The Man Behind You* by Carl Bode. Reprinted by permission of the publisher.

HOUGHTON MIFFLIN COMPANY. Poems by Anne Sexton, from *To Bedlam and Part Way Back*, 1960; *All My Pretty Ones*, 1962.

TED HUGHES. "Dark Women," "New Moon in January," "Encounter," "Wodwo."

INFERNO PRESS EDITIONS. Four poems from Gil Orlovitz, *Selected Poems*, 1960.

ALFRED A. KNOPF, INC. Poems from *Heart's Needle* by W. D. Snodgrass, by permission of Alfred A. Knopf, Inc. "Orpheus," copyright, 1956 by W. D. Snodgrass; "The Marsh," copyright, 1957 by W. D. Snodgrass; "September in the Park," copyright, 1959 by W. D. Snodgrass; "The Operation," copyright, 1959 by W. D. Snodgrass; "Home Town," copyright, 1959 by W. D. Snodgrass; "The Campus on the Hill," copyright, 1958 by W. D. Snodgrass; "These Trees Stand . . . ," copyright, 1956 by W. D. Snodgrass.

PHILIP LARKIN. [One man walking a deserted platform] and [Heaviest of flowers, the head] from *The North Ship*, 1945.

MICHAEL LEBECK. Gil Orlovitz, numbers XXXIII, XXIX, IX, from *Art of the Sonnet*.

DENISE LEVERTOV. "The Gypsy's Window," "Laying the Dust," from *Here and Now*.

MACMILLAN & CO., LTD. (London). "This Above All is Precious and Remarkable," "Anniversary," "Apology for Understatement," "Brooklyn Heights," "A Song about Major Eatherly," from John Wain, *Weep Before God*, 1961.

THE MACMILLAN COMPANY (New York). Quotation from *The Autobiography of William Butler Yeats*, 1953, pp. 101–2.

THE MARVELL PRESS. "Wires," "Going," "Reasons for Attendance," "Wedding-Wind," "Maiden Name," "Poetry of Departures," "If, My Darling," "Lines on a Young Lady's Photograph Album," and "Church Going" are reprinted from

ACKNOWLEDGMENTS

The Less Deceived by permission of The Marvell Press, Hessle, Yorkshire, England.

ROBERT MEZEY. "You Could Say," "After Hours," "No Country You Remember."

WILLIAM MORROW & COMPANY, INC. "Bombay Arrival," "The Edge of Day," "Sunken Evening," "Home from Abroad," "Town Owl," "Scot in the Desert," "Long Summer," from *My Many-Coated Man* by Laurie Lee, copyright 1961, by permission of William Morrow and Company, Inc.

HOWARD NEMEROV. "Brainstorm," "Runes," from *New & Selected Poems.* "A Spell before Winter," "Human Things," "De Anima," "The Dial Tones," from *The Next Room of the Dream.*

NEW DIRECTIONS. "August," "The Stranger," from William Everson, *The Residual Years.* Copyright 1948 by New Directions. Reprinted by permission of New Directions, Publishers. Numbers 2, 8, 15, 28, and "Dog" from Lawrence Ferlinghetti, *A Coney Island of the Mind,* copyright 1955, © 1958 by Lawrence Ferlinghetti. "The Great Chinese Dragon," from *Starting from San Francisco,* copyright © 1958, 1961 by Lawrence Ferlinghetti. Reprinted by permission of New Directions, Publishers. "With Eyes at the Back of Our Heads," "The Quarry Pool," "To the Snake," from Denise Levertov, *With Eyes at the Back of Our Heads,* © 1958, 1959 by Denise Levertov Goodman. "A Map of the Western Part of the County of Essex in England," "Resting Figure," "The Jacob's Ladder," "Matins," "Merritt Parkway," "Illustrious Ancestors," from Denise Levertov, *The Jacob's Ladder,* © 1958, 1961 by Denise Levertov Goodman. Reprinted by permission of New Directions, Publishers. Following poems by Kenneth Patchen: "Do I Not Deal with Angels?" and "The New Being," from *The Teeth of the Lion,* copyright 1942 by Kenneth Patchen; "O When I Take My Love Out Walking," from *Red Wine & Yellow Hair,* copyright 1949 by Kenneth Patchen; "In a Crumbling Majesty," "The Great Sled-Makers," from *The Famous Boating Party,* copyright 1954 by Kenneth Patchen; "O She Is as Lovely-Often," "O Now the Drenched Land Wakes," from *When We Were Here Together,* copyright 1957 by Kenneth Patchen; "Because He Liked to be at Home," "Because My Hands Hear the Flowers Thinking," from *Because It Is,* copyright 1960 by New Directions. All reprinted by permission of New Directions, Publishers. The poems by Dylan Thomas, from *The Collected Poems of Dylan Thomas,* Copyright 1939, 1942, 1946, © 1957 by New Directions. Reprinted by permission of New Directions, Publishers.

THE NEW YORKER. Theodore Roethke, "In a Dark Time," © 1960 The New Yorker Magazine, Inc. James Dickey, "The Dusk of Horses," © 1962 The New Yorker Magazine, Inc.; "The Poisoned Man," © 1962 The New Yorker Magazine, Inc.; "The Scarred Girl," © 1963 The New Yorker Magazine, Inc.

THE OBSERVER. Thom Gunn, "The Goddess."

GIL ORLOVITZ. His poems included in this anthology.

OXFORD UNIVERSITY PRESS, INC. "The Ground Hog," " 'Now is the Air Made of Chiming Balls'," "The Soul Longs to Return Whence It Came," " 'If I Could Only Live at the Pitch That is Near Madness'," "The Fury of Aerial Bombardment," "The Horse Chestnut Tree," "The Tobacconist of Eighth Street,"

viii

ACKNOWLEDGMENTS

"The Cancer Cells," "Cousin Florence," "Off Spectacle Island," "Attitudes," "A Ship Burning and a Comet All in One Day," from *Collected Poems, 1930–1960* by Richard Eberhart. © Richard Eberhart 1960. Reprinted by permission of Oxford University Press, Inc. "The Spider," "Hark Back," "Am I My Neighbor's Keeper?" from *The Quarry* by Richard Eberhart. © Richard Eberhart 1964. Reprinted by permission of Oxford University Press, Inc. Four lines from "Hurrahing in Harvest," taken from *Poems of Gerard Manley Hopkins*, 3rd ed., 1948, p. 74.

THE PARTISAN REVIEW. Theodore Roethke, "Otto."

KENNETH PATCHEN. Various poems.

PUTNAM & CO. LTD. (London). Poems from Howard Sergeant, *The Headlands*, 1953.

RANDOM HOUSE, INC. "Elegy for a Dead Soldier" (*V-Letter and Other Poems*), Karl Shapiro. Copyright 1944 by Karl Shapiro. Reprinted from *Poems 1940–1953*, by Karl Shapiro, by permission of Random House, Inc. "Love for a Hand" (*Poems 1940–1953*), Karl Shapiro. Copyright 1952 by Karl Shapiro. Reprinted from *Poems 1940–1953*, by Karl Shapiro, by permission of Random House, Inc. Originally appeared in *The New Yorker*. "Poet" (*Person, Place and Thing*), Karl Shapiro. Copyright 1942 by Karl Jay Shapiro. Reprinted from *Poems 1940–1953*, by Karl Shapiro, by permission of Random House, Inc. "The Potomac" (*Poems 1940–1953*), Karl Shapiro. Copyright 1941 by Karl Shapiro. Reprinted from *Poems 1940–1953*, by Karl Shapiro, by permission of Random House, Inc. Part II, "The Recognition of Eve," from "Adam and Eve" (*Poems 1940–1953*), Karl Shapiro. From "Adam and Eve," Copyright 1951 by Karl Shapiro. Reprinted from *Poems 1940–1953*, by Karl Shapiro, by permission of Random House, Inc. "Jew" (*V-Letter and Other Poems*), Karl Shapiro. Copyright 1943 by Karl Shapiro. Reprinted from *Poems of a Jew*, by Karl Shapiro, by permission of Random House, Inc. "August Saturday Night on the Negro Street" (*The Bourgeois Poet*), Karl Shapiro. © Copyright 1962 by Karl Shapiro. Reprinted from *The Bourgeois Poet*, by Karl Shapiro, by permission of Random House, Inc.

THEODORE ROETHKE. "The Far Field," "Light Listened," "Otto," "In a Dark Time."

ROUTLEDGE & KEGAN PAUL, LTD. "Reason for Not Writing Orthodox Nature Poetry," from John Wain, *A Word Carved on a Sill*, 1956.

RUTGERS UNIVERSITY PRESS. Various poems by John Ciardi. Copyright 1950, 1951, 1952, 1953, 1954, 1955, 1956, 1957, 1958, 1959, 1960, 1961, 1962. Reprinted by permission of the author and of the Trustees of Rutgers, the State University of New Jersey.

ST MARTIN'S PRESS, INCORPORATED. John Wain, "Reasons for Not Writing Orthodox Nature Poetry," from *A Word Carved on a Sill*, Macmillan & Company Ltd., and St Martin's Press, Inc. John Wain, "This Above All is Precious and Remarkable," "Anniversary," "Apology for Understatement," "Brooklyn Heights," "A Song About Major Eatherly," from *Weep Before God*, Macmillan & Company Ltd., and St Martin's Press, Inc.

SATURDAY REVIEW. Richard Eberhart, "Am I My Neighbor's Keeper?"

SCIAMACHY. Gil Orlovitz, "Homage to Charles Laughton."

CHARLES SCRIBNER'S SONS. Poems by Robert Creeley. Reprinted with the permission of Charles Scribner's Sons from *For Love* by Robert Creeley. Copyright © 1962 Robert Creeley.

THE SEWANEE REVIEW. Theodore Roethke, "The Far Field." First published in *The Sewanee Review*, Autumn 1962. Copyright © by The University of the South.

TRACE 45. Gil Orlovitz, "Masterindex 23."

JOHN WAIN. "Sestina to Khasan Israelov."

A. P. WATT & SON. Quotation from *The Autobiography of William Butler Yeats*. With the kind permission also of Mrs. Yeats and The Macmillan Co. of Canada.

WESLEYAN UNIVERSITY PRESS. "The Heaven of Animals," copyright © 1961 by James Dickey, "In the Tree House at Night," copyright © 1961 by James Dickey, "In the Lupanar at Pompeii," copyright © 1961, all reprinted from *Drowning with Others* by permission of Wesleyan University Press. "The Dusk of Horses," copyright © by James Dickey, "The Scarred Girl," copyright © 1963 by James Dickey, "The Poisoned Man," copyright © by James Dickey, all reprinted from *Helmets* by permission of Wesleyan University Press. "The New Icarus," "Adam's Footprint," "Bout with Burning," "Fantasy on the Resurrection," "The Final Hunger," "No Return," all copyright © 1956 by Vassar Miller, reprinted from *Wage War on Silence* by permission of Wesleyan University Press. "Ballad of the Unmiraculous Miracle," "Song for a Marriage," "The Whooping Crane," "In Consolation," "Return," "For Instruction," all copyright © 1960 by Vassar Miller, reprinted from *Wage War on Silence* by permission of Wesleyan University Press. "Love's Eschatology," "Protest," "From an Old Maid," all copyright © 1963 by Vassar Miller, reprinted from *My Bones Being Wiser* by permission of Wesleyan University Press.

MRS. W. B. YEATS and THE MACMILLAN CO. OF CANADA for the quotation from W. B. Yeats, *Autobiographies*, on page 14.

THE YORKSHIRE POST. Richard Eberhart, "To Laughter, to Leering."

CONTENTS

EDITOR'S PREFACE

Toward a Redefinition of "MODERN POETRY"

Fifty years ago it made sense to begin anthologies of "modern poetry" with Walt Whitman (1819–92), Emily Dickinson (1830–86), Gerard Manley Hopkins (1844–89), or Thomas Hardy (1840–1928). What made sense then has become a senseless tradition. Half a century of new poetry has now been written. Anthologies grow bigger and bigger until they resemble two-volume encyclopedias. Even so, the real Moderns get short shrift. The most recent anthologies of "modern poetry" typically devote less than a fourth of their space to poets born in this century. The result: major contemporary poets represented by a few pages, many important poets omitted altogether.

One might defend the traditional starting points by saying that Whitman, Dickinson, Hardy, and Hopkins are pioneers who prepared the way for the poets now writing. Granted. But the same is true of John Donne (1572–1631). Contemporary poetry is what it is because of all of the major and some of the minor poets that have preceded it. The influence of Donne is alive; so is that of Shakespeare, Chaucer, and the anonymous author of *Beowulf*.

The only practical expedient is to fix arbitrarily on a date, and let it be the dividing line between "modern poetry" and what has gone before. In the process, a new set of labels will be needed. From Walt Whitman to, say, W. H. Auden, one might speak of the Early Moderns, the Turn-of-the-Century Poets, or the *Transitional* Poets. That period has a certain integrity. During it occurred most of the poetic mutations that still largely shape the poetry of today. The great technical experiments were made; the shifts in poetic sensibility took place. Though some of the major figures of the Transitional Period are alive and very much alive, they already securely belong to literary history, and have earned their place in the general anthologies of English-language verse "from Beowulf to W. H. Auden." The term *modern poetry* can now be conveniently limited to the still newer generation of poets. It would be schematically pleasing to define this group as poets born in the present century. The practical disadvantage is that this would include W. H. Auden himself and a number of poets from the first decade of the century who are already abundantly represented in the usual anthologies of "modern poetry." For this practical reason, I have chosen 1910 as my beginning point, except that I have included three poets from the first decade simply because the anthologists have rarely accorded their work the attention it merits.

Today's Poets is therefore a collection of poets, British and American, who have come to the fore in the last three or four decades. Thirty-three are represented in all. Each has sufficient space so that some balanced idea can be formed of his scope and achievements.

The primary criterion has been quality. It would be absurd to assert, "These are the thirty-three best modern poets," but I would simply maintain that all of them are excellent, and some more than merely excellent.

The second criterion has been variety. The whole spectrum, from Beats to Academics, is on display here. Many of the poets blessedly refuse to fit into any critical pigeonhole. Nor are all of them well-known figures. I am happy to include certain poets who are among the most interesting, but who too rarely or never have been anthologized: Carl Bode, Bink Noll, Gil Orlovitz, Howard Sergeant, R. S. Thomas, Derek Walcott, to name a few.

I hope the general reader will experience some of the excitement that gripped me as I worked on this anthology. Here are the real voices of our times, the poets who can uniquely speak to our present condition, in all their untamable variety—speaking sometimes in low cultivated voices, sometimes raising their voices to a shrill shout, but never dull.

Today's Poets should be of particular use in universities and colleges. It is the first anthology that brings within one set of covers an adequate representation of the "real Moderns," British and American, conservative and experimental alike. It provides sufficient material for a course in contemporary poetry, or can serve to supplement the traditional anthologies in those courses that begin with Whitman and come down to the present.

The section, "Notes on the Poets," gives basic biographical and bibliographical information. It is followed by an alphabetical "Index of Authors, Titles, and First Lines" for quick reference. Untitled poems are given under the first line, enclosed in square brackets.

I owe thanks to many more persons than I can mention by name. First of all, my gratitude to many of the poets themselves who not only cooperated by giving permission but frequently suggested particular poems for inclusion, or provided me with previously unpublished poems. My thanks also to a great number of scholars, editors, poets, and critics in Great Britain and the United States who counseled with me and sometimes called my attention to poets whose work I might otherwise have overlooked. A special word of thanks is due to Wilbur S. Scott, Philip Durham, Carl Bode, Howard Sergeant, and George MacBeth, who read the Introduction in rough draft and made invaluable suggestions; they are not to be held responsible for anything I say, but the Introduction is the better for their painstaking criticism. My work on the British poets was greatly facilitated by The Poetry Society which gave me free run of its London library. Last but not least: my thanks to my daughters, Sarah-Lindsay, Alison, and Damaris McGuire, who typed long and faithfully to help me, and my thanks to my friends at Charles Scribner's Sons, whose patience and enthusiasm were unfailing during the whole time I was working on *Today's Poets.*

I must record two disappointments. I had hoped to include the poetry of Robert Duncan. For reasons which I respect—but regret— he declined to give me permission. I also wished to represent Robert Lowell with special fullness, but the American publisher of *Life Studies* imposes a strict limitation on the amount of poetry from that book that can be included in an anthology. For this reason, I have not been able to represent Mr. Lowell's later work as completely as I wished.

Beloit College   C.W.
October, 1964

INTRODUCTION

A Sampling of Moderns

It is intriguing to imagine what the most respected Victorian poets would make of the poetry written in Britain and America during the past thirty years. One suspects that if, by some time-warp or other device of science fiction, Tennyson and Longfellow could wander unobserved through the modern poetry collection in the Harvard Lamont library, or turn through the pages of this present anthology, their initial reaction would be a mixture of recognition, surprise, bewilderment, indignation, and excitement. Here are the opening lines from six poems of our times.[1]

> Trying to chop mother down is like
> hunting deer inside Russia
> with phalangists for hat-pins.
>
> FROM "She Went to Stay," by Robert Creeley

> My wife asleep, her soft face turned from me,
> My children sleeping in their rooms as well,
> I get up, drawn to the window, to see what I must see:
> Silver, and black and silver. There is almost a silver smell.
>
> FROM "Sonnet: The Window," by Carl Bode

[1] For the poems in their entirety, see Index of Authors and Titles.

1

the rooster crows in my belly
an old hangout for the billiard cues of the morning
and table-hopping hail hail the ganglias all here
after sunset like a mouthwash last yesterlight
and the white tails of the gorillas on television
and that liberal politician stumping for twilight supremacy
down by that old
           shill
           stream
As I buttonholed the Ancient Auctioneer
how goes America going
             going
              FROM "The Rooster," by Gil Orlovitz

From what I am, to be what I am not,
To be what once I was, from plan and plot
To learn to take no thought,
I go, my God, to Thee.
              FROM "Return," by Vassar Miller

A spider in the bath. The image noted:
Significant maybe but surely cryptic.
A creature motionless and rather bloated,
The barriers shining, vertical and white:
Passing concern, and pity mixed with spite.
              FROM "The Image," by Roy Fuller

Farmer, you were young once.
And she was there, waiting, the unique flower
That only you could find in the wild moor
Of your experience.
Gathered, she grew to the warm woman
Your hands had imagined
Fondling soil in the spring fields.
              FROM "Age," by R. S. Thomas

FAMILIAR AND STRANGE

There is much in the six poems that would seem perfectly familiar and natural to Tennyson and Longfellow. They would note that poets still write about religious experience and love of a woman. Some of the poetry would also seem ordinary enough in its technical aspects. The Victorians wrote sonnets, and so does Carl Bode. Iambic meter, the rhythm-of-all-work, serves Vassar Miller and Roy Fuller as faithfully as it served Tennyson or Longfellow.

Not everything is strange. But much is. A typical Victorian poet would sense that he was plunged into a poetic world where the familiar and the odd, even the distasteful, were all mixed together. How would he take a phrase like Creeley's "Trying to chop mother down"? Gil Orlovitz' "The Rooster" would baffle him—what exactly is the poet *trying to say* and why is he doing such queer things with language? Then Roy Fuller uses as his symbol a creature that the Victorians rarely associated with poetry, a spider.

In short, modern poetry has enough continuity with Victorian poetry so that Longfellow and Tennyson would find themselves partially at home. At the same time, they would feel that they had stepped into a universe created by Kafka, where some things are familiar and others are bizarre, and even the familiar things, on closer examination, turn out to have an odd twist.

Continuity and change: these are the two key concepts to be kept in mind when reading the poetry of our times and comparing it with that of earlier centuries.

THE LINEAGE OF REVOLUTION

No period has a monopoly of poetic innovations. When old English alliterative and accentual verse yielded to rhymed and metrical stanzas, it was a revolution. The introduction of blank verse in the sixteenth century was another revolution. The seventeenth century saw John Donne and the other Metaphysicals writing a poetry in which the sacred and the profane, the lovely and the grotesque, were combined into a violent dislocation of what the Elizabethans had called poetry. With the coming of Romanticism, Keats and Wordsworth were berated by the reviewers as though their names were Pound and Eliot; they were accused of wilful obscurity, lines that did not scan, and substituting sound for sense.

The history of poetry is one revolution after another, but every revolution leaves much unchanged. As will become clear later on, the

3

subject matter—and indeed the technique—of modern poetry is not as radically different from that of a hundred years ago as many of the friends, and enemies, of contemporary verse would contend.

If poetry, while maintaining its continuity in a long and living tradition, is always in process of mutating into new forms and new sensibilities, the late nineteenth and early twentieth centuries cannot claim to be unique. All the period can reasonably assert, with substantial evidence, is that the mutations have been unusually frequent and violent, so that Longfellow might have more trouble reading Gil Orlovitz than Alexander Pope would have had reading Longfellow.

LONGFELLOW AND ROBERT LOWELL

Everything one can say about "Modern Poetry" may be disproved by singling out this poem or that, but certain generalizations *can* be made, in a broad, almost statistical way. For example, it is extremely unlikely that any modern poet would write a poem like Longfellow's "The Jewish Cemetery at Newport," and it is equally unlikely that any Victorian (with the possible exception of Hopkins) would have written Robert Lowell's "The Quaker Graveyard in Nantucket." The first poem typifies what the Victorians meant by the word poetry; the second is highly representative of modern poetry at its best. The opening sections of the two poems are as follows:

THE JEWISH CEMETERY AT NEWPORT

How strange it seems! These Hebrews in their graves,
    Close by the street of this fair seaport town,
Silent beside the never-silent waves,
    At rest in all this moving up and down!

The trees are white with dust, that o'er their sleep
    Wave their broad curtains in the southwind's breath,
While underneath these leafy tents they keep
    The long, mysterious Exodus of Death.

And these sepulchral stones, so old and brown,
    That pave with level flags their burial-place,
Seem like the tablets of the Law, thrown down
    And broken by Moses at the mountain's base.

4

> The very names recorded here are strange,
>   Of foreign accent, and of different climes;
> Alvares and Rivera interchange
>   With Abraham and Jacob of old times.

THE QUAKER GRAVEYARD IN NANTUCKET

A brackish reach of shoal off Madaket,—
The sea was still breaking violently and night
Had steamed into our North Atlantic Fleet,
When the drowned sailor clutched the drag-net. Light
Flashed from his matted head and marble feet,
He grappled at the net
With the coiled, hurdling muscles of his thighs:
The corpse was bloodless, a botch of reds and whites,
Its open, staring eyes
Were lustreless dead-lights
Or cabin-windows on a stranded hulk
Heavy with sand. We weight the body, close
Its eyes and heave it seaward whence it came,
Where the heel-headed dogfish barks its nose
On Ahab's void and forehead; and the name
Is blocked in yellow chalk.
Sailors, who pitch this portent at the sea
Where dreadnaughts shall confess
Its hell-bent deity,
When you are powerless
To sand-bag this Atlantic bulwark, faced
By the earth-shaker, green, unwearied, chaste
In his steel scales: ask for no Orphean lute
To pluck life back. The guns of the steeled fleet
Recoil and then repeat
The hoarse salute.

Even on a first reading, some of the differences are obvious. One is the relatively superficial fact that Longfellow shows traces of a standardized "poetic diction" (*o'er, climes*), whereas Lowell's language is that of normal but intense prose. More importantly, Longfellow tells the reader from the beginning how he should respond: "How strange it seems!" Lowell gradually evokes the reader's response

5

by indirect means as the poem goes along. Longfellow's poem is very regular in its form—lines of iambic pentameter, rhyming *abab*. Lowell's rhythm is basically iambic pentameter, but filled with deliberate irregularities and rough combinations of syllables. The line length varies, perhaps according to some pattern, but if so the pattern is not transparent. Longfellow uses straight rhyme. Lowell employs a series of modulations between pure rhyme and various sorts of half rhyme (*Madaket, night, Fleet, lute,* etc., which have in common the same terminal consonant, *t*).

"The Jewish Cemetery at Newport" pictures the fact of death in broad, general, gentle strokes. "The Quaker Graveyard" has the realism of a medical student's first experience in anatomy laboratory ("a botch of reds and whites, / Its open, staring eyes"). The figurative language of Longfellow's poem is readily grasped and seems merely an extra ornament rather than an essential part of the poem. For instance, "Exodus of Death" is a striking phrase and might have been expanded so as to create the structure of the entire poem, but Longfellow simply uses it for its momentary beauty and then drops it. The allusion to *Moby Dick* in Lowell's phrase, "Ahab's void and forehead," is not an incidental adornment; it is further developed as the poem progresses and is a structural part of the whole work.

Longfellow's poem is much more relaxed; he is in no hurry, and has no compulsion to make every word work hard. A line can say very little but say it pleasantly—"At rest in all this moving up and down!" where the words after "rest" add little to the thought or mental picture, since the previous line with its phrase "never-silent waves" has already implied the up and down motion. Lowell's poem is more compressed, having scarcely a word that could be bluepenciled without destroying some essential fact, idea, or image.

Finally, Longfellow pretty much says it straight. His poem is like an essay written in verse. It demands little effort on the reader's part. Lowell's poem is devious, and would be extremely difficult to convert into a prose paraphrase. The reader is not always sure what is literally true and what is figure of speech. Certain inversions of fact, such as "When the drowned sailor clutched the drag-net," are curiously powerful in the context of the poem, but how do they correspond to what was actually happening? The paradoxical result of this and the other differences is that Longfellow, who followed the familiar traditions of

6

poetry faithfully, has written a poem that is closer akin to prose than is the freewheeling but fiercely poetic poem by Lowell.

Lowell is far from being the most "modern" of the moderns in his way of writing. And Longfellow is not a straw man. He is a considerably better poet than most recent critics have granted, and "The Jewish Cemetery" is one of his best poems. The two are discussed here not to encourage that self-congratulation in which every literary period likes to indulge, but simply to set in contrast a good poem, typical of the nineteenth century, and a good poem, typical of the present.

Mutations

If Tennyson and Longfellow were the prototypal poets of a hundred years ago, as Yeats, Eliot, Pound, and Auden, were during the transitional period to modern poetry, and Lowell perhaps is today, the question arises: What has happened meanwhile?

The answer is simply that poetry has undergone a series of mutations, some of which produced brief-lived monsters, while others were so successful that they succeeded in the Darwinian struggle for poetic survival. It remains to look at a few of the poets in whom these mutations are evident. There is no space here to discuss any poet in detail. Many readers will know them already. The most that can be attempted is a brief listing of the particular ways in which certain poets broke ground for the future. This is useful background for looking at the poets in this anthology. They are what they are, in part at least, because of their predecessors.

POE AS PIONEER

A complete survey would have to begin with the anonymous poets of the Old English period and come up to the present. A more modest one would certainly take as its starting point Wordsworth, Coleridge, and others of their period—modern poetry is irradicably stamped with the spirit of Romantic individualism. But for present purposes, Edgar Allan Poe (1809–49) will serve for a beginning. The first American poet who was also a major literary critic, Poe's example in his verse and perhaps still more the impact of his critical theories make him a living influence still. He is, for one thing, a great-great-grandfather of the New Criticism and its more recent developments. In a time when poetry was commonly considered a pleasant ornament of life, or else the handmaiden of country, God, morals, and patriotism, he insisted that a poem is a thing in its own right, an esthetic construct. It is not designed to make men good or happy; it cannot be measured by external standards. This craftsman's eye view of poetry naturally involved an extreme and highly technical interest in technique itself. Along with this, in Poe's poetry as well as his criticism, was a strong psychological bent, the desire to present feelings and emotions in a chemically pure state.

Poe profoundly excited the French poet, Baudelaire, and through him the influence of Poe passed into the mainstream of French symbolism, to suffer various sea-changes there and be re-exported later to the English-speaking countries, via Eliot and Pound among others. Poe is thus, indirectly at least, one of the many reasons that "The Jewish Cemetery," excellent as it is, could scarcely be written by any poet living today.

THE MANY WHITMANS

Walt Whitman (1819–92) is the next revolutionary. It is important to distinguish between the various Whitmans. Subsequent poets have picked and chosen among the protean aspects of his poetry. Some have been mainly attracted by the strutting, he-man pretensions of Whitman's verse and the conscious pose of the poet himself, who along the way shortened his name from Walter to Walt, saw to it that he was pictured with open collar minus necktie, and wrote anonymous reviews of his own work in which he hinted at his devilish lustfulness. It is not hard to see the he-man Whitman alive in Sandburg's glorification of Chicago's tough hogbutchers, and in much of the masculine posturing of the Beats.

Whitman the two hundred per cent male—in his poetry if not in his real life—is the least significant Whitman. To any American poet he offered something more important: America itself as the subject matter of poetry. He took the day-by-day contemporary America and made poetry of it: cab drivers, prostitutes, swarms of immigrants in the great cities, the lonely farms, the pioneers in their wagons moving westward, still westward. America was to him not merely the new

8

world, but the new humanity—vital, democratic, advancing toward an ultimate brotherhood.

This sense of the living America is one of Whitman's major breakthroughs in poetic sensibility. His explorations of poetic subject matter have permanently affected American poetry, and to some extent poetry beyond these shores. To American poets, he offered the real America. To all poets he offered a subject matter in which plain people and ordinary experiences are as worthy of the poet's attention as the limited range of "poetic subjects" hitherto acceptable. Sandburg, Edgar Lee Masters, Vachel Lindsay, Hart Crane, William Carlos Williams, and Stephen Vincent Benét are only a few of the poets who carried on his discovery of America and the common man.

Whitman was a later and more radical Wordsworth in his expansion of subject matter; he was also a Wordsworth when he set out to free himself from a stylized "poetic diction," and raise the language of ordinary speech to the intensity of poetry. Like Wordsworth, he partially succeeded and partially failed. He floundered about amid colloquialisms and a linguistic hodgepodge of words grabbed wherever he could find them—"These from me, O Democracy, to serve you, ma femme!"—and he constantly slipped back into the hackneyed language of the poetasters—"Then dearest child, mournest thou only for Jupiter?", "O Threat! O throbbing heart!" At his best, however, he did for daily language what he did also for daily life, revealing the poetry in both. Most poets of the twentieth century have maintained, at least in theory, that a word is in itself neither poetic nor prosy, that the context in which it is placed determines whether it is poetic. It was Whitman's achievement to demonstrate at least in scattered parts of his poetry that this is so.

Whitman also set about to liberate himself from conventional scansion. He was a pioneer in free verse. This term was subsequently to be abused and cheapened by a great horde of poets, particularly around the time of World War I, who took the term to mean that anything goes: prose chopped up into lines of varying length becomes, by some alchemy of the printer, poetry. Whitman's free verse was not merely a negative thing, a declaration of independence against anapests and dactyls; rather, it was an effort to discover other rhythms—the cadence of breath groups, the natural rhythm that thought and feeling produce when they are purified and raised to the excitement of poetry. Each poem, when approached by the poet in this spirit, becomes a new problem (this is why good free verse is fantastically hard to write), demanding that the poet create *for it* the type of rhythm that would be organically related to the content and mood of the poem itself. It means tailored-to-measure rhythm, not ready-made rhythms hanging on the poetic rack ready for use.

The lasting legacy of Whitman's experiments in free verse is that the poet has a bigger tool kit. He may choose—many do choose—not to use the tools that Whitman proposed, but at least they are there. Just as Whitman expanded the scope of poetry, he expanded and diversified the devices that make for rhythm and the sense of poetic form.

One part of Whitman's legacy has only just begun to be recognized clearly. Many readers have been puzzled at Whitman's colossal egotism combined with his consuming passion for the masses and the grasses. The key seems to be that Whitman was, before everything else, a mystic. Perhaps a Taoist would understand his poetry better than a Thomist would. In his creedless perception of whatever is ultimate, Whitman was constantly reworking some primal and intensely personal experience—the direct awareness of the unity of all things. Thus the egoistic "I" is no longer mere egotism; "I" and America are one; America and mankind are one; mankind and a blade of grass are one. This Whitman has been poorly understood and rarely imitated; the vision is too personal to be meaningful except to the poet who has had a similar one, and in that case he does not need the example of Whitman.

DICKINSON

One other American poet calls for attention at this point, Emily Dickinson (1830–86). At its worst her poetry can be offensively cute, too pertly cozy with God. But at its best, and most of it is at its best, it is—and this may be claiming too little—the greatest poetry written by any American woman.

From a technical viewpoint, Dickinson's stanza forms seem at first to present little that is new. Most of her poems could be sung to the hymn tunes that were intoned weekly in Amherst. On a more careful reading, the freedom of rhythm within the traditional patterns becomes evident; she could vary and "rough up" her meters in as boldly modern a way as Robert Lowell.

One minor technical innovation was fostered, if not invented, by Dickinson—the deliberate use of imperfect rhymes, such as those noted earlier in "The Quaker Graveyard." This has been a useful legacy to modern poets, who freely use pure rhyme, half rhyme, or modulate between the two. Other and more important aspects of Dickinson's poetry point first of all toward the modern rediscovery of the "Metaphysical" poets of the seventeenth century. There is in Dickinson the same willingness to see unsuspected resemblances between things usually put in different conceptual pigeonholes.

> Bring me the sunset in a cup,
> Reckon the morning's flagons up,
>   And say how many dew;
> Tell me how far the morning leaps,
> Tell me what time the weaver sleeps
>   Who spun the breadths of blue!

Most of all, her poetry points toward the frame of mind that crystalized in the Imagist movement around the time of World War I. Dickinson hates to say abstract things abstractly; she suggests them obliquely by quick phrases that bring up an evocative sensory image:

> Inebriate of air am I,
> And debauchee of dew,
> Reeling, through endless summer days,
> From inns of molten blue.

If nineteenth century poetry tended to be long-winded and patiently explicit, Dickinson represents the revolt toward compressed, indirect statement. She did not meet her reader nine-tenths of the way as Longfellow did. She was willing to communicate, but only on her own terms, which meant that the reader would have to throw off his easy assumptions about the nature of poetry and re-educate himself by reading her work, one poem at a time. This stubborn determination not to spoonfeed the reader lies back of much "modern obscurity."

HOPKINS AND TODAY'S POETRY

The next great source of poetic mutations is the English Jesuit priest, Gerard Manley Hopkins (1844–89), whose influence, like that of Dickinson, was posthumous. A younger contemporary of Tennyson's, Hopkins was in some curious ways the poetic cousin of Whitman. For one thing, he loosened the traditional patterns of meter. This he did not by free verse but by evolving what he called "sprung rhythm." The number of stressed syllables in a line creates the beat; the unstressed syllables may vary in number and position. For example, the opening stanza of "Hurrahing in Harvest" has five heavy stresses to each line, but no ingenuity of scansion can torture the lines into iambic pentameter or any other standard meter:

> Summer ends now; now, barbarous in beauty, the stooks arise
> Around; up above, what wind-walks! what lovely behaviour
> Of silk-sack clouds! has wilder, willful-wavier
> Meal-drift moulded ever and melted across skies?

The influence of sprung rhythm has been considerable, reinforcing the example of free verse by suggesting another and somewhat more disciplined means of achieving a perceptible beat without being fettered by traditional meters.

Like Whitman also—and like Dickinson in her more elusive way—Hopkins had a vision. An orthodox Catholic Christian, he interpreted the vision in the terms of traditional theology, seeing the splendor of all things as a reflection or manifestation of God the Creator—"The world is charged with the grandeur of God. / It will flame out, like shining from shook foil." His poetic concern is to behold, to glorify in words, to give thanks. In giving thanks, he pushes and compresses language to the point where it seems it will break under the weight of glory. Conventional syntax is brushed aside, weak words like articles and pronouns are discarded. Great clusters of vividly expressive words are created: "stallion stalwart," "very-violet-sweet," "the dappled-with-damson west," "daylight's Dauphin, dapple-dawn-drawn Falcon, in his riding / Of the rolling level underneath him steady air . . ."

Hopkins' technical experiments live on in the resources available to any modern poet; his spirit, so far as it can be recaptured, is visible in much of the work of such poets as Brother Antoninus and Ned O'Gorman.

OUT OF IRELAND

The Irish poet William Butler Yeats (1865–1939) is in himself almost a history of late nineteenth and early twentieth century poetry, for he evolved from the dreamy, Celtic-twilight softness of his earlier verse to the leaner, more intellectual, and exceeding complex poetry of his later period.

Yeats was not a great technical innovator. His rhythms, his stanza forms are not too different from those of the Victorian period during which he was born and wrote his first poems. Nor is his greatest contribution the use he made of Irish folklore in his early poetry. His delicate Celtic twilight was imitated, mostly badly, by many Irish poets and some honorary Irishmen, but Cuchulain and Oisin have not replaced Odysseus and Sweeney in the modern treasurehouse of symbols.

His importance is first of all that he was one of the poets to fall strongly under the spell of the French Symbolists. This is a catch-all term that commonly includes Baudelaire, Verlaine, Laforgue, Rimbaud, Mallarmé, and the Belgian, Maeterlinck. With all their diversity, they had a certain approach in common. They aimed at indirect suggestion rather than explicit statement; they sought symbols that would evoke a particular emotion or perception by a sudden flash of empathy and insight on the reader's part. Their poetry tended away from formal, logical presentation, toward a teasing ambiguity, a mysterious vagueness of surface. They were the exact opposite of those poets who have used an essay style of verse; they were the antithesis of a Longfellow. Sometimes they have been compared in their complexity and deviousness to the English Metaphysicals, but the latter had in addition a passionate cerebral quality. Later, in the work of T. S. Eliot, the influence of the French Symbolists was to combine with that of the Metaphysicals and jointly contribute a large share of the obscurity for which modern poetry has been roundly damned.

Yeats was also one of the first poets to face the characteristic dilemma of the modern poet—what frame of reference to use when society as a whole has no universal and coherent set of beliefs. The nineteenth century clung to the fiction that society was Christian, but by the time of Yeats' maturity it was evident that Christianity is simply one alternative among many that the individual may choose in order to make sense of his experience. It is not a poet's proper job to create a pattern of beliefs and values, but he needs one inside of which he can write poetry. Much of the poetry of this century has been a desperate quest for something to believe, even if the belief can sometimes be only "as if it were true."

13

Certain poets have experienced a conversion or reconversion to some established faith—Eliot and Auden who turned to orthodox Christianity, the Marxist converts of the 1930's, etc. In doing so, they have found themselves with a frame of reference. Others have felt as Yeats did in his famous autobiographical statement:

> I was unlike others of my generation in one thing only. I am very religious, and deprived by Huxley and Tyndall, whom I detested, of the simple-minded religion of my childhood, I had made a new religion, almost an infallible church of poetic tradition, of a fardel of stories, and of personages, and of emotions, inseparable from their first expression, passed on from generation to generation by poets and painters with some help from philosophers and theologians . . . I had even created a dogma: "Because those imaginary people are created out of the deepest instinct of man, to be his measure and his norm, whatever I can imagine those mouths speaking may be the nearest I can go to truth." [1]

Yeats' "as if" faith was a strange and wonderful composite, but it made possible some of the greatest poems of the century. At the same time it set an example. The poet without a traditional faith is emboldened to ransack other times and cultures, take what he likes, add any contributions from his own imagination, and thus create a substitute faith. From this a great deal of the obscurity of modern poetry arises, as separate private faiths replace a public one.

THE QUESTION OF FROST

The next poet presents a problem. Robert Frost (1874–1963) is unquestionably a major poet—among the American-born, he ranks with Whitman, Dickinson, and Eliot—but is he a seminal poet? Does his poetry represent a mutation and therefore an influence on later poets? The scholars and critics have been slow in getting around to Frost. The lovable but deceptive mask of the well-adjusted, normal rustic American that he wore deceived them for a time into thinking his poetry was simple. The man was not simple; neither is the poetry.

One strand of Frost's verse has a kinship with Ralph Waldo Emerson (1803–82). This comes out in his quietly meditative poems, particularly those with a country setting, where the facts of

---

[1] *The Autobiography of William Butler Yeats,* The Macmillan Company, New York, 1953, pp. 101–2.

14

nature serve as a kind of allegory or commentary on human affairs. But—despite Frost's jibes about free verse—there is a strain of the Whitman in him. Whitman aimed at being the poet of the common man, writing in the common language. He only partially succeeded in both attempts; his common men remain curiously generalized and abstract, and his language of common speech is a *mélange* that no common man ever spoke. Whether or not Frost was in any way influenced by Whitman, he achieved in large measure what Whitman had set out to do. In poem after poem he presents ordinary people, sharply individualized, and presents them as though he identifies himself with them. Better than either Wordsworth or Whitman, he coaxes everyday language into yielding its poetry. In these ways, and in his ability to make a fragment of narrative serve as a moral or philosophic parable, he has offered a model to poets whose inclinations are *not* toward French symbolism and its Anglo-Saxon derivatives. One suspects—it is very difficult to pin it down—that Frost has quietly influenced a number of the modern poets, including Louis Coxe, Richard Wilbur, and Richard Eberhart, and that it may eventually be found that he has infiltrated the poetic tradition and shaped it as surely as Eliot, Pound, and the other poets most frequently mentioned. Perhaps the evident movement in recent poetry back to relative clarity and apparent simplicity owes a great but largely unrecognized debt to Frost.

OUT OF IDAHO

Next, out of Hailey, Idaho, came Ezra Pound (1885–) who was to be the impressario of the "new poetry." Armed with a lofty view of his own gifts and the poet's role as cultural savior, he arrived in England in 1908, and soon was correcting Yeats' manuscripts, as later he was to bluepencil the rough draft of Eliot's *The Waste Land*.

At the time of Pound's arrival, English poetry was tending toward a kind of verse later called Georgian, from the anthologies issued between 1912–22. The term embraced poets as diverse as John Masefield, W. H. Davies, Harold Monro, James Stephens, and Robert Graves, but—for a time at any rate—they seemed to have in common a quiet lyricism, a love of nature, a bias in favor of rustic settings. Their poetry was nearly always pleasant, rarely startling.

Pound had not crossed the Atlantic to become a dutiful Georgian. The English soon recognized in him a dynamo of ideas and energy, and the ability to organize a literary campaign as though it were the capture of a military bridgehead. Such a campaign was the Imagist Movement, whose first anthology was issued in 1914 under Pound's impetus. The credo of Imagism finally crystalized to include: the language of common speech, the *exact* word, the free use of new rhythms when suitable, absolute freedom in choice of subject, the use of imagistic instead of generalized or abstract language, concentration. These principles scarcely appear revolutionary now, but at their time, against the Georgian backdrop, they were.

Poetry: A Magazine of Verse was established in Chicago by Harriet Monroe about this time, and it proved a convenient American outlet for the new movement. Meanwhile, Pound soon quarreled with his transatlantic assistant, Amy Lowell, and in pique pulled out of the organized movement, leaving its leadership to her.

There is no time here to trace the later career of Pound and the movements and controversies in which he has been involved. His most obvious importance is simply that for years he kept things stirred up. He was always discovering new poets, finding publishers for them, issuing manifestoes and challenging the poetic assumptions of the past.

His own career as a poet is curiously broken and fragmentary. After a brilliant start he yielded more and more to poetic and personal eccentricities, powerfully aided and abetted by his later infatuation with Mussolini's doctrines. The *Cantos*, on which he is presumably still working in Italy, are a magnificent series of fragments, a hodgepodge of doggerel, smart aleck verse, intellectual pretentiousness, crudity, and soaring bits of poetry, all held together by the force of certain key ideas of social philosophy and further given form by the poetic convention that all times and cultures exist simultaneously for the poet; a Chinese philosopher can discuss usury with Thomas Jefferson.

Pound was yet another transmission belt for the influence of the nineteenth-century French Symbolists. In general, he has been an all-purpose transmission belt, with his translations and adaptations from Old English, Provençal, Latin, Chinese, Italian, and French poetry. He represents cultural eclecticism, an outlook powerful in all the modern arts.

Commonly Pound is grouped with Eliot and Yeats as an ancestor of the modern tradition of highly learned and cerebral verse. It might also be argued that he stands partly in the Whitman tradition and has broadened it and passed it along, much modified, one grants. In the *Cantos* he uses colloquial rhythms as freely as a Whitman, and puts on the same mantle of bard and prophet. Hart Crane attempted a similar combination of the cerebral and the bardic. Most of the subsequent poets have leaned one way or the other. Some have leaned a third way, their own.

At any rate, Pound's achievements have been so varied that his example points in half a dozen different directions at once. Almost every later poet has felt the direct or indirect influence of one Pound or the other.

Finally, Pound is the clearest example of the lover's quarrel between poet and society. This has been more a rule than an exception since the Romantic Movement. One of the recurrent themes of poetry is, "Where does poetry—and the poet—fit in?" Some poets, like Pound, have seriously elected themselves the legislators of the world, and have turned bitter and destructive when society did not ratify the election. Others have merely lamented their isolation or wittily satirized philistine society; some have holed up in their privacy and written poetry for other poets to read in *their* privacy.

POET AND CRITIC

Another American arrived in England in 1914 and remained there to become a British subject. He was a gentleman already from his upper-class New England background, though by accident of history he had been born in St. Louis. T. S. Eliot (1888–) scarcely needs detailed discussion. Not only has his literary criticism been the greatest modern fountainhead for thinking about poetry, but his poetic example has been the single largest influence in shaping the contemporary poetic tradition. Even the poets now in rebellion against "grandfather" find their rebellion shaped and colored by the inescapable fact of Eliot and the Eliot influence.

Afflicted from the start with a brooding horror of the meaninglessness of life in the depersonalized world of the modern wasteland, Eliot sought and found in certain strands of French Symbolism the poetic tools that would enable him to capture, express, and thereby transcend the emptiness of futility. Later his quest, essentially religious as well as esthetic, was to lead him to Classicism, Crown, and Church, but in the earlier poetry, such as *Prufrock*, one finds the horror, the

17

sense of paralysis and unreality, in its purest state. One sees also the characteristic Eliot devices that were to become part of the tool kit of contemporary verse. There is the free use of historical, literary, and mythological allusions from all periods to throw light on the present moment. There is the tendency to organize a poem not by some logical progression, but by psychological states or free association—in *Prufrock* the reader is never sure just what happens when, or whether it all happens in the mind of Prufrock—but what he does know is the contents of Prufrock's mind. With Eliot the strong tendency of poetry to be psychological becomes stronger.

One item of Eliot's critical theory is of particular importance— the doctrine of the "objective correlative," which he defines as "a set of objects, a situation, a chain of events which shall be the formula of that particular emotion; such that, when the external facts, which must terminate in sensory experience, are given, the emotion is immediately evoked." Prufrock does not say, "I have wasted my life in trivial experiences"; he says, "I have measured out my life with coffee spoons." He does not say, "I wish I could live purely by instinct"; he says, "I should have been a pair of ragged claws / Scuttling across the floors of silent seas," evoking a picture of primitive, mindless savagery.

Eliot was also one of the great rediscoverers of the English metaphysical tradition, supremely John Donne, with its serious punning, its refusal to be over-solemn, its oblique and frequently bizarre comparisons, in general its insistence that poetry is not concerned only with the obviously "beautiful" but can create its effects by the skilful juxtaposition of wildly assorted elements of experience and observation. All in all, the influence of Eliot has been against "saying it straight," and toward "saying it indirectly, saying it deviously, so that you can say it more powerfully and evocatively and more exactly."

That Eliot caught the consciousness of his times is now evident. Almost any college Freshman knows that "April is the cruellest month" and *The Waste Land*, once derided as an impossibly difficult pastiche, now seems almost obvious to an intelligent reader. The mood of the literate public, its sensibility, has caught up with Eliot, and meanwhile his technical innovations have become the stock-in-trade of the poetic community.

THE 'THIRTIES

One could almost end at this point and say that Eliot was the last great source of poetic mutations, and there remains only a series of minor adaptations of a rich and varied tradition. Almost, but not quite. Deeply as W. H. Auden shows the influence of Eliot, he is an innovator and influence in his own right—the seminal poet of the 1930's, a period when politics and international relations pressed so inescapably on the consciousness of everyone that poetry itself was inevitably drawn to social themes.

Auden is a member and chief theorician of a so-called group (sometimes styled the "Pylon Poets") consisting of himself, Louis MacNeice, C. Day Lewis, and Stephen Spender. Because they partially overlapped at Oxford, the journalists invested them with a cohesion they never possessed. (The four never sat together in the same room till one day after World War II, Mr. Auden assures me.) In Auden's early poetry there is a mixture of Freud and Marx that seemed to offer a modern substitute for the vanished Christian certainties of an earlier time; later he was to return to the Church as an Anglo-Catholic *cum* Kierkegaard, though this return was not to mark any loss of the sharp eye for the social scene.

As versatile a poet as Dryden, Auden is from a technical viewpoint the great eclectic and experimenter. He can turn out a ballad or mimic the rhythms of music hall tunes; from the sonnet and the sestina to the alliterative verse of the Old English period he is completely the master. But his versatility goes beyond mere technique. He is the peculiarly modern man, finding images and implications in the detective story, exploring Dante's territory in a New York bar, impartially writing elegies for Marx, Freud, and Yeats. One feels that he travels by his poetic wits, that he has never evolved a standard approach and style. Each poem is an occasion for inspired improvisation, rather than the application of some tried-and-true formula. In him the poetic buffoon and the prophet are inseparably united; he cavorts and in cavorting says some of the more profound and compelling things that the verse of this century has uttered.

Before concluding this all too cursory sketch of the transitional period between Victorian and modern poetry, one other thing should be mentioned: irony. Not all the poets have practiced it. (One finds it hard to imagine Whitman's being ironical.) But it has been a common tone or attitude in much of the poetry of this century, and is very evident in Eliot and Auden, as well as in the well-made and muted verse of many gifted younger poets. Perhaps irony flourishes when there is no longer one faith uniting society; perhaps it stems in part from the "as if" beliefs that some poets profess, and their implied pact with the reader that he will "suspend his disbelief" so as to respond to their work. Whatever its complex sources, irony is more in evidence in this century than in the preceding one. Even when the poet is expressing what he literally believes (e.g., Auden's Christian poetry) there is likely to be a tone implying that not all men share these assumptions. Earlier it was suggested that the Victorians tended to "play it straight." The prevalence of irony is one way in which modern poetry does not play it straight.

Innovation and Achievement

In the preceding survey no attempt has been made to provide a systematic history of late nineteenth and early twentieth century poetry. The quest was for seminal poets, whose work embodies the "mutations" that have been modified and developed in modern poetry. The poets singled out have been those that broke new ground for the future. Certain poets have achieved impressive stature and a permanent place in quieter ways. It is doubtful that E. A. Robinson, Thomas Hardy, or Robert Graves can be called important innovators, but they are important poets. There is no one-to-one relation between the greatness of a poet and his fame as a poetic experimenter. It has been cogently argued that Shakespeare merely did better, with conventional poetic and dramatic tools, what other playwrights were already doing.

In a longer and more systematic discussion, several dozen additional poets would demand detailed treatment, either for their inherent worth, their influence, or both. (It seems odd indeed to have reached this point without at least a passing mention of Wallace Stevens!) But enough has been said to indicate some of the striking mutations that have taken place during the past hundred years.

STUBBORN INDIVIDUALITY

It is, of course, merely a handy figure of speech to talk of poetry as though it evolves like some species of reptile. Every poet is a bundle of personal mutations, no matter how much he may have been influenced by the poets before him and the poetic climate they have collectively bequeathed to him. In addition, if two poets could have identical talents, temperaments, and intellects, but lived in different periods of time, their poetry would be different for that very reason. A poet responds to the world around him: its sights, its problems, its unspoken assumptions, the great events that are transpiring. The outer world not merely gives subject matter but colors the poet's sensibility. On the other hand, two poets living in the same place and period may—because no two persons *are* identical in talent, temperament, and intellect—respond in utterly different ways to the outer world. The massive fact of the Industrial Revolution has been with us since Blake, but the poets do not agree on how to take it. Auden made poetry out of abandoned mine pits and rusty sidings; Frost chose to be a lone striker and concentrate on the rural world from which he could cast shrewd glances at the tumult and chaos outside.

POET AND PUBLIC

Looking backward now at the changes in poetry from Poe to Auden, the total impression is twofold: enlargement and eclecticism. The poet has been liberated to use or create any form and any type of language; he can be as psychological as an analyst or as theological as a Thomist; he can ransack exotic literatures, mythologies, the anthropological journals for his purposes; he can create a private faith or adopt a public one or write from a stance of atheistic existentialism; he can be as obscure as he chooses to be and let the public be damned, or he can appoint himself bard to the public.

This immense liberty has been won at a price, which is the partial loss of a public. The ordinary man, in so far as he concerns himself with the arts, is conservative; he reacts with both esthetic and moral indignation against novelties. The pace of poetic mutation has been too fast for him. The same is true with all the arts; the philistine of today is just reaching the point where he praises nineteenth-century Impressionism as a means of condemning twentieth-century Abstract Expressionism.

Nonetheless, the alienation between poet and public has never been absolute. Some poets of the nineteenth century—Tennyson, Longfellow, even the "difficult" Browning—succeeded in winning substantial publics. In our own century, Robert Frost became an uncrowned laureate. Lawrence Ferlinghetti may not be invited to read at bankers' conventions, but he has a vast public in university audiences. Other poets have tried to meet the public halfway but failed;

such was Vachel Lindsay who in discouragement eventually drank the Lysol of defeat. Still other poets have written for themselves, for other poets, and for a handful of passionate lovers of poetry.

The cleavage between the poet and the public is commonly attributed to the obscurity of modern verse. This is undoubtedly a factor, but not the only one. Not all modern poets are obscure. The man who refuses to read Dylan Thomas usually does not read W. D. Snodgrass or Vassar Miller either, yet he could understand either of them almost as readily as the Wordsworth he memorized in grade school.

The alienation of the poet is matched by the alienation of other artists, and in every case it seems to date from the late eighteenth or early nineteenth century, when the factory chimneys began to belch, a new social class rose to dominance, and literature and the arts entered into their "Romantic" phase. The poet had usually been on easy terms with the old aristocrat, who was frequently his patron. The ascetic capitalists of Birmingham and Manchester—often rising from a background of little culture—had less interest in the frivolities of life. True, they learned to read, if they did not already possess the art, and they educated their children, and in time literacy became generally available to almost everyone in Britain and the United States. A vast reading public was created, and it became collectively the new patron of the poets.[1] This public, recently introduced to literature, wanted poetry that was easy to understand, moralistic, comforting. It was willing to pay for it by buying books. Some poets and novelists adapted themselves to the new literacy and flourished in public esteem. Others would have nothing to do with it. The showdown was perhaps the rise of the Naturalistic novelists toward the end of the century, when these writers had to choose between outraging the general public or being false to their own vision of reality. Most of them chose to be honest. The present century, with some exceptions, has seen the poet going his own way, writing for whoever is willing to take him on his own terms. This intransigence of the poet is gradually creating and educating a public, still small but growing, that is ready to meet the poet where *he* is.

A poet is not always a comfortable citizen to have around. He has a way of saying things the public prefers not to hear. He is often in the position of Winston Churchill when the latter was in the politi-

---

[1] Here, as in several other places in this Introduction, I am indebted to my good friend, Professor Wilbur S. Scott, for certain lines of thought.

cal wilderness, prophesying war to a generation that believed in peace in our time. Poets sometimes dig too deep for comfort. Those of to-day, living in a century of world wars, genocide, hydrogen bombs, and population explosion, do not often specialize in metrical peace of mind.

POETRY AND LITERARY CRITICISM

So much for poet and public. Before turning to the poets repre-sented in this anthology, one other factor in the evolution of modern verse deserves mention. This is the rise of literary criticism. The New Criticism, which includes such critics as T. S. Eliot, I. A. Richards, John Crowe Ransom, and Allen Tate, has produced a body of probing and highly technical analyses of poetry that has no parallel in any earlier period. Its specialty is the *"explication de texte,"* the minute examination of a poem line by line, word by word. It is strong on levels of meaning, ambiguity, poetic texture. In a way it is a poet's criticism of poetry, for it sees poetry as an autonomous art, subject only to its own inner laws. As such, it has a powerful appeal. Many poets are also critics. Sometimes they write poetry as though they were preparing it for analysis in a graduate seminar on literary criti-cism. The result *can* be a precious self-consciousness, and a fear of letting one's self go. But on balance, the impact of modern literary criticism on the writing of poetry has probably been good. It has certainly given the poets a sophisticated awareness of how each ele-ment in a poem contributes to the total effect, and has made them aware of all the technical resources of their art.

At any rate, thanks to the poetic pioneers and their analytical allies, the critics, the poet's tool kit since the 1930's has been full to bursting. Possibly still other important gadgets have been added since that time and we are too close to recognize their worth, but in general it appears that the present period is more one of picking-and-choosing and refining familiar techniques and approaches, rather than a quest for startling novelties.

The Polarization of American Poetry

The recent evolution of American poetry has been in two diver-gent directions. The Eliot-Pound-Yeats tradition, as modified by Stevens, Auden, and others, has been the standard point of departure for many beginning poets. These have been the poets most often honored with Guggenheims and other awards, and published in the literary quarterlies. They constitute a kind of "poetic establishment." Some of them are connected with publishing houses; some edit quarterlies; many teach. Links of personal friendship and mutual admiration bind certain of them together. All in all, the poets of this tradition have occupied the sunny and civilized uplands of contemporary poetry.

It would be very false to think of them as mechanically writing in the manner of the great transitional poets. That tradition has become progressively modified, toned down, the rough edges rubbed off. The result is a kind of poetry that usually seems less startling than the early work of Eliot or Pound. It is likely to be tastefully modern, exquisitely competent in technique, urbane, sometimes too civilized.

These poets carrying on the generalized but progressively modified heritage of the great poetic revolutionaires are found more and more on the university and college campus. A typical life cycle is college, a summer at a writer's workshop, very likely a master's degree but more rarely a Ph.D., a first book of poetry, perhaps a Lamont award or a Guggenheim, eventually a position on some campus teaching poetry, criticism, and creative writing, more books of poetry, occasional readings on other campuses, often an editorial connection with a literary periodical.

The schools have thus become the new patrons. The final evaluation of this relationship is not available yet. A highly experimental young artist once said to me, "Here I am, teaching students how to paint crazy pictures—for three hours academic credit." He feared that his own work would become too self-conscious, too refined. Certainly, a teaching job provides a livelihood and pleasantly stimulating surroundings; it may also tend to domesticate the poet. At any rate, it has become almost the general pattern among the younger American poets who stand in this mainline of poetic evolution, and comparable things are happening in Great Britain.

THE UNDERGROUND

Meanwhile, an underground current of poetry has survived in America and finally come to the surface with publicity and fanfare. This current is that of the barbaric yawp; its many ancestors include Whitman, certain aspects of Pound, W. C. Williams, Lindsay, Sandburg, with today frequently a strong dash of Zen. Until recently few of these poets received important awards, and they were rarely employed on campuses.

This underground poetic current survived during its lean years in Black Mountain College, in San Francisco, among certain poets in New York, and among others scattered over the country and united by tiny magazines and tinier presses. The rise of the Beats [1] in the mid 1950's first brought the diffuse poetic underground to general notice, and since then the two broad streams of American poetry have enjoyed something closer to an equality in the book reviews and major publishing houses.

Obviously, many of the best poets do not fit comfortably in either pigeonhole, and others are assimilating what is useful to them in each tradition, and then setting forth on their separate and lonely ways. To see how arbitrary all labels are, one need only dip into the conservative anthology, *New Poets of England and America*, and its opposite number, *The New American Poetry, 1945–1960*. In the first are included a number of the American poets in this present anthology: Mezey, Miller, Nemerov, Snodgrass, Wilbur, Lowell. It would be a rash critic who tried to prove that they are merely variations of a common tradition. Likewise, the poets in the other collection—for example, Antoninus, Creeley, Ferlinghetti—are sharply individual, unmistakably themselves. Still, in a rough way the generalization holds. The "academics" and the "wild men"—call them what you will—represent the two poles of current American verse.

The British Scene

In Great Britain the recent picture has been somewhat different, mainly because poetic wild men are there in short supply. It is true that in the mid 1930's Dylan Thomas rose like some elemental force in Wales and produced a poetry of Dionysian savagery and magnificence, which was imitated, always with baleful results, by many beginning poets. Thomas is a major figure, one of the few unquestion-

---

[1] The label, Beat, was never very precise, but has been most often applied to such poets as Allen Ginsberg, Jack Kerouac, Gregory Corso, Gary Snyder, and Philip Whalen. Not all poets of the "underground" or "anti-establishment" are Beats.

ably major poets of the period covered by this anthology. But from the start his work was widely misunderstood. Many readers, bewitched and shaken by his power, his mystic evocation of instinct, transported into a Celtic sensibility where the sources of life seem magically revealed, overlooked the important fact that he was one of the great craftsmen of his times, writing and rewriting his poems, systematically creating the technical structures through which he expressed the wildest insights. Unlike some of the poetic wild men, who boast of their semi-automatic methods of composition and assert that they blot fewer lines than Shakespeare ever did, Thomas worked at it. His highly rational mind was put to the service of his intuitions. The combination of patient intelligence and intuitive grasp of life produced a kind of poetry impossible to imitate.

Apart from Thomas, British poetry has been in a relatively quiet period, enlivened by occasional manifestoes, factional anthologies, and "movements" sparked by the journalists with the tacit cooperation of young poets yearning for a place in the sun. Movements come more easily in England than in America because of the centralization of cultural life. The great training grounds of poetry are still Oxford and Cambridge, though sometimes a redbrick university serves, and an occasional poet emerges elsewhere. The publishers and the BBC are concentrated in London, to which a large number of the poets gravitate. It is not literally true that everyone knows everyone, but it is much closer to the truth than in sprawling America. Thus a "movement" can be started overnight and quickly warmed up in *The Spectator* and over the BBC. Whether all this constitutes a "poetic establishment" is much debated. The English writer with a university degree is likely to say *No,* and his colleague who has scrambled ahead without a degree votes *Yes.* Except for the greater degree of centralization, the situation is actually akin to that in the United States, where poets of the first category (the "Academics") profit from a network of important connections, and those with a different background have to struggle harder for equal recognition.

"THE MOVEMENT"

Some movements have more enduring consequences than others. The 1940's saw a brief-lived Apocalyptic Movement, complete with its own anthology. It was neo-Romantic in tone; there were touches of surrealism, and a taste of Dylan Thomas. It proved a poetic dead-

26

end. Its main importance was the negative one of helping prepare the way for what curiously came to be called simply "The Movement," and which was a revolt against many strands of twentieth century poetry, including the Apocalyptic.

The Movement, whose anthology, *New Lines*, appeared in 1956, was the doing of young poets from Oxford and Cambridge, the majority of whom were academics by profession. Some were influenced by the austere intellectual quality of Empson's poetry, but still more they were swayed by their antipathies. They were in rebellion against the dream magnificence of Dylan Thomas, the chaos and obscurity of the Apocalyptics, even against the old masters, Eliot, Pound, and Auden. They tended to admire Robert Graves, who was gradually emerging into critical attention. They argued that poetry should speak to the ordinary intelligent reader: it should not be too private, too queer, too personal, too loaded down with esoteric symbols. In their theories they were the Alexander Popes of their times, trying to reclaim for poetry a role in the lives of cultivated citizens. They were strong on the importance of poetic discipline and form, and indeed took such particular relish in composing *terza rima* and sestinas that they often overlooked other interesting forms. Implied as much as expressed in their stance was a feeling that the bloodstream of English poetry had become contaminated by foreign influences: Eliot and Pound, and the seductive lures of French Symbolism. The Movement was thus in many ways a back-to-the-native-roots movement.

New Lines contained the work of nine poets—Elizabeth Jennings, John Holloway, Philip Larkin, Thom Gunn, Kingsley Amis, D. J. Enright, Donald Davie, Robert Conquest, and John Wain. Of these, Larkin has been truest to the original purposes of the Movement, and his poetry demonstrates the real though limited achievements possible with such a concept of poetry.

The Movement involved a lowering of sights, a more modest view of what poetry can do. It was a wholesome clean-up operation, banishing a great deal of fuzzy romanticism and uninspired symbol-chasing and cosmic muttering, but its inhibitions soon became evident, even to most of the poets involved. It was too matter-of-fact, too commonsensical, too drab, too completely British. It was in fact an attempt to make British poetry a cozy world of its own that any British university student could appreciate; there was something anachronistic about the way it turned aside from the broader currents of poetry flowing throughout the world. It produced a great number of extremely competent poems, and very few that have the ultimate ring of major poetry.

THE MAVERICKS

New Lines was promptly followed by a counterattack, a rival anthology, *Mavericks* (1957). Including the work of J. C. Hall, David Wright, Vernon Scannell, Dannie Abse, Michael Hamburger, John Smith, Anthony Cronin, W. Price Turner, and Jon Silkin, the foreword attacked the Movement as fundamentally anti-poetic in spirit and argued for more spontaneity, for the Dionysian and the Romantic.

Movement poets and Mavericks alike have subsequently stuck to their desks and written their poems and developed in individual directions, with little regard for the critical and journalistic labels they originally wore.[1]

The most striking difference between current British and American poetry may be summed up under two headings. First, the Yeats-Eliot-Pound influence is more evident in America than England. It is not completely dead overseas, and some poets, such as Charles Tomlinson, openly acknowledge and defend it. But the Movement was a step away from it. In America, the tradition, toned down and infinitely modified, is still alive, especially but not exclusively in the work of the more "Academic" poets. The language of American poetry (even with some of the "wild men") bears the marks of this tradition, in a way seldom found in the latest British poets.

In the second place, Great Britain has nothing fully corresponding to the "wild man" school of poetry. There is, indeed, a small-scale poetry-and-jazz movement, much like its San Francisco predecessors and centered in Soho under the devoted leadership of Mike Horovitz, who also publishes *New Departures*. Most of these poets are young and it is too early to say what mark they will make. For a time they were so assiduously ignored by the rest of the poetic world that it took some literary detective work to discover their existence. The "poetic establishment," if one exists, finally recognized them in 1962

---

[1] In 1963 Robert Conquest published *New Lines 2*. John Holloway has been dropped, and such Mavericks as Vernon Scannell have been brought in, together with various other poets—Richard Kell, George MacBeth, Hilary Corke, etc. The new *New Lines* is thus a more general type of anthology, and marks the blurring of factional lines.

and they have since appeared several times on the BBC and been commissioned to perform at festivals. They remain very peripheral, as compared to the equivalent movement in America.

FROM THE FRINGES

The tightly-knit poetic life centered in London has its advantages and disadvantages. Poets can achieve early recognition, but become too self-conscious and addicted to literary politics in the process. Several of the most promising poets to emerge recently have lived far from the center. One is the Welsh parson, R. S. Thomas. For years he has served one obscure Welsh parish or another; for a long time he published his poetry privately. Eventually the BBC discovered him, and his collected verse was published by a London house, with a laudatory introduction by John Betjeman. He then stood revealed as perhaps the most individual talent of his times. Another is the West Indian, Derek Walcott, who has lived in England but has his permanent home in Trinidad. The individuality and vitality of his poetry point toward a future achievement that may render meaningless the pettifogging debates between the warring manifestoes.

The advantages of centralization should not be underrated. Poets abound in London, and can get together easily, for mutual comfort and stimulation. One group meets periodically in a Dulwich pub to hear readings by visiting poets; the same group makes appearances elsewhere on invitation, to read their own work. Another circle, operating more like a writer's workshop, is the one started originally by Philip Hobsbaum and now organized by Edward Lucie-Smith. Ted Hughes is an early alumnus of the group. The members mimeograph poems in advance; six are discussed and analyzed at each meeting. Several books of individual poetry have already been published by members, and a joint anthology was issued in 1963. Out of such a continuing group, new talents continue to appear.

Cautious Generalizations

It is time now to have an impressionistic overall look at the poets in this present book, and see what conclusions one can draw about them as a whole. The first generalization is that all generalizations are partial lies. A poet is a poet first of all because of a stubborn and individual talent. He is not the mere product of "influences," literary or external. Brother Antoninus, Roy Fuller, Karl Shapiro, Gil Orlovitz, and John Ciardi were all born in the second decade of this century, all experienced the Depression, the War, and the Cold War, all are acquainted with the sweep of English and American poetry, but no one would confuse one man's work with another's.

THE IMPACT OF SOCIETY AND HISTORY

At the same time, no poet lives in a vacuum. The great events of history, the social circumstances of his times, the things that are happening in poetry and the other arts, do have an effect on him and leave a mark on his poetry. For example, in the 1930's when great numbers of British and American poets were socially concious by duty as well as inclination, the poet who deliberately chose to turn inward and forget the problems of the outer world did it with a different, perhaps a defiant tone, that would not have been provoked in another period.

It is extremely difficult to generalize about the total impact of depression, war, cold war, hydrogen bomb, racial problems, etc., on the poetry of recent decades. Shapiro's early verse was mostly "war poetry," but he never considered himself a "war poet." Almost every poet shows at least an oblique awareness of the shattering events of the century, but this awareness is more often expressed indirectly, through nuances of tone, rather than by odes on a soup kitchen or even elegies for Hiroshima.

After the depression poetry of the 1930's and the war poetry of the 1940's, many of the poets seem to have turned inward, concentrating on personal, psychological, sometimes religious themes, without explicit reference to the chaotic and threatening deeds of the outer world. Comparable trends can be discerned in the contemporary novel. Perhaps Ferlinghetti is right when he asserts that the next big movement in poetry will not be any revolution in technique, but a wholehearted return to the poet's role as social observer, participant, and critic.

CHANGE AND CONTINUITY

So much by way of preliminary cautions. I shall be frankly personal and impressionistic in my remaining comments. When I re-read the manuscript of this anthology, I am struck not as much by the radical difference of modern poetry as by its continuity with English-language poetry of the past. The more extreme experiments of recent decades have been assimilated and partly domesticated. The poetry emerging today is less "queer" than forty years ago, a shade more public. As such, it looks not like a violent mutation from nineteenth century standards, but rather a logical evolution. Compared to art with its abstract expressionism, drama with the theater of the absurd, and music with its atonal experiments and electronic music, it appears that poetry has, in its technical and formal aspects, pursued a relatively moderate course. It has created new tools, enlarged the usefulness of the old ones, but all this is simply part of the steady evolution of the poetic tradition.

So far as subject matter is concerned, the continuity is still more striking. Man and woman and sex and love have not lost their charm for the poet, though more often than his nineteenth century predecessor he tosses in a strong dash of bitters. A large number of the best poems are religious. Poets can be religious in several ways, by praising God or by scolding Him for not existing, but on the whole they seem more God-haunted than the novelists. Nature poetry is also alive, though not as abundant as in earlier times. There are poems about nuclear fission and race problems, but not as many as one would expect. In general, poets today, like poets of all times, write about what moves them personally, and that turns out to be among other things love, death, beauty, anxiety. Not too much has changed here.

THE MAJOR FIGURES

The inevitable question arises: Who are the giants in this group? The answer must be an evasive one—that it is difficult to spot a giant while he is still alive. Robert Frost was widely read for years before the critics and scholars began to take him with real seriousness. Others, such as Carl Sandburg, have been prematurely hailed as giants. Still, some giants have been recognized early. Though as late as the 1930's many college courses in recent poetry featured Sara Teasdale or Edgar Lee Masters rather than T. S. Eliot, the latter's greatness was evident to the more discerning even before *The Waste Land*.

Are there any giants here? Dylan Thomas in his own unique way. Robert Lowell, whose work is still in process of an exciting evolution. Any others? I suspect the late Theodore Roethke, who was doing his

31

best work at the time of his death, will loom larger than even his admirers have suspected. Of the remaining poets, Richard Eberhart's fantastic productivity makes him an uneven poet but when his work is winnowed by time the surviving poems will be among the most moving and memorable of this period. Other poets that may have the spark of greatness are Brother Antoninus, Gil Orlovitz, Derek Walcott, and John Wain. I could name several others from this anthology. Meanwhile, in an obscure corner of Great Britain or the United States, some poet—not included here—is probably hard at work, creating the poems that will mark him as the major figure of this half century.

Three Pitfalls

I reach this point with the awareness that I have been doing three things, all of which I deplore. In the last few paragraphs I have been trying to rank poets, or talk of them as though they are racehorses on which one puts a modest bet. There is something insufferable about the attempt; any anthologist should content himself with the modest statement that he finds the poets in his collection interesting and worth reading, and leave it at that. Let the future with its slowly forming concensus of critical judgment take care of naming the winners. Indeed I must go further and insist that the whole critical and evaluative frame of mind, if permitted to dominate one's response to poetry, can get between reader and poem and keep him from full enjoyment and appreciation of what he finds on the printed page. The reader should forget about various degrees of "greatness" (as though each poet had to pass a sort of CEB examination and be graded from 200 to 800) and simply take each poem as it comes, for what it is.

PIGEONHOLES

In the second place, this Introduction has encouraged the reader to group poets into categories, as though they were members of different political parties or religious denominations. It is difficult to talk about modern poetry at all unless this is done, but always one must bear in mind how awkwardly any poet fits into the category proposed for him. "Wild men" and "Academics," "Movement poets" and

"Mavericks"—these terms oversimplify and distort as much as they clarify. After the terms have served their very limited purpose, they are best discarded or used with the most extreme caution and humility. Each of the thirty-three poets here represented is so stubbornly and completely himself that only a complete set of thirty-three pigeonholes could render them justice. Indeed, thirty-three would not be enough, for many of the poets are in process of far-reaching developments and changes, moving away from one style and sensibility toward the new and the unpredictable.

LITERARY DETERMINISM

Finally, most of this Introduction has been historical, tracing the transition from the Victorians to the Moderns. This approach helps anyone understand many aspects of modern poetry—technique, attitudes toward subject matter, the language of poetry, etc.—but it encourages a baleful and benighted kind of literary determinism, as though a poet were "nothing but" the sum total of his literary heredity and the environmental influences around him. Here again one comes back to the intractable and glorious individuality of each poet. What makes him a poet is also what renders him capable of picking and choosing from the poetic past and from his environment. Each poet is also a source of new "mutations" in his own work. To talk of a poet as though he were merely the product of poetic "heredity" and "environment" is like saying you can understand President de Gaulle by checking on his menu and analyzing the air he breathes.

The historical study of poetry is simply another scholarly tool, useful if not carried too far, an obstacle between reader and poem if allowed to become an explain-all. The historical background that this Introduction has briefly presented is best kept in reserve, to be used where it sheds light on any poet or poem, but not to be the pair of spectacles through which one gazes at one poem after another.

THE PATRIMONY OF POETRY

I come back to the glorious variety of these thirty-three poets. Bink Noll and W. D. Snodgrass both write of family life and its poignantly personal moments, but how utterly different their poems are. God is celebrated by many of the poets, but no one would mistake the long, cadenced lines of Brother Antoninus, and his passion of agony and adoration, for the sonnets of Vassar Miller, in which religious feeling beats against the tight walls of form; neither would be confused with Carl Bode's sonnets and lyrics in which the dialogue between the things of spirit and the things of body is celebrated. And who would confuse Robert Lowell's early religious poetry with the work of any poet, living or dead?

Many of the poets have a quarrel, loving or not, with society, and some of them wage a war in poem after poem, but again each poet is unmistakable. Kenneth Patchen, who has been compared to Blake, writes with the innocence of one who sees but can scarcely believe the horror and the triviality about him; Gil Orlovitz goes into a marvel of controlled frenzy; R. S. Thomas sees the narrowness of Welsh country life but soberly identifies himself with it; Lawrence Ferlinghetti pokes poetic fun at mass culture and conformity.

It would be easy to go down the list, demonstrating that each poet is himself and not somebody else. The poems demonstrate that better than a prose commentary.

Conclusion

The future can take care of passing any permanent judgments on the poets in this anthology. It can say which are giants and which are merely tall for their times. Meanwhile, one fact is clear. Few periods of British or American poetry have produced a larger number of poems so excellent that it would diminish mankind's patrimony if they were allowed to lie forgotten in magazines and slender books of verse. This anthology is merely a sampling of the poetic riches created in the past three or four decades. It demonstrates that those poets who rightly bear the title of modern are faithful but not slavish heirs of a great tradition. They are adding new and unique wealth, year by year, to the heritage.

Beloit College   C.W.

RICHARD EBERHART

(1904–)

The Groundhog

In June, amid the golden fields,
I saw a groundhog lying dead.
Dead lay he; my senses shook,
And mind outshot our naked frailty.
There lowly in the vigorous summer
His form began its senseless change,
And made my senses waver dim
Seeing nature ferocious in him.
Inspecting close his maggots' might
And seething cauldron of his being,
Half with loathing, half with a strange love,
I poked him with an angry stick.
The fever arose, became a flame
And Vigour circumscribed the skies,
Immense energy in the sun,
And through my frame a sunless trembling.
My stick had done nor good nor harm.
Then stood I silent in the day
Watching the object, as before;
And kept my reverence for knowledge
Trying for control, to be still,
To quell the passion of the blood;

Until I had bent down on my knees
Praying for joy in the sight of decay.
And so I left; and I returned
In Autumn strict of eye, to see
The sap gone out of the groundhog,
But the bony sodden hulk remained.
But the year had lost its meaning,
And in intellectual chains
I lost both love and loathing,
Mured up in the wall of wisdom.
Another summer took the fields again
Massive and burning, full of life,
But when I chanced upon the spot
There was only a little hair left,
And bones bleaching in the sunlight
Beautiful as architecture;
I watched them like a geometer,
And cut a walking stick from a birch.
It has been three years, now.
There is no sign of the groundhog.
I stood there in the whirling summer,
My hand capped a withered heart,
And thought of China and of Greece,
Of Alexander in his tent;
Of Montaigne in his tower,
Of Saint Theresa in her wild lament.

'Now Is the Air Made of Chiming Balls'

Now is the air made of chiming balls.
The stormcloud, wizened, has rolled its rind away.
Now is the eye with hill and valley laved
And the seeds, assuaged, peep from the nested spray.
The bluebird drops from a bough. The speckled meadow-lark
Springs in his lithe array. Fresh air
Blesses the vanished tear; the bunched anguish.
The laughing balls their joyful pleasure tear.

Renewed is the whole world and the sun
Begins to dress with warmth again every thing.
The lettuce in pale burn; the burdock tightening;
And naked necks of craning fledglings.

The Soul Longs to Return Whence It Came

I drove up to the graveyard, which
Used to frighten me as a boy,
When I walked down the river past it,
And evening was coming on. I'd make sure
I came home from the woods early enough.
I drove in, I found to the place, I
Left the motor running. My eyes hurried,
To recognize the great oak tree
On the little slope, among the stones.
It was a high day, a crisp day,
The cleanest kind of Autumn day,
With brisk intoxicating air, a
Little wind that frisked, yet there was
Old age in the atmosphere, nostalgia,
The subtle heaviness of the Fall.
I stilled the motor. I walked a few paces;
It was good, the tree; the friendliness of it.
I touched it, I thought of the roots;
They would have pierced her seven years.
O all peoples! O mighty shadows!
My eyes opened along the avenue
Of tombstones, the common land of death.
Humiliation of all loves lost,
That might have had full meaning in any
Plot of ground, come, hear the silence,
See the quivering light. My mind worked
Almost imperceptibly, I
In the command, I the wilful ponderer.
I must have stood silent and thoughtful
There. A host of dry leaves

37

Danced on the ground in the wind.
They startled, they curved up from the ground,
There was a dry rustling, rattling.
The sun was motionless and brittle.
I felt the blood darken in my cheeks
And burn. Like running. My eyes
Telescoped on decay, I out of command.
Fear, tenderness, they seized me.
My eyes were hot, I dared not look
At the leaves. A pagan urge swept me.
Multitudes, O multitudes in one.
The urge of the earth, the titan
Wild and primitive lust, fused
On the ground of her grave.
I was a being of feeling alone.
I flung myself down on the earth
Full length on the great earth, full length,
I wept out the dark load of human love.
In pagan adoration I adored her.
I felt the actual earth of her.
Victor and victim of humility,
I closed in the wordless ecstasy
Of mystery: where there is no thought
But feeling lost in itself forever,
Profound, remote, immediate, and calm.
Frightened, I stood up, I looked about
Suspiciously, hurriedly (a rustling),
As if the sun, the air, the trees
Were human, might not understand.
I drew breath, it made a sound,
I stepped gingerly away. Then
The mind came like a fire, it
Tortured man, I thought of madness.
The mind will not accept the blood.
The sun and sky, the trees and grasses,
And the whispering leaves, took on
Their usual characters. I went away,
Slowly, tingling, elated, saying, saying
Mother, Great Being, O Source of Life

To whom in wisdom we return,
Accept this humble servant evermore.

'If I Could Only Live at the Pitch That Is Near Madness'

If I could only live at the pitch that is near madness
When everything is as it was in my childhood
Violent, vivid, and of infinite possibility:
That the sun and the moon broke over my head.

Then I cast time out of the trees and fields,
Then I stood immaculate in the Ego;
Then I eyed the world with all delight,
Reality was the perfection of my sight.

And time has big handles on the hands,
Fields and trees a way of being themselves.
I saw battalions of the race of mankind
Standing stolid, demanding a moral answer.

I gave the moral answer and I died
And into a realm of complexity came
Where nothing is possible but necessity
And the truth wailing there like a red babe.

The Fury of Aerial Bombardment

You would think the fury of aerial bombardment
Would rouse God to relent; the infinite spaces
Are still silent. He looks on shock-pried faces.
History, even, does not know what is meant.

You would feel that after so many centuries
God would give man to repent; yet he can kill
As Cain could, but with multitudinous will,
No farther advanced than in his ancient furies.

Was man made stupid to see his own stupidity?
Is God by definition indifferent, beyond us all?
Is the eternal truth man's fighting soul
Wherein the Beast ravens in its own avidity?

Of Van Wettering I speak, and Averill,
Names on a list, whose faces I do not recall
But they are gone to early death, who late in school
Distinguished the belt feed lever from the belt holding pawl.

The Horse Chestnut Tree

Boys in sporadic but tenacious droves
Come with sticks, as certainly as Autumn,
To assault the great horse chestnut tree.

There is a law governs their lawlessness.
Desire is in them for a shining amulet
And the best are those that are highest up.

They will not pick them easily from the ground.
With shrill arms they fling to the higher branches,
To hurry the work of nature for their pleasure.

I have seen them trooping down the street
Their pockets stuffed with chestnuts shucked, unshucked.
It is only evening keeps them from their wish.

Sometimes I run out in a kind of rage
To chase the boys away: I catch an arm,
Maybe, and laugh to think of being the lawgiver.

I was once such a young sprout myself
And fingered in my pocket the prize and trophy.
But still I moralize upon the day

And see that we, outlaws on God's property,
Fling out imagination beyond the skies,
Wishing a tangible good from the unknown.

And likewise death will drive us from the scene
With the great flowering world unbroken yet,
Which we held in idea, a little handful.

The Tobacconist of Eighth Street

I saw a querulous old man, the tobacconist of Eighth Street.
Scales he had, and he would mix tobacco with his hands
And pour the fragrance in a paper bag.
You walked out selfishly upon the city.

Some ten years I watched him. Fields of Eire
Or of Arabia were in his voice. He strove to please.
The weights of age, of fear were in his eyes,
And on his neck time's cutting edge.

One year I crossed his door. Time had crossed before.
Collapse had come upon him, the collapse of affairs.
He was sick with revolution,
Crepitant with revelation.

And I went howling into the crooked streets,
Smashed with recognition: for him I flayed the air,
For him cried out, and sent a useless prayer
To the disjointed stones that were his only name:

Such insight is one's own death rattling past.

The Cancer Cells

Today I saw a picture of the cancer cells,
Sinister shapes with menacing attitudes.
They had outgrown their test-tube and advanced,
Sinister shapes with menacing attitudes,

Into a world beyond, a virulent laughing gang.
They looked like art itself, like the artist's mind,
Powerful shaker, and the taker of new forms.
Some are revulsed to see these spiky shapes;
It is the world of the future too come to.
Nothing could be more vivid than their language,
Lethal, sparkling and irregular stars,
The murderous design of the universe,
The hectic dance of the passionate cancer cells.
O just phenomena to the calculating eye,
Originals of imagination. I flew
With them in a piled exuberance of time,
My own malignance in their racy, beautiful gestures
Quick and lean: and in their riot too
I saw the stance of the artist's make,
The fixed form in the massive fluxion.

I think Leonardo would have in his disinterest
Enjoyed them precisely with a sharp pencil.

Cousin Florence

There it is, a block of leaping marble
Given to me by an ancestor.
The hands that passed it held down ninety years.
She got it in the love-time of Swinburne.

This woman with her stalwart mien,
More like a Roman than a Greek,
Fumbled among old bags of rubble
For something indomitable that she could seek.

She saw the light of ancient days around her,
Calling in the hip-cracked hospital.
She chose at last. Then the clear light
Of reason stood up strong and tall.

With a pure, commanding grace
She handed me a piece of the Parthenon,
Saying, this I broke with my own hands,
And gave me the imagination of the Greeks.

I thought the spirit of this woman
The tallest that I had ever seen,
Stronger than the marble that I have,
Who was herself imagination's dream

By the moment of such sacrament,
A pure force transmitting love,
Endurance, steadfastness, her calm,
Her Roman heart, to mine, of dream.

I would rather keep her noble acts,
The blood of her powerful character, a mind
As good as any of her time, than search
My upward years for such a stone that leaps.

Off Spectacle Island

Seals and porpoises present
A vivid bestiary
Delightful and odd against the mariner's chart.

The sea bells do not locate them,
Nor lights, nor the starred ledges;
We are unprotected from their lyricism.

They play in the blue bay, in day,
Or whoosh under the midnight moonlight;
We go from point to point where we are going.

I would rather see them playing,
I would rather hear them course
Than reach for Folly from Pride's Light.

Attitudes

IRISH CATHOLIC

After the long wake, when many were drunk,
Pat struggled out to the tracks, seething
Blinded, was struck by a train,
Died too. The funeral was for the mother and son.

The Catholic music soared to the high stones,
Hundreds swayed to the long, compulsive ritual.
As the mourners followed the caskets out
Wave followed wave of misery, of pure release.

NEW ENGLAND PROTESTANT

When Aunt Emily died, her husband would not look at her.
Uncle Peter, inarticulate in his cold intelligence,
Conceded few flowers, arranged the simplest service.
Only the intimate members of the family came.

Then the small procession went to the family grave.
No word was spoken but the parson's solemn few.
Silence, order, a prim dryness, not a tear.
We left the old man standing alone there.

A Ship Burning and a Comet All in One Day

When the tide was out
And the sea was quiet,
We hauled the boat to the edge,
On a fair day in August,
As who, all believing,
Would give decent burial
To the life of a used boat,
Not leave a corpse above ground.

And some, setting fires
On the old and broken deck,
Poured on the kerosene
With a stately quietude,
Measuring out departure,
And others brought libations
In red glasses to the sea's edge,
And all held one in hand.

Then the Captain arose
And poured spirit over the prow
And the sparks flew upward
And consigned her with fierce
Cry and fervent prayer
To immortal transubstantiation.
And the pure nature of air
Received her grace and charm.

And evening came on the sea
As the whole company
Sat upon the harsh rocks
Watching the tide come in
And take the last debris,
And when it became dark
A great comet appeared in the sky
With a star in its nether tail.

Am I My Neighbor's Keeper?

The poetry of tragedy is never dead.
If it were not so I would not dream
On principles so deep they have no ending,
Nor on the ambiguity of what things ever seem.

The truth is hid and shaped in veils of error
Rich, unanswerable, the profound caught in plain air.
Centuries after tragedy sought out Socrates
Its inexplicable essence visits us in our lair,

Say here, on a remote New Hampshire farm.
The taciturn farmer disappeared in pre-dawn.
He had beaten his handyman, but no great harm.
Light spoke vengeance and bloodstains on the lawn.
His trussed corpse later under the dam
Gives to this day no answer, says I am.

Hark Back

To have stepped lightly among European marbles
Dwelling in a pantheon of air;

To have altered the gods in a fact of being;

To have envisaged the marriage
Of everything new with the old,

And sprung a free spirit in the world

Is to have caught my own spirit
On a bicycle in the morning

Riding out of Paris,
Heading South.

My flesh felt so good
I was my own god.

To Laughter, to Leering

When the rigors of the world assail you,
Answer them with gaiety, irreverence, and daring.
When your hope, that grew with morning,
Seems a mockery of life at evening,
Answer hope with laughter and with leering.

46

When love that seemed the best of all
Turned into love of someone else but you,
    Call a mask the seeming true,
Say all is mud and moiling blood and gall,
Seek the heavens for something new and true.

When betrayal in life-situations seems the norm,
Seek hell if it has any tales to tell,
    Burn in dark fires, hear hideous yells,
Say, this is the very ecstasy of form;
Arise again in faith from where you fell.

When the suicide groans, and gives up the ghost,
Lying in great enigma on the floor,
    Throw tears like flowers before the fastened door,
Raise your voice in prayer to the Host,
For did he know what he was dying for?

When you see the new-born baby smiling
Think, the universe asked not your permission
    For continuing, in its startling revision,
Mystery and shrouds compounding and compiling;
Laugh and leer at the child's prevision.

The Spider

I

The spider expects the cold of winter.
When the shadows fall in long Autumn
He congeals in a nest of paper, prepares
The least and minimal existence,
Obedient to nature. No other course
Is his; no other availed him when
In high summer he spun and furled
The gaudy catches. I am that spider,
Caught in nature, summer and winter.
You are the symbol of the seasons too.

II

Now to expatiate and temporize
This artful brag. I never saw so quieting
A sight as the dawn, dew-clenched foot-
Wide web hung on summer barn-eaves, spangled.
It moves to zephyrs that is tough as steel.
I never saw so finely-legged a creature
Walk so accurate a stretch as he,
Proud, capable, patient, confident.
To the eye he gave close penetration
Into real myth, the myth of you, of me.

III

Yet, by moving eyesight off from this
There is another dimension. Near the barn,
Down meadow to shingle, no place for spiders,
The sea in large blue breathes in brainstorm tides,
Pirates itself away to ancient Spain,
Pirouettes past Purgatory to Paradise.
Do I feed deeper on a spider,
A close-hauled view upon windless meaning,
Or deeper a day or dance or doom bestride
On ocean's long reach, on parables of God?

WILLIAM EMPSON

(1906–)

The World's End

"Fly with me then to all's and the world's end
And plumb for safety down the gaps of stars;
Let the last gulf or topless cliff befriend,
What tyrant there our variance debars?"

Alas, how hope for freedom, no bars bind;
Space is like earth, rounded, a padded cell;
Plumb the stars' depth, your lead bumps you behind;
Blind Satan's voice rattled the whole of Hell.

On cushioned air what is such metal worth
To pierce to the gulf that lies so snugly curled?
Each tangent plain touches one top of earth,
Each point in one direction ends the world.

Apple of knowledge and forgetful mere
From Tantalus too differential bend.
The shadow clings. The world's end is here.
This place's curvature precludes its end.

To an Old Lady

Ripeness is all; her in her cooling planet
Revere; do not presume to think her wasted.
Project her no projectile, plan nor man it;
Gods cool in turn, by the sun long outlasted.

Our earth alone given no name of god
Gives, too, no hold for such a leap to aid her;
Landing, you break some palace and seem odd;
Bees sting their need, the keeper's queen invader.

No, to your telescope; spy out the land;
Watch while her ritual is still to see,
Still stand her temples emptying in the sand
Whose waves o'erthrew their crumbled tracery;

Still stand uncalled-on her soul's appanage;
Much social detail whose successor fades,
Wit used to run a house and to play Bridge,
And tragic fervour, to dismiss her maids.

Years her precession do not throw from gear.
She reads a compass certain of her pole;
Confident, finds no confines on her sphere,
Whose failing crops are in her sole control.

Stars how much further from me fill my night.
Strange that she too should be inaccessible,
Who shares my sun. He curtains her from sight,
And but in darkness is she visible.

Camping Out

And now she cleans her teeth into the lake:
Gives it (God's grace) for her own bounty's sake

What morning's pale and the crisp mist debars:
Its glass of the divine (that Will could break)
Restores, beyond Nature: or lets Heaven take
(Itself being dimmed) her pattern, who half awake
Milks between rocks a straddled sky of stars.

Soap tension the star pattern magnifies.
Smoothly Madonna through-assumes the skies
Whose vaults are opened to achieve the Lord.
No, it is we soaring explore galaxies,
Our bullet boat light's speed by thousands flies.
Who moves so among stars their frame unties;
See where they blur, and die, and are outsoared.

Legal Fiction

Law makes long spokes of the short stakes of men.
Your well fenced out real estate of mind
No high flat of the nomad citizen
Looks over, or train leaves behind.

Your rights extend under and above your claim
Without bound; you own land in Heaven and Hell;
Your part of earth's surface and mass the same,
Of all cosmos' volume, and all stars as well.

Your rights reach down where all owners meet, in Hell's
Pointed exclusive conclave, at earth's centre
(Your spun farm's root still on that axis dwells);
And up, through galaxies, a growing sector.

You are nomad yet; the lighthouse beam you own
Flashes, like Lucifer, through the firmament.
Earth's axis varies; your dark central cone
Wavers, a candle's shadow, at the end.

This Last Pain

This last pain for the damned the Fathers found:
"They knew the bliss with which they were not
      crowned."
  Such, but on earth, let me foretell,
  Is all, of heaven or of hell.

Man, as the prying housemaid of the soul,
May know her happiness by eye to hole:
  He's safe; the key is lost; he knows
  Door will not open, nor hole close.

"What is conceivable can happen too,"
Said Wittgenstein, who had not dreamt of you;
  But wisely; if we worked it long
  We should forget where it was wrong.

Those thorns are crowns which, woven into knots,
Crackle under and soon boil fool's pots;
  And no man's watching, wise and long,
  Would ever stare them into song.

Thorns burn to a consistent ash, like man;
A splendid cleanser for the frying-pan:
  And those who leap from pan to fire
  Should this brave opposite admire.

All those large dreams by which men long live well
Are magic-lanterned on the smoke of hell;
  This then is real, I have implied,
  A painted, small, transparent slide.

These the inventive can hand-paint at leisure,
Or most emporia would stock our measure;
  And feasting in their dappled shade
  We should forget how they were made.

Feign then what's by a decent tact believed
And act that state is only so conceived,
    And build an edifice of form
    For house where phantoms may keep warm.

Imagine, then, by miracle, with me,
(Ambiguous gifts, as what gods give must be)
    What could not possibly be there,
    And learn a style from a despair.

Note on Local Flora

There is a tree native in Turkestan,
Or further east towards the Tree of Heaven,
Whose hard cold cones, not being wards to time,
Will leave their mother only for good cause;
Will ripen only in a forest fire;
Wait, to be fathered as was Bacchus once,
Through men's long lives, that image of time's end.
I knew the Phoenix was a vegetable.
So Semele desired her deity
As this in Kew thirsts for the Red Dawn.

Doctrinal Point

The god approached dissolves into the air.

Magnolias, for instance, when in bud,
Are right in doing anything they can think of;
Free by predestination in the blood,
Saved by their own sap, shed for themselves,
Their texture can impose their architecture;
Their sapient matter is always already informed.

Whether they burgeon, massed wax flames, or flare
Plump spaced-out saints, in their gross prime, at prayer,

Or leave the sooted branches bare
To sag at tip from a sole blossom there
They know no act that will not make them fair.

Professor Eddington with the same insolence
Called all physics one tautology;
If you describe things with the right tensors
All law becomes the fact that they can be described with
    them;
This is the Assumption of the description.
The duality of choice becomes the singularity of existence;
The effort of virtue the unconsciousness of foreknowledge.

That over-all that Solomon should wear
Gives these no cope who cannot know of care.
They have no gap to spare that they should share
The rare calyx we stare at in despair.
They have no other that they should compare.
Their arch of promise the wide Heaviside layer
They rise above a vault into the the air.

Your Teeth Are Ivory Towers

There are some critics say our verse is bad
Because Piaget's babies had the same affection,
Proved by interview. These young were mad,

They spoke not to Piaget but to themselves. Protection
Indeed may safely grow less frank; a Ba
Cordial in more than one direction

Can speak well to itself and yet please Pa.
So too Escape Verse has grown mortal sin.
This gives just one advantage; a moral Ha

Can now be retorted in kind. Panoplied in
Virtuous indignation, gnawing his bone,
A man like Leavis plans an Escape. To begin

With brickbats as your basis of the known
Is to lose ground, and these ones were compiled
From a larger building: The safety valve alone

Knows the worst truth about the engine; only the child
Has not yet been misled. You say you hate
Your valve or child? You may be wise or mild.

The claim is that no final judge can state
The truth between you; there is no such man.
This leads to anarchy; we must deliberate.

We could once carry anarchy, when we ran
Christ and the magnificent milord
As rival pets; the thing is, if we still can

Lacking either. Or take Faust, who could afford
"All things that move between the quiet poles"
To be made his own. He had them all on board.

The poles define the surface and it rolls
Between their warring virtues; the spry arts
Can keep a steady hold on the controls

By seeming to evade. But if it parts
Into uncommunicable spacetimes, few
Will hint or ogle, when the stoutest heart's

Best direct yell will never reach; though you
Look through the very corners of your eyes
Still you will find no star behind the blue;

This gives no scope for trickwork. He who tries
Talk must always plot and then sustain,
Talk to himself until the star replies,

Or in despair that it could speak again
Assume what answers any wits have found
In evening dress on rafts upon the main,
Not therefore uneventful or soon drowned.

Aubade

Hours before dawn we were woken by the quake.
My house was on a cliff. The thing could take
Bookloads off shelves, break bottles in a row.
Then the long pause and then the bigger shake.
It seemed the best thing to be up and go.

And far too large for my feet to step by.
I hoped that various buildings were brought low.
The heart of standing is you cannot fly.

It seemed quite safe till she got up and dressed.
The guarded tourist makes the guide the test.
Then I said The Garden? Laughing she said No.
Taxi for her and for me healthy rest.
It seemed the best thing to be up and go.

The language problem but you have to try.
Some solid ground for lying could she show?
The heart of standing is you cannot fly.

None of these deaths were her point at all.
The thing was that being woken he would bawl
And finding her not in earshot he would know.
I tried saying Half an Hour to pay this call.
It seemed the best thing to be up and go.

I slept, and blank as that I would yet lie.
Till you have seen what a threat holds below
The heart of standing is you cannot fly.

Tell me again about Europe and her pains,
Who's tortured by the drought, who by the rains.
Glut me with floods where only the swine can row
Who cuts his throat and let him count his gains.
It seemed the best thing to be up and go.

A bedshift flight to a Far Eastern sky.
Only the same war on a stronger toe.
The heart of standing is you cannot fly.

Tell me more quickly what I lost by this,
Or tell me with less drama what they miss
Who call no die a god for a good throw,
Who say after two aliens had one kiss
It seemed the best thing to be up and go.

But as to risings, I can tell you why.
It is on contradiction that they grow.
It seemed the best thing to be up and go.
Up was the heartening and the strong reply.
The heart of standing is we cannot fly.

Four Legs, Three Legs, Two Legs

Delphic and Theban and Corinthian,
Three lines, by the odd chance, met at a point,
The delta zero, the case trivial.

A young man's cross-road but a shady one.
Killing a mistaken black cat in the dark
He had no other metaphysical trait.

God walks in a mysterious way
Neither delighteth he in any man's legs.

The wrecked girl, still raddled with Napoleon's paint,
Nose eaten by a less clear conqueror,
Still orientated to the average dawn,
Behind, Sahara, before, Nile and man
A toy abandoned, sure, after so many,
That the next sun will take her for a walk,
Still lifts a touching dog's face eager for a sign.

Not one for generalising his solutions
Oedipus placed the riddle with a name.
Another triumph for the commonplace.
While too much to pretend she fell and burst
It is a comfort that the Sphinx took such an answer.

Reflection from Rochester

"But wretched Man is still in arms for Fear."

"From fear to fear, successively betrayed"—
By making risks to give a cause for fear
(Feeling safe with causes, and from birth afraid),

By climbing higher not to look down, by mere
Destruction of the accustomed because strange
(Too complex a loved system, or too clear),

By needing change but not too great a change
And therefore a new fear—man has achieved
All the advantage of a wider range,

Successfully has the first fear deceived,
Thought the wheels run on sleepers. This is not
The law of nature it has been believed.

Increasing power (it has increased a lot)
Embarrasses "attempted suicides,"
Narrows their margin. Policies that got

"Virility from war" get much besides;
The mind, as well in mining as in gas
War's parallel, now less easily decides

On a good root-confusion to amass
Much safety from irrelevant despair.
Mere change in numbers made the process crass.

We now turn blank eyes for a pattern there
Where first the race of armament was made;
Where a less involute compulsion played.
"For hunger or for love they bite and tear."

Ignorance of Death

Then there is this civilising love of death, by which
Even music and painting tell you what else to love.
Buddhists and Christians contrive to agree about death

Making death their ideal basis for different ideals.
The Communists however disapprove of death
Except when practical. The people who dig up

Corpses and rape them are I understand not reported.
The Freudians regard the death-wish as fundamental,
Though "the clamour of life" proceeds from its rival "Eros."

Whether you are to admire a given case for making less clamour
Is not their story. Liberal hopefulness
Regards death as a mere border to an improving picture.

Because we have neither hereditary nor direct knowledge of death
It is the trigger of the literary man's biggest gun
And we are happy to equate it to any conceived calm.

Heaven me, when a man is ready to die about something
Other than himself, and is in fact ready because of that,
Not because of himself, that is something clear about himself.

Otherwise I feel very blank upon this topic,
And think that though important, and proper for anyone to bring up,
It is one that most people should be prepared to be blank upon.

Success

I have mislaid the torment and the fear.
You should be praised for taking them away.
Those that doubt drugs, let them doubt which was here.

Well are they doubted for they turn out dear.
I feed on flatness and am last to leave.
Verse likes despair. Blame it upon the beer
I have mislaid the torment and the fear.

All losses haunt us. It was a reprieve
Made Dostoevsky talk out queer and clear.

Those stay most haunting that most soon deceive

And turn out no loss of the various Zoo
The public spirits or the private play.
Praised once for having taken these away
What is it else then such a thing can do?

Lose is Find with great marsh lights like you.
Those that doubt drugs, let them doubt which was here
When this leaves the green afterlight of day.
Nor they nor I know what we shall believe.
You should be praised for taking them away.

Just a Smack at Auden

Waiting for the end, boys, waiting for the end.
What is there to be or do?
What's become of me or you?
Are we kind or are we true?
Sitting two and two, boys, waiting for the end.

Shall I build a tower, boys, knowing it will rend
Crack upon the hour, boys, waiting for the end?

Shall I pluck a flower, boys, shall I save or spend?
All turns sour, boys, waiting for the end.

Shall I send a wire, boys? Where is there to send?
All are under fire, boys, waiting for the end.
Shall I turn a sire, boys? Shall I choose a friend?
The fat is in the pyre, boys, waiting for the end.

Shall I make it clear, boys, for all to apprehend,
Those that will not hear, boys, waiting for the end,
Knowing it is near, boys, trying to pretend,
Sitting in cold fear, boys, waiting for the end?

Shall we send a cable, boys, accurately penned,
Knowing we are able, boys, waiting for the end,
Via the Tower of Babel, boys? Christ will not ascend.
He's hiding in his stable, boys, waiting for the end.

Shall we blow a bubble, boys, glittering to distend,
Hiding from our trouble, boys, waiting for the end?
When you build on rubble, boys, Nature will append
Double and re-double, boys, waiting for the end.

Shall we make a tale, boys, that things are sure to mend,
Playing bluff and hale, boys, waiting for the end?
It will be born stale, boys, stinking to offend,
Dying ere it fail, boys, waiting for the end.

Shall we go all wild, boys, waste and make them lend,
Playing at the child, boys, waiting for the end?
It has all been filed, boys, history has a trend,
Each of us enisled, boys, waiting for the end.

What was said by Marx, boys, what did he perpend?
No good being sparks, boys, waiting for the end.
Treason of the clerks, boys, curtains that descend,
Lights becoming darks, boys, waiting for the end.

Waiting for the end, boys, waiting for the end.
Not a chance of blend, boys, things have got to tend.
Think of those who vend, boys, think of how we wend,
Waiting for the end, boys, waiting for the end.

Sonnet

Not wrongly moved by this dismaying scene
  The thinkers like the nations getting caught
  Joined in the organising that they fought
To scorch all earth of all but one machine.

It can be swung, is what these hopers mean,
  For all the loony hooters can be bought
  On the small ball. It can then all be taught
And reconverted to be kind and clean.

A more heartening fact about the cultures of man
  Is their appalling stubbornness. The sea
Is always calm ten fathoms down. The gigan-

  tic anthropological circus riotously
Holds open all its booths. The pygmy plan
  Is one note each and the tune goes out free.

Chinese Ballad

Now he has seen the girl Hsiang-Hsiang,
  Now back to the guerrilla band;
And she goes with him down the vale
  And pauses at the strand.

The mud is yellow, deep, and thick,
  And their feet stick, where the stream turns.
"Make me two models out of this,
  That clutches as it yearns.

"Make one of me and one of you,
      And both shall be alive.
Were there no magic in the dolls
      The children could not thrive.

"When you have made them smash them back:
      They yet shall live again.
Again make dolls of you and me
      But mix them grain by grain.

"So your flesh shall be part of mine
      And part of mine be yours.
Brother and sister we shall be
      Whose unity endures.

"Always the sister doll will cry,
      Made in these careful ways,
Cry on and on, Come back to me,
      Come back, in a few days."

THEODORE ROETHKE

(1908–63)

The Cycle

Dark water, underground,
Beneath the rock and clay,
Beneath the roots of trees,
Moved into common day,
Rose from a mossy mound
In mist that sun could seize.

The fine rain coiled in a cloud
Turned by revolving air
Far from that colder source
Where elements cohere
Dense in the central stone.
The air grew loose and loud.

Then, with diminished force,
The full rain fell straight down,
Tunneled with lapsing sound
Under even the rock-shut ground,
Under a river's source,
Under primeval stone.

A *Field of Light*

1

Came to lakes; came to dead water,
Ponds with moss and leaves floating,
Planks sunk in the sand.

A log turned at the touch of a foot;
A long weed floated upward;
An eye tilted.

    Small winds made
    A chilly noise;
    The softest cove
    Cried for sound.

    Reached for a grape
    And the leaves changed;
    A stone's shape
    Became a clam.

    A fine rain fell
    On fat leaves;
    I was there alone
    In a watery drowse.

2

Angel within me, I asked,
Did I ever curse the sun?
Speak and abide.

    Under, under the sheaves,
    Under the blackened leaves,
    Behind the green viscid trellis,
    In the deep grass at the edge of a field,
    Along the low ground dry only in August,—

Was it dust I was kissing?
A sigh came far.

Alone, I kissed the skin of a stone;
Marrow-soft, danced in the sand.

3

The dirt left my hand, visitor.
I could feel the mare's nose.
A path went walking.
The sun glittered on a small rapids.
Some morning thing came, beating its wings.
The great elm filled with birds.

Listen, love,
The fat lark sang in the field;
I touched the ground, the ground warmed by the killdeer,
The salt laughed and the stones;
The ferns had their ways, and the pulsing lizards,
And the new plants, still awkward in their soil,
The lovely diminutives.

I could watch! I could watch!
I saw the separateness of all things!
My heart lifted up with the great grasses;
The weeds believed me, and the nesting birds.
There were clouds making a rout of shapes crossing a windbreak of
        cedars,
And a bee shaking drops from a rain-soaked honeysuckle.
The worms were delighted as wrens.
And I walked, I walked through the light air;
I moved with the morning.

Praise to the End!

1

It's dark in this wood, soft mocker.
For whom have I swelled like a seed?
What a bone-ache I have.
Father of tensions, I'm down to my skin at last.

66

It's a great day for the mice.
Prickle-me, tickle-me, close stems.
Bumpkin, he can dance alone.
Ooh, ooh, I'm a duke of eels.

Arch my back, pretty-bones, I'm dead at both ends.
Softly softly, you'll wake the clams.
I'll feed the ghost alone.
Father, forgive my hands.

The rings have gone from the pond.
The river's alone with its water.
All risings
Fall.

2

Where are you now, my bonny beating gristle,
My blue original dandy, numb with sugar?
Once I fished from the banks, leaf-light and happy:
On the rocks south of quiet, in the close regions of kissing,
I romped, lithe as a child, down the summery streets of my veins,
Strict as a seed, nippy and twiggy.
Now the water's low. The weeds exceed me.
It's necessary, among the flies and bananas, to keep a constant vigil,
For the attacks of false humility take sudden turns for the worse.
Lacking the candor of dogs, I kiss the departing air;
I'm untrue to my own excesses.

Rock me to sleep, the weather's wrong.
Speak to me, frosty beard.
Sing to me, sweet.

Mips and ma the mooly moo,
The likes of him is biting who,
A cow's a care and who's a coo?—
What footie does is final.

My dearest dear my fairest fair,
Your father tossed a cat in air,

67

Though neither you nor I was there,—
What footie does is final.

Be large as an owl, be slick as a frog,
Be good as a goose, be big as a dog,
Be sleek as a heifer, be long as a hog,—
What footie will do will be final.

I conclude! I conclude!
My dearest dust, I can't stay here.
I'm undone by the flip-flap of odious pillows.
An exact fall of waters has rendered me impotent.
I've been asleep in a bower of dead skin.
It's a piece of a prince I ate.
This salt can't warm a stone.
These lazy ashes.

3

The stones were sharp,
The wind came at my back;
Walked along the highway,
Mincing like a cat.

The sun came out;
The lake turned green;
Romped upon the goldy grass,
Aged thirteen.

The sky cracked open
The world I knew;
Lay like the cats do
Sniffing the dew.

I dreamt I was all bones;
The dead slept in my sleeve;
Sweet Jesus tossed me back:
I wore the sun with ease.

The several sounds were low;
The river ebbed and flowed:
Desire was winter-calm,
A moon away.

Such owly pleasures! Fish come first, sweet bird.
Skin's the least of me. Kiss this.
Is the eternal near, fondling?
I hear the sound of hands.

Can the bones breathe? This grave has an ear.
It's still enough for the knock of a worm.

I feel more than a fish.
Ghost, come closer.

4

Arch of air, my heart's original knock,
I'm awake all over:
I've crawled from the mire, alert as a saint or a dog;
I know the back-stream's joy, and the stone's eternal pulseless longing.
Felicity I cannot hoard.
My friend, the rat in the wall, brings me the clearest messages;
I bask in the bower of change;
The plants wave me in, and the summer apples;
My palm-sweat flashes gold;
Many astounds before, I lost my identity to a pebble;
The minnows love me, and the humped and spitting creatures.

I believe! I believe!—
In the sparrow, happy on gravel;
In the winter-wasp, pulsing its wings in the sunlight;
I have been somewhere else; I remember the sea-faced uncles.
I hear, clearly, the heart of another singing,
Lighter than bells,
Softer than water.

Wherefore, O birds and small fish, surround me.
Lave me, ultimate waters.
The dark showed me a face.
My ghosts are all gay.
The light becomes me.

The Waking

I wake to sleep, and take my waking slow.
I feel my fate in what I cannot fear.
I learn by going where I have to go.

We think by feeling. What is there to know?
I hear my being dance from ear to ear.
I wake to sleep, and take my waking slow.

Of those so close beside me, which are you?
God bless the Ground! I shall walk softly there,
And learn by going where I have to go.

Light takes the Tree; but who can tell us how?
The lowly worm climbs up a winding stair;
I wake to sleep, and take my waking slow.

Great Nature has another thing to do
To you and me; so take the lively air,
And, lovely, learn by going where to go.

This shaking keeps me steady. I should know.
What falls away is always. And is near.
I wake to sleep, and take my waking slow.
I learn by going where I have to go.

I Knew a Woman

I knew a woman, lovely in her bones,
When small birds sighed, she would sigh back at them;

Ah, when she moved, she moved more ways than one:
The shapes a bright container can contain!
Of her choice virtues only gods should speak,
Or English poets who grew up on Greek
(I'd have them sing in chorus, cheek to cheek).

How well her wishes went! She stroked my chin,
She taught me Turn, and Counter-turn, and Stand;
She taught me Touch, that undulant white skin;
I nibbled meekly from her proffered hand;
She was the sickle; I, poor I, the rake,
Coming behind her for her pretty sake
(But what prodigious mowing we did make).

Love likes a gander, and adores a goose:
Her full lips pursed, the errant note to seize;
She played it quick, she played it light and loose;
My eyes, they dazzled at her flowing knees;
Her several parts could keep a pure repose,
Or one hip quiver with a mobile nose
(She moved in circles, and those circles moved).

Let seed be grass, and grass turn into hay:
I'm martyr to a motion not my own;
What's freedom for? To know eternity.
I swear she cast a shadow white as stone.
But who would count eternity in days?
These old bones live to learn her wanton ways:
(I measure time by how a body sways).

The Far Field

I

I dream of journeys repeatedly:
Of flying like a bat deep into a narrowing tunnel,
Of driving alone, without luggage, out a long peninsula,

The road lined with snow-laden second growth,
A fine dry snow ticking the windshield,
Alternate snow and sleet, no on-coming traffic,
And no lights behind, in the blurred side-mirror,
The road changing from glazed tarface to a rubble of stone,
Ending at last in a hopeless sand-rut,
Where the car stalls,
Churning in a snowdrift
Until the headlights darken.

II

At the field's end, in the corner missed by the mower,
Where the turf drops off into a grass-hidden culvert,
Haunt of the cat-bird, nesting-place of the field-mouse,
Not too far away from the ever-changing flower-dump,
Among the tin cans, tires, rusted pipes, broken machinery,—
One learned of the eternal;
And in the shrunken face of a dead rat, eaten by rain and ground-
    beetles
(I found it lying among the rubble of an old coal bin)
And the tom-cat, caught near the pheasant-run,
Its entrails strewn over the half-grown flowers,
Blasted to death by the night watchman.

I suffered for birds, for young rabbits caught in the mower,
My grief was not excessive.
For to come upon warblers in early May
Was to forget time and death:
How they filled the oriole's elm, a twittering restless cloud, all one
    morning,
And I watched and watched till my eyes blurred from the bird shapes,—
Cape May, Blackburnian, Cerulean,—
Moving, elusive as fish, fearless,
Hanging, bunched like young fruit, bending the end branches,
Still for a moment,
Then pitching away in half-flight,
Lighter than finches,
While the wrens bickered and sang in the half-green hedgerows,
And the flicker drummed from his dead tree in the chicken-yard.

—Or to lie naked in sand,
In the silted shallows of a slow river,
Fingering a shell,
Thinking:
Once I was something like this, mindless,
Or perhaps with another mind, less peculiar;
Or to sink down to the hips in a mossy quagmire;
Or, with skinny knees, to sit astride a wet log,
Believing:
I'll return again,
As a snake or a raucous bird,
Or, with luck, as a lion.

I learned not to fear infinity,
The far field, the windy cliffs of forever,
The dying of time in the white light of tomorrow,
The wheel turning away from itself,
The sprawl of the wave,
The on-coming water.

III

The river turns on itself,
The tree retreats into its own shadow.
I feel a weightless change, a moving forward
As of water quickening before a narrowing channel
When banks converge, and the wide river whitens;
Or when two rivers combine, the blue glacial torrent
And the yellowish-green from the mountainy upland,—
At first a swift rippling between rocks,
Then a long running over flat stones
Before descending to the alluvial plain,
To the clay banks, and the wild grapes hanging from the elmtrees,
The slightly trembling water
Dropping a fine yellow silt where the sun stays;
And the crabs bask near the edge,
The weedy edge, alive with small snakes and bloodsuckers,—

I have come to a still, but not a deep center,
A point outside the glittering current;

My eyes stare at the bottom of a river,
At the irregular stones, iridescent sandgrains,
My mind moves in more than one place,
In a country half-land, half-water.

I am renewed by death, thought of my death,
The dry scent of a dying garden in September,
The wind fanning the ash of a low fire.
What I love is near at hand,
Always, in earth and air.

IV

The lost self changes,
Turning toward the sea,
A sea-shape turning around,—
An old man with his feet before the fire,
In robes of green, in garments of adieu.

A man faced with his own immensity
Wakes all the waves, all their loose wandering fire.
The murmur of the absolute, the why
Of being born fails on his naked ears.
His spirit moves like monumental wind
That gentles on a sunny blue plateau.
He is the end of things, the final man.

All finite things reveal infinitude:
The mountain with its singular bright shade
Like the blue shine on freshly frozen snow,
The after-light upon ice-burdened pines;
Odor of basswood on a mountain-slope,
A scent beloved of bees;
Silence of water above a sunken tree:
The pure serene of memory in one man,—
A ripple widening from a single stone
Winding around the waters of the world.

Light Listened

O what could be more nice
Than her ways with a man?
She kissed me more than twice
Once we were left alone.
Who'd look when he could feel?
She'd more sides than a seal.

The close air faintly stirred.
Light deepened to a bell,
The love-beat of a bird.
She kept her body still
And watched the weather flow.
We live by what we do.

All's known, all, all around:
The shape of things to be;
A green thing loves the green
And loves the living ground.
The deep shade gathers night;
She changed with changing light.

We met to leave again
The time we broke from time;
A cold air brought its rain,
The singing of a stem.
She sang a final song;
Light listened when she sang.

Otto

I

He was the youngest son of a strange brood,
A Prussian who learned early to be rude

To fools and frauds: He does not put on airs
Who lived above a potting shed for years.
I think of him, and I think of his men,
As close to him as any kith or kin.
Max Laurisch had the greenest thumb of all.
A florist does not woo the beautiful:
He potted plants as if he hated them.
What root of his ever denied its stem?
When flowers grew, their bloom extended him.

II

His hand could fit into a woman's glove,
And in a wood he knew whatever moved;
Once when he saw two poachers on his land,
He threw his rifle over with one hand;
Dry bark flew in their faces from his shot,—
He always knew what he was aiming at.
They stood there with their guns; he walked toward,
Without his rifle, and slapped each one hard;
It was no random act, for those two men
Had slaughtered game, and cut young fir trees down.
I was no more than seven at the time.

III

A house for flowers! House upon house they built,
Whether for love or out of obscure guilt
For ancestors who loved a warlike show,
Or Frenchmen killed a hundred years ago,
And yet still violent men, whose stacked-up guns
Killed every cat that neared their pheasant runs;
When Hattie Wright's angora died as well,
My father took it to her, by the tail.
Who loves the small can be both saint and boor,
(And some grow out of shape, their seed impure;)
The Indians loved him, and the Polish poor.

IV

In my mind's eye I see those fields of glass,
As I looked out at them from the high house,
Riding beneath the moon, hid from the moon,
Then slowly breaking whiter in the dawn;
When George the watchman's lantern dropped from sight
The long pipes knocked: it was the end of night.
I'd stand upon my bed, a sleepless child
Watching the waking of my father's world,—
O world so far away! O my lost world!

In a Dark Time

In a dark time, the eye begins to see.
I meet my shadow in the deepening shade;
I hear my echo in the echoing wood—
A lord of nature weeping to a tree.
I live between the heron and the wren,
Beasts of the hill and serpents of the den.

What's madness but nobility of soul
At odds with circumstance? The day's on fire!
I know the purity of pure despair,
My shadow pinned against a sweating wall.
That place among the rocks—is it a cave,
Or winding path? The edge is what I have.

A steady storm of correspondences!
A night flowing with birds, a ragged moon,
And in broad day the midnight comes again!
A man goes far to find out what he is—

77

Death of the self in a long, tearless night,
All natural shapes blazing unnatural light.

Dark, dark my light, and darker my desire.
My soul, like some heat-maddened summer fly,
Keeps buzzing at the sill. Which I is I?
A fallen man, I climb out of my fear.
The mind enters itself, and God the mind,
And one is One, free in the tearing wind.

CARL BODE

(1911–)

from "THE SACRED SEASONS"

III: Feast of Saint Andrew the Apostle

The splendid arc of fishnet cast wide upon the sea
Involves no school; the subtle fish stay free.
The cords reticulate the water in inter-angled swells,
With brown lines patterning over the stately wells.
The men who man the boat refuse to understand
That of the oaken boat submerged by sand
Only the sheathed bottom and the ribs are left.
They stare; they wonder of what they are bereft.

That net was cast by no one; yet who is really free?
The net, itself surrounded, all too soon will be
Twisted, torn of cordage, warped, and ragged of weft;
And though the flashing fish are dialectic, swift and deft
They still will gasp upon the sand—within the sunken boat—
While the torpid fishers of men hold freedom by the throat.

XII: Eastertide

Oh stupid miracle of my own devising,
To be seen in spite of soot flakes floating down,

Spring shall be here—only through my arising
Into this deadened town.

The last snow in the street has just dried away,
Leaving its little drifts of dirt behind.
The squares of lawn before each house are grey
And the windows are blind.

Shortly, some people will come to look for me;
But, till now, the only sign of life anywhere
Has been some chimney smoke rising quietly
Into the vacant air.

Now, having lain in a cellar three blank days,
I arise. But it is my own new life I put
Into the renascent town . . . My own face greys
Under the last flecks of soot.

from ''LONDON SONNETS''

III: The City Considered as a Tulip Tree

On the smooth steep escalator, four storeys'
Rise or fall, see the nimble people run;
From tube to tube their hats or skirts are blown
Their filaments stream undone

And yet such strands will seldom tangle; eyes
Avoid eyes and fix upon a moving stair
That takes them to the tulip beds strict yet
Supple in the English air.

A purple almost black, an honest pink,
Globed yellow cupped with its own aquamarine;
Bed after partied bed. The escalators
Stop now steeped in decent green.

The breeze dies, the colours hold their place,
Watched by watchers stilled of face.

VI: *Who Calls the English Cold?*

Who calls the English cold? Eros is
Everywhere: lying on Hyde Park's summer lawn
The couples of young London touch; beyond
The bole of every tree there peeps the faun.

Canes tap on the gravelled walk, old ladies
Pass close by, skiffs skim the Serpentine
Yet there is only mouth on mouth
And a quickening as arms entwine.

Alone the visitor keeps the bench, having
Briskly walked nowhere; head back and eyes aslant
He regards the guttering day and hears the
Words of love as Hyde Park orators' rant.

Seizing his cane or skiff, louring at the faun,
He strides the swelling lawn up to the road above
Where his orator proclaims
Universal love.

XV: *Covent Garden Market*

By God I hate to grow old.
Resignation, pushcart philosophy,
White dry film, geraniums drowned in tea;
Each hair lost or greyed turns me cold,
Lines scored on my face do not need to bleed;
Beyond the Covent Gardener hawking fruit,
Black apples, melons, berries, turned to suit
The epicure, who feeds on maggots as the maggots feed.

What can deceive me? The mind itself, the very soul,
Wears through; the peddler falls across his cart,
Yellow and limp, soon for someone else to push
    Away—no tipping at the Burning Bush—
    Stand and deliver at the crumbling hole!
Let no black-coated fool dare take my part
And mumble over me that everything that stops must start.

Personal Letter to the Ephesians

    Breaking through the sandy soil
    The bony finger rises, then
    Grows into an arm;
    And all can see the bony mouth
    Fixed on the word Alarm.

    But none can taste the salt
    Of terror, not having died
    Themselves, not having known
    The smothering grave nor
    The crushing weight of stone.

    But these bones of John the Baptist
    Will flower into flesh
    And he will walk anointed
    With oils of fragrant hawthorn,
    Bright bleeding-heart and pointed

    Valentine. There is no life
    Without a death, perhaps no
    Peace without a terror.
    Beware of crying out the truth
    Unless, O men of Ephesus,
    You also speak in error.

The Bad Children

The children of light—mongoloid,
Hydrocephalic, crazed, awry—
Will build their glass houses
Out of shards of pale sky
Or brittle splinters of causes.

Their names will be biblical,
Esther, Naomi, Levi, Moses,
Or else cheap blue plastic,
Charlene, Joni, Sondra, Elvis.
Their minds will be lame or spastic,

Their hearts futile. While they
Play with their impossible toys
Their parents, aching, will stand
And watch them. Outside, the healthy noise
Of other children, playing Pretend,

Joyously aping the children of light,
Will meet the ears of the wordless
Parents. And they will stop and ponder
The rich health of the children of darkness,
Who deny God. And they will wonder

(The fathers turning to the mothers),
They will wonder as they try to measure
Sure causes against clumsy effects,
Which is worse, God's displeasure
In this world or the next?

Requiem

So. They and I are back from the outside.
Sitting in the cold sunlight of the parlour

We agree, with no pride,
That we never saw so many lovely flowers.
Petals still lie on the rug; the heavy scent has not died.

There is not much else for us to talk
About really—not much to say or do,
Except to get up and walk
Around in the cold, scented sunlight; so I sit
Looking down, and pull into strands a piece of flower stalk.

I think, of course, of that night last year
When I dreamt that you need not have died, so that my
Mind was filled with a dull, queer
Kind of loneliness which would not go away for
A long while; I remember it well as I sit here.

And I well remember those flowers,
Thick leaves with dust on them, coarse hairy stems
Forced by late summer showers.
The blooms were large and had a flat, metallic
Odour. They were bouquets of love, they were ours.

The Burial of Terror

How green the green at Salem is,
The lawn below the sea,
So lay a lace upon the face,
The face no longer his
Nor like to be,

A gauze upon the curious gaze
And then in sea-green fear
At the trees bent over the lawn
Let him go his curious ways,
Or far or near,

To the richness of the water. Why,
Peace has never been here.
Yet who can say where it has gone?
Who has seen it disappear?

Sonnet: Head Next to Mine

Head next to mine but turned aside, you lie
As if you had to listen to make love—
As if the central sense were sound, not touch,
As if a brittle word were an impatient shove;

But too as if the smallest sigh came from
The finger lightly laid upon your hair;
Or from a tense embrace, wave after wave
Of subtle resonance along the air.

What do you hear? Brows knit, eyes anxiously
Intent, your face shows that the oncoming sound
Must be austere or shrill; and I myself
No longer feel—or hear—my pulses pound;

Until I feel your mouth answer my seeking—
And then I know lips were not made for speaking.

Sonnet: The Window

My wife asleep, her soft face turned from me,
My children sleeping in their rooms as well,
I get up, drawn to the window, to see what I must see:
Silver, and black and silver. There is almost a silver smell.

The moon on this burnished California hill,
The stars with their sober silver spark.
I know. And the savor of the night through the patch of dill.
If I could drink aromatics or take eucalyptus bark,

If I could drink sense and have its glow to keep,
Or even if I could bathe the folded shapes of words
With any light of mine this once, then I could sleep.
Straining, I stand and can hear no sound, no wind, no birds . . .

But all at once there comes the howl of a far-off hound
And all that I want to say is said in that single sound.

Variation on a Theme by Dylan Thomas

Why, everyone speaks Welsh; the stipple sheen;
Of pink. Black stitching through the opal floor;
You ask aghast, what do those people mean
And each brick-bombast wall becomes a door.

Before that, though, the empyrean opens up,
Tongues of angels tickled at their tips,
Coal miners filing down the valleys for to sup
Never even swipe their blackened lips.

And earlier still, the public wife has stood
Where billows beat against the robbing line.
What she has done was for the public good—
Water for arid Wales, surcease at the mine.

And earliest of all, the lush green lay,
The loving, easy land where no one went away.

The Planet

The solid ocean and the liquid land:
On both—free from my cage of ribs, dressed
In my Sunday best—I steadfast stand
Or sailing sing hosannas which call me blest.

86

Onward the ritual winds, the vestments sway.
Through the church windows the rain shines down
In lucent drops upon the sunny day.
And I—I die indefinitely of brown.

I rise; to ponder puzzles or to peer
At the prettiest girls in church. I sit;
And stare at the blonde one kneeling near.
I kneel; and undress her lovingly, bit by bit.

Until at last, the benediction done,
I bolt; and see you beckoning in the sun.

The Nocturne

Why the hell do you use all that black
In your painting, my neighbor asks across the fence.
I thumb my canvases, the oboes going slack,
Flutes elegantly wailing, the colors colors of elegance.

Of course the concert stops; the composer done,
He wipes his hands upon a greasy rag of fire
Replying flatly that he was only having fun
And who the hell are you, may I inquire?

I crane my neck upon the latest night.
It shapes and opens up into arcades
And avenues and pergolas of light.
My eye, now leading its battalions on, invades
The widening valleys, the martial music bright
With scimitars; and everywhere the neighbors lean on spades.

KENNETH PATCHEN

(1911–)

At the New Year

In the shape of this night, in the still fall
    of snow, Father
In all that is defenseless and lost, even as
    the lives of your children
In everything that moves tonight, the trolleys
    and the lovers, Father
In the great hush of fields, in the ugly noise
    of our cities
In this frosty gaze of stars, in those trenches
    where the slain are, Father
In all this wide land waiting, in the great liners
    pitching toy-like upon the shroud-cold sea
In all that has been said honestly, in all that is
    petty and mean at this hour, Father
In all that is good and lovely, in every house
    where sham and hatred are
In the name of those who wait without hope, in the
    sound of angry voices, Father
Before the bells ring, O before this tiny moment
    has become swollen with the grief of a world
Before it becomes as guilt-soiled and hideous as the
    lives of your children, Father
O there is this high clean singing in the air

O forever this sorrowful human face in eternity's window
And there are other bells that we would ring, Father
O there are other bells that we would ring!

'Do I Not Deal with Angels'

Do I not deal with angels
When her lips I touch

So gentle, *so warm and sweet*—falsity
Has no sight of her
O the world is a place of veils and roses
When she is there

I am come to her wonder
Like a boy finding a star in a haymow
And there is nothing cruel or mad or evil
Anywhere

What the Grecian Earns

I do not count the day
Unless something proves life.

The sick who sauce their doings with God
Will not rank an apple with an emperor;
Little more can I distinguish between the garments
Of fortune and what fools wear—because
Heaven's pitchmen can sell me anything.

I am willing to be gentle.
I am willing to be gathered into my place.
What hurried over the womb I was in
Won't lack for speed to leave me now.
I shall not be divided by the angels
Who float about in flimsy nightshirts on wet clouds.

89

What gives scope to summer made the continents
Of greed and murder; put man in his little box
And slammed tight the lid. But my wound
Does not ask salve from cannibals, nor do I expect
Fleece to grow on doorknobs—because
The world's pitchmen can sell me nothing.

I am willing to be shaped.
I am willing to be shipped on the first celestial jaunt.

'The Carts of the Wee Blind Lass'

The carts of the wee blind lass
Were covered with silvery wool
That shone on the road
Like sheep walking with God.
Her hair was caught in a fine knot
At the toe of her brain, and her eyes
Had been painted over by imps of heaven.
She held her name in a little dish,
And always at crossings she cried it.

The carts were pulled by horses
Fashioned of mountain-bones
And the anger of yellow eagles.
Their wheels rolled on a single track
That led a little above the air.

And what sell ye, my pretty?
It is nothing I sell, true sir.

Then what do ye bring? lassie say . . .
It is apples I bring. Yet none for you.

Now tell me short the name of this good lad
That I may send him spinning . . .

Then spin the devil, my happy wit;
For my apples are for him.
O take my pretty apples, Mr. Dark!
O all my juicy ripe apples are for thee!

'Rest, Heart of the Tired World'

Rest, heart of the tired world.
Hush . . . go to sleep.
Men and cities keep their cold terrible watches,
And the ocean frets at these naked lands of pain.
O hushabye . . . and go to sleep.

This red rain . . .
To breathe . . .
To weep . . .
To love where only murder has been lain . . .
To find youth, and faith, and all their quick kin,
Buried deep in talking halls of horror . . .
No.
It is that we cannot see,
That we cannot hear,
That we cannot smell,
Or taste, or feel, or think;
For surely no will in heaven or earth
Could endure what we seem to possess;
We live in the shadow of a greater shadow—
But there is the sun!
And from him man shall have life,
And he shall have redress from the crimes
Of his most brutal habitation . . .

O rest, heart of the tired world.
Hush . . . and go to sleep.
There is a beautiful work for all men to do,
And we shall at last wake into the sun.

Now I Went Down to the Ringside and Little Henry Armstrong Was There

They've got some pretty horses up in the long dark mountains.
Get him, boy!

They've got some nifty riders away yonder on that big sad road.
Get him, boy!

They've got some tall talk off in that damn fine garden.
Get him, boy!

When you can't use your left, then let the right go.
When your arms get tired, hit him with a wing.
When you can't see very good, smell where he is.

They've got some juicy steaks in that nice sweet by-and-by.
Get him, boy!

They've got a lot of poor black lads in that crummy old jailhouse.
Get him, boy!

O they've got a lot of clean bunks up in their big wide blue sky.
That's his number, boy!

'Christ! Christ! Christ! That the World'

Christ! Christ! Christ! that the world
Should be so dark and cold for many!
That there should be hungry and sick and homeless
In every land on earth . . .

My heart fills with pity and anger . . .
Goddamn all these filthy butchering swine!

O that there should be maimed and broken and mad
In every land on this beautiful earth . . .

Christ! Christ! Christ! that the world
Should be so dark and cold for so many!

Land of the Never-Ending Heart

Lights of people shandle holiness . . .
    and in the noon herds of birds
    wanker over a bluement that
    peaceables the flower and the flow
    of days and trees and the haunted
High walking of the dead shakes
Its white harness out upon the whiteness
That has no stain. O larks
Of women sing at doors
    and in the twilight lanes of darks
    hurry to their sparkling chores.

Pale fish nudge sleepily through ferns pale
As breasts . . . as crests
Of forgotten legends ponder mysteries
    which have slain and have given
    grace to men. Then lace of wonder
    clothes heaven's unfrolicking kings
Who have lain there very long.

O hills of spirits guard each pure thing . . .
And in its singing find their song.

'O When I Take My Love Out Walking'

O when I take my love out walking
In the soft frosted stillness of this summer moon

Then are the mysteries all around us
O what can I say!

    the ever-known, the ever-new
    like her they seem
O lully, lullay
    only this little moment is real
Here at the edge of the world
    and the throne. The rest's a lie
    which shadows scheme.

Now gentle flowers are awash on the sleeping hill
And as I bend to kiss her opened lips
O then do the wonders and the sparklings seem
A shabby tinsel show for my dear queen.

The New Being

They'd make you believe that your problem is one of sex,
That men and women have mysteriously become
Strange and fearful to one another—sick, diseased, cold—
And that is true. But no loss of a father-image or of
Any other image, did this. Why don't you face the truth for once?
You have accepted the whole filthy, murderous swindle without
A word of protest, hated whomever you were told to hate,
Slaughtered whomever you were told to slaughter; you've lied,
Cheated, made the earth stink with your very presence—Why
Shouldn't you despise and hate one another? Why shouldn't
Your flesh crawl everytime you touch one another?
Why should you expect to make 'love' in a bed fouled with corpses?

Oh, you poor, weak little frauds, sucking around
Frantically for something to ease your guilt—
Why don't you face it?
Your birthright, liferight,
Deathright, and now your
Sexright, you've lost. What
Did you expect? How
Else could it be? You've
Made property and money your only gods—

Well, this is their rule,
This is what you wanted.
And now they'll wipe you out.
Why don't you face it?
Stop sucking around.
Your pet witch-doctors can't help you,
They're all sick from the same thing.
Your pompous intellectuals can't help you,
They're all sick from the same thing.
Your sly, vicious statesmen can't help you,
They're all sick from the same thing.
Why don't you face it?

No, your problem is not one of sex—
Your problem is that you have betrayed your animal
Into hands as cruel and bloody as your own.
Man is dead.
I don't know what kind of thing you are.

In the Moonlight

They step through the moonlight
The cool snowy curtains
Of the moonlight
Brushing over them like wings

Of some chaste insect

And their heads
Their arching necks and flowering antlers
Are like a music
Like chimes in the moonlight

Sounding down the ghostly

Forest paths
Like trumpets made of water

Kings
Announcing a dream savior
To a world of shadows
See, they
Stride through the moonlight

Specters of the moonlight

For Miriam

As beautiful as the hands
Of a winter tree
And as holy
O base are they beside thee

As dross beside thee

O green birds
That sing the earth to wakefulness
As tides the sea
O drab are they beside thee

As tinsel beside thee

O pure
And fair as the clouds
Wandering
Over a summer field
They are crass beside thee
Hands that
Move through the starhair

O tawdry are they beside thee

An Easy Decision

I had finished my dinner
Gone for a walk
It was fine
Out and I started whistling

It wasn't long before

I met a
Man and his wife riding on
A pony with seven
Kids running along beside them

I said hello and

Went on
Pretty soon I met another
Couple
This time with nineteen
Kids and all of them
Riding on
A big smiling hippopotamus

I invited them home

In a Crumbling

Majesty of horns sweeps in the stagtide . . .

After such glory . . . the glory of that vast frosty wood there
. . . O the belling of that glory bringing a face to each of night's cold
windows—this defeat, this death, this petty corruption . . . He stumbled to his knees, and the proud forehead of his running broke upon
the sand like an egg.

(Ah, the angry, lung-colored stain that flowered at his bridle, that spilled like a cottony cheese over his withers and harness-buckling . . . that raged like a tattering doom of flags above the chariot there . . . that rose like the grim pale frost of an agony above the decaying splinter of wheels . . .)

The stain widens, briefly . . . hesitates . . . then drains back without trace.

The Great Sled-Makers

They get drunk, these Great Sled-Makers. Their copper mugs, around which their fingers easily circle once, and once again, hold what's called a "quart handsome" (about five and ⅜s gallons mirke-measure).

The Great Sled-Makers get drunk like other people do hopeless. An hour or two old they demand whiskey, and poor slap–hoppy brute the mother who'd not lay them lovely on . . . all pink-fuzzy, ah, happy little belchers, rest ye well in between the worlds, as you might say.

Seven sees most married. Typically they live above saloons, their sole furniture a firehouse pole.

For, you must understand, it doesn't take a few hours or even a few days to make a Great-Sled; it takes closer to a thousand years.

Eleven have been built so far, not counting of course those which slip away from time to time (no doubt you've heard of tidal waves and earthquakes). Each is heavier than all the mountains placed together on a table having proper equipment for weighing of this sort; each requires a highway of at least a million lanes . . . at the very least. In other words, the Great-Sleds are not small. Just picture them! with their runners of molten silver, their golden bodies painted a screaming red under a zigzag of yellow and buff stripes. The effect is quite nice. Only so far, you've probably guessed by now, nobody's bought nary a one.—*Whh-iskey, bo-oy!*

Where?

> There's a place the man always say
> Come in here, child
> No cause you should weep
> Wolf never catch the rabbit
> Golden hair never turn white with grief
> Come in here, child
> No cause you should moan
> Brother never hurt his brother
> Nobody here ever wander without a home
> There must be some such place somewhere
> But I never heard of it

O She is as Lovely-Often

O she is as lovely-often as every day; the day following the day . . . the day of our lives, the brief day

Within this moving room, this shadowy oftenness of days where the hurry of our lives is said . . . O as lovely-often as the moving wing of a bird.

But ah, alas, sooner or later each of us must stand before that grim Roman Court, and be judged free of even such lies as I have told about the imperishable beauty of her hair. But that time is not now, and even such lies as I told about the enduring wonder of her grace, are lies that contain within them the only truth by which a man may live in this world.

O she is as lovely-often as every day; the day following the day . . . the day of our lives, ah, alas, the brief day.

'O Now the Drenched Land Wakes'

> O now the drenched land wakes;
> Birds from their sleep call

Fitfully, and are still.
Clouds like milky wounds
Float across the moon.

O love, none may
Turn away long
From this white grove
Where all nouns grieve.

Because He Liked to Be at Home

He usually managed to be there when
He arrived. A horse, his name was
Hunry Fencewaver Walkins—he'd sometimes
Be almost too tired to make it;
Because, since he also hated being alone,
He was always on the alert to pop forth
At a full run whenever the door opened.
Then one day it happened—
He didn't get there in time!
Of course he couldn't risk opening the door—
So, panting, he just stood there in the hall—
And listened to the terrible sound of himself weeping
In that room he could never, never enter again.

Because My Hands Hear the Flowers Thinking

I scooped up the moon's footprints but
The ground climbed past with a sky
And a dove and a bent vapor.
The other half of cling together wove by
In the breath of the willows: O fall in
Fall in! sang eagle ox ferret elm and riverbank . . .
And we, O we too must learn to live here!
To usefully use what we are! O fall in
Fall in beside our brothers! For only in giving

Love may we achieve trust and true community. O
Of these wondrous likenesses, none, O none at all
Can we know unless we take the giving of love
As our pledge and only law! O in this lion-leaf,
This glory of a son's unseeking belief that soars
Over every road where his mother walks in the
Splendor and mystery of birth-death . . . O there!
In that known unknown country . . . O there may we
See with the eyes of grass; hear our own voices
In the speaking of the trees; and touch our lives
With hands of rock and hurrying mountains . . . O on
The floor of the seas, and at the back of this dead
Bird's radiant face, our lives are watching us—
I think they are not lived in this world

BROTHER ANTONINUS
(1912–)

August

Smoke color:
Haze thinly over the hills, low hanging,
But the sky steel, the sky shiny as steel, and the sun shouting.
The vineyard: in August the green-deep and heat-loving vines
Without motion grow heavy with grapes.
And he in the shining, on the turned earth, loose-lying,
The muscles clean and the limbs golden, turns to the sun the
    lips and the eyes;
As the virgin yields, impersonally passionate,
From the bone core and the aching flesh, the offering.

He has found the power and come to the glory.
He has turned clean-hearted to the last god, the symbolic sun.
With earth on his hands, bearing shoulder and arm the light's
    touch, he has come.
And having seen, the mind loosens, the nerve lengthens,
All the haunting abstractions slip free and are gone;
And the peace is enormous.

The Stranger

    Pity this girl.
    At callow sixteen,

Glib in the press of rapt companions,
She bruits her smatter,
Her bed-lore brag.
She prattles the lip-learned, light-love list.
In the new itch and squirm of sex,
How can she foresee?

How can she foresee the thick stranger,
Over the hills from Omaha,
Who will break her across a hired bed,
Open the loins,
Rive the breach,
And set the foetus wailing within the womb,
To hunch toward the knowledge of its disease,
And shamble down time to doomsday?

Hospice of the Word

Maurin House, Fifth & Washington, Oakland

In the ventless room,
Over the beds at the hour of rising,
Hangs now the smother and stench of the crude flesh;
And at the grimed sink
We fill the basin of our mutual use,
Where our forty faces, rinsed daily,
Leaves each its common trace,

Is it then in this?
In this alone, then, that we find our oneness?
Who never in cleanliness, never in purity
Have ever truly met?

O my brothers! Each brings his sin-deforméd face
To the greasy pan! Is it not a terrible thing
To come upon our lives, here in each other?
In the inalienable commonality of our grosser selves?

And found there, that sign and testimonial
Of our secret hearts! Could it not have been other?
A true revealment of the soul's intent,
A freer gift, welcomed, and most dear?

Far off, in clefted rocks and dells, the springwater
Throbs out the faultless pulse of earth,
A lucent flow.

And God's sheer daylight
Pours through our shafted sky
To proffer again
The still occasion of His grace
Where we might meet each other.

II

But the stain remains, ubiquitous, under the thumb,
In the crease of the knuckle or about the wrist,
Or there where the lice-suck leaves its tracing along the rib.
As I too, at night undressing, my body, its odor
Lifts like a sigh of the utter flesh:
The common breath of the poor.

"Could it not have been other?"
Moan of the scrupulous self,
Wrung outcry of the oppressed heart
Thrown back to God.

But how else and where?
Not in the urbane apartments, surely,
The suburban mansions,
Nor the luxurious hotels.

For in the crucible of revulsion
Love is made whole. St. Francis
Ran on gooseflesh toward the leper's sore:
He saw His God. Improbable and rare,
Most priceless ingredient,

It lurks behind the stubble beards;
And night after night, under the hovering breath of hundreds,
It is there; and morning after morning,
In the innominate faces soused at the shallow pan,
That in this has become like that makeshift dish
Seized up in haste without foreknowledge
That April afternoon, toward three,
When the oblique lance, upthrust,
Unloosed the floodgates of the Redemption—
How many faces, rinsed there,
Might rise, like mine, from the Bloodbath,
Almost whole? The bowl where Pilate
Damped his mincing fingers and the immortal Dish
Under the crossbeam, merge here, where the Christ-gaze
Focusses and holds. Of love, tortured and serene,
It stares from the visage of all men,
Unsanctioning, its immense pity and its terrible grief!
Or there on the nail above the sink
Where the townswoman's culled linen, smutched,
Gives back the Divine Face!
How many times each day is not that impetuous brow
Thrusted into my sight, saying always:
"Not these but *this*. Look! It is I!"

O Lord and Sacrificer! I turn to meet,
But the dead sin of the inordinate self
Tentacles my heart! Take now my wrong!

And very fast, a movement
Shifting forthright through the nimbus
Of a veiled withholdance, His look
Lances, and His unbelievable mouth,
Torrent of joy, pressed home,
Shudders the rapt heart.

Gustate, et videte quoniam suavis est Dominus!

A Canticle to the Christ in the Holy Eucharist

*Written on the Feast of St. Therese of the Child Jesus, Virgin and
Contemplative, 1953*

And the many days and the many nights that I lay as one barren,
As the barren doe lies on in the laurel under the slope of Mt. Tamal-
pais.
The fallow doe in the deep madrone, in the tall grove of the redwoods,
Curling her knees on the moist earth where the spring died out of the
mountain.
Her udder is dry. Her dugs are dry as the fallen leaves of the laurel,
Where she keeps her bed in the laurel clump on the slope of Tamal-
pais.

Sudden as wind that breaks east out of dawn this morning you struck,
As wind that poured from the wound of dawn in the valley of my
beginning.
Your look rang like the strident quail, like the buck that stamps in the
thicket.
Your face was the flame. Your mouth was the rinse of wine. Your
tongue, the torrent.

I fed on that terror as hunger is stanched on meat, the taste and the
trembling.
In the pang of my dread you smiled and swept to my heart.
As the eagle eats so I ate, as the hawk takes flesh from his talon,
As the mountain lion clings and kills, I clung and was killed.

This kill was thy name. In the wound of my heart thy voice was the
cling,
Like honey out of the broken rock thy name and the stroke of thy kiss.
The heart wound and the hovering kiss they looked to each other,
As the lovers gaze in their clasp, the grave embrace of love.

This name and the wound of my heart partook of each other.
They had no use but to feed, the grazing of love.
Thy name and the gaze of my heart they made one wound together.
This wound-made-one was their thought, the means of their knowledge.

There is nothing known like this wound, this knowledge of love.
In what love? In which wounds, such words? In what touch? In whose
  coming?
You gazed. Like the voice of the quail. Like the buck that stamps in
  the thicket.
You gave. You found the gulf, the goal. On my tongue you were meek.

In my heart you were might. And thy word was the running of rain
That rinses October. And the sweetwater spring in the rock. And the
  brook in the crevice.
Thy word in my heart was the start of the buck that is sourced in the
  doe.
Thy word was the milk that will be in her dugs, the stir of new life in
  them.
You gazed. I stood barren for days, lay fallow for nights.
Thy look was the movement of life, the milk in the young breasts of
  mothers.

My mouth was the babe's. You had stamped like the buck in the man-
  zanita.
My heart was dry as the dugs of the doe in the fall of the year on
  Tamalpais.
I sucked thy wound as the fawn sucks milk from the crowning breast
  of its mother.
The flow of thy voice in my shrunken heart was the cling of wild
  honey,
The honey that bled from the broken comb in the cleft of Tamalpais.

The quick of thy kiss lives on in my heart with the strike, the wound
  you inflicted,
Like the print of the hind feet of the buck in the earth of Tamalpais.
You left thy look like a blaze on my heart, the sudden gash in the
  granite,
The blow that broke the honeycomb in the rock of Tamalpais.

And the blaze of the buck is left in the doe, his seal that none may
  have her.
She is bred. She takes his sign to the laurel clump, and will not be seen.
She will lie under laurel and never be seen. She will keep his secret.

She will guard in her womb his planted pang. She will prove her token.
She will hold the sign that set her trust, the seal of her communion.

I will feed thy kiss: as the doe seeks out the laurel clump and feeds her
    treasure.
I will nurse in my heart the wound you made, the gash of thy delivery.
I will bear that blaze in my struck soul, in my body bring it.
It keeps in me now as the sign in the doe, the new life in the mother.

For each in that wound is each, and quick is quick, and we gaze,
A look that lives unslaked in the wound that it inflicted.
My gaze and thine, thy gaze and mine, in these the troth is taken.
The double gaze and the double name in the sign of the quenchless
    wound,
The wound that throbs like wakening milk in the winter dugs of the
    doe,
Like honey out of the broken comb in the rock of Tamalpais.

Thou art gone. I will keep thy wound till you show. I will wait in the
    laurel.
I know as the knowledge is of the doe where she lies on Tamalpais.
In the deep madrone. In the oak. In the tall grove of the redwoods.
Where she lies in laurel and proves the wound on the slope of Mt.
    Tamalpais.

A *Siege of Silence*

> A siege of silence? Thy meaning-moving voice
> Hushed in the heart's crypt, thine eye
> Shut in unreckoning slumber—
> God? God? What storms of the dredgèd deep
> Your absence lets, the rock-croppage mind,
> Kelp-girthed, sunken under swell,
> All seas of the unislanded soul
> Typhooned, hurricaned to hell!
>
> God! God! A place of eels and octopuses
> Opens down under! Hell-stench

Sulphurs the waters, the drench of madness
Gags my plunged head! Death's belly rips!
The Devil's ruptured fundament,
Fawning with reechy kisses,
Strokes my lips!

God, to purge the memory pure
What cautery is needful?
To ease the soul of rancor,
Quench its hate?
God, God of the paradisal heart
I wait!

What Birds Were There

Wheresoever the body is, thither will the eagles be gathered together.

—SAINT LUKE'S GOSPEL

I dream that I am leaving the scene of an execution. Night has fallen, and I am walking slowly through deserted country. The execution has been awesome rather than terrifying, and as I meditate on what has happened, it is as if I can see about me, in the night-shapes of bushes, the dark figures of various great birds, which, as I pass between them, settle into the contours of human heads. I become aware that these are the faces of the executioners, hardening as they transform into abstract and hieratic projections, without personality, serving to represent fixation points of human nature, utterly inflexible in their particular constellations of consciousness, and I know they will never relent. I think how sad it is that nature cannot reject the logic of its own determinism. Then I come out upon a clearing, and notice on my left a hill of graves, and an owl, like that of Minerva, perched upon a stone. Looking west I see the moon, with the face of a diseased woman, sinking into the sea.

Two magpies under the cypresses.
And what birds were there then I wonder,
To make a graveness in the afternoon
When the nailing was done to the cross hilt,
The man-act centered on the heart of God, irrevocable?
Sparrows, to be sure, scratching about in the street offal,

Yes, curb-brawlers, common as fleas,
Picking right and left for barley seed in the horse manure.
Doubtless a meadowlark off on a fence,
V-breasted, his splendor-drenched throat
Reaved on the spontaneous uprush
Of a rapture unremarked.
Or perhaps that treetop dandy the oriole,
Spinner of gestures, withdrawn now deep in his solitary covert,
His dulcet song, like rich contralto,
Unnoticed on that air.
Say rather, and more to the point,
Two gyrfalcons for outriders sweeping the cross quarter,
Circling, kleeing their strict sabbatical cries,
Imprecational and severe as executioners,
A curse on all triflers. Say further,
The mountain raven, malevolent prophet,
Utterer of virulent indictive oaths,
Imperious from the lodgepole pine,
Damnation drawn down out of the black beak inexorable.
Say too the appalled roadrunner,
Off in a fright scandalized over the stubble patch,
The town curs yelping after. Say most significantly
That grim gliding keeper of appointments, that dark
Ceremonial purist the vulture, a frown on the sky,
Methodical as an undertaker, adaptative
And deferential as the old woman of griefs
Who wraps up the dead.

But this does not mean, small birds of a feather,
That you, in your earnest beneficent presences,
Were somehow inapposite: linnets and speckled finches,
Fleet swallows, sheer swifts of the chimney;
Nor may it impeach your own most consonant
Purling evocative condolence, rain doves of the roof.
Better than those who thumbed sharp iron and plaited thorn!
Better than those who rattled dice for a stranger's shirt
And sponged galled water! Better than those
Who palmed hard silver to close a deal and slunk off after,

Too guilty to haggle! Oh, better by far
Than any of these were you, were you, flit messengers,
Arrived at that place all unbeknownst of what was toward,
But quietly there, not come but *sent*, keeping a tryst
After friend and foe had all alike gone over the hill,
Back down to man's dearth, man's glib and man's madness,
Nor left any light, the owl only upon the slab
To mourn the ruse when the moon sagged out, exhausted,
Her face demented, her jaw half gone,
Till the fierce star of morning
Pierced like the inner eye of God that scorning cloud,
Birthmarked that dawn!

In All These Acts

Cleave the wood and thou shalt find Me, lift the rock and I am there!

—THE GOSPEL ACCORDING TO THOMAS

Dawn cried out: the brutal voice of a bird
Flattened the seaglaze. Treading that surf
Hunch-headed fishers toed small agates,
Their delicate legs, iridescent, stilting the ripples.
Suddenly the cloud closed. They heard big wind
Boom back on the cliff, crunch timber along the ridge.
They shook up their wings, crying; terror flustered their pinions.
Then hemlock, tall, torn by the roots, went crazily down,
The staggering gyrations of splintered kindling.
Flung out of bracken, fleet mule deer bolted;
But the great elk, caught midway between two scissoring logs,
Arched belly-up and died, the snapped spine
Half torn out of his peeled back, his hind legs
Jerking that gasped convulsion, the kick of spasmed life,
Paunch plowed open, purple entrails
Disgorged from the basketwork ribs
Erupting out, splashed sideways, wrapping him,
Gouted in blood, flecked with the brittle silver of bone.
Frenzied, the terrible head

Thrashed off its antlered fuzz in that rubble
And then fell still, the great tongue
That had bugled in rut, calling the cow-elk up from the glades,
Thrust agonized out, the maimed member
Bloodily stiff in the stone-smashed teeth . . .

                                      Far down below,
The mountain torrent, that once having started
Could never be stopped, scooped up that avalanchial wrack
And strung it along, a riddle of bubble and littered duff
Spun down its thread. At the gorged river mouth
The sea plunged violently in, gasping its potholes,
Sucked and panted, answering itself in its spume.
The river, spent at last, beating driftwood up and down
In a frenzy of capitulation, pumped out its life,
Destroying itself in the mother sea,
There where the mammoth sea-grown salmon
Lurk immemorial, roe in their hulls, about to begin.
They will beat that barbarous beauty out
On those high-stacked shallows, those headwater claims,
Back where they were born. Along that upward-racing trek
Time springs through all its loops and flanges,
The many-faced splendor and the music of the leaf,
The copulation of beasts and the watery laughter of drakes,
Too few the grave witnesses, the wakeful, vengeful beauty,
Devolving itself of its whole constraint,
Erupting as it goes.

                  In all these acts
Christ crouches and seethes, pitched forward
On the crucifying stroke, juvescent, that will spring Him
Out of the germ, out of the belly of the dying buck,
Out of the father-phallus and the torn-up root.
These are the modes of His forth-showing,
His serene agonization. In the clicking teeth of otters
Over and over He dies and is born,
Shaping the weasel's jaw in His leap
And the staggering rush of the bass.

LAWRENCE DURRELL

(1912–)

Conon in Exile

I

Three women have slept with my books,
Penelope among admirers of the ballads,
Let down her hair over my exercises
But was hardly aware of me; an author
Of tunes which made men like performing dogs;
She did not die but left me for a singer in a wig.

II

Later Ariadne read of *The Universe,*
Made a journey under the islands from her own
Green home, husband, house with olive trees.
She lay with my words and let me breathe
Upon her face; later fell like a gull from the
Great ledge in Scio. Relations touched her body
Warm and rosy from the oil like a scented loaf,
Not human any more—but not divine as they had hoped.

III

You who pass the islands will perhaps remember
The lovely Ion, harmless, patient and in love.
Our quarrels disturbed the swallows in the eaves,
The wild bees could not work in the vine;

Shaken and ill, one of true love's experiments,
It was she who lay in the stone bath dry-eyed,
Having the impression that her body had become
A huge tear about to drop from the eye of the world.
We never learned that marriage is a kind of architecture,
The nursery virtues were missing, all of them,
So nobody could tell us why we suffered.

IV

It would be untrue to say that *The Art of Marriage*
And the others: *Of Peace in the Self* and *Of Love*
Brought me no women; I remember bodies, arms, faces,
But I have forgotten their names.

V

Finally I am here. Conon in exile on Andros
Like a spider in a bottle writing the immortal
Of Love and Death, through the bodies of those
Who slept with my words but did not know me.
An old man with a skinful of wine
Living from pillow to poke under a vine.

At night the sea roars under the cliffs.
The past harms no one who lies close to the Gods.
Even in these notes upon myself I see
I have put down women's names like some
Philosophical proposition. At last I understand
They were only forms for my own ideas,
With names and mouths and different voices.
In them I lay with myself, my style of life,
Knowing only coitus with the shadows,
By our blue Aegean which forever
Washes and pardons and brings us home.

Alexandria

To the lucky now who have lovers or friends,
Who move to their sweet undiscovered ends,

Or whom the great conspiracy deceives,
I wish these whirling autumn leaves:
Promontories splashed by the salty sea,
Groaned on in darkness by the tram
To horizons of love or good luck or more love—
As for me I now move
Through many negatives to what I am.

Here at the last cold Pharos between Greece
And all I love, the lights confide
A deeper darkness to the rubbing tide;
Doors shut, and we the living are locked inside
Between the shadows and the thoughts of peace:
And so in furnished rooms revise
The index of our lovers and our friends
From gestures possibly forgotten, but the ends
Of longings like unconnected nerves,
And in this quiet rehearsal of their acts
We dream of them and cherish them as Facts.

Now when the sea grows restless as a conscript,
Excited by fresh wind, climbs the sea-wall,
I walk by it and think about you all:
B. with his respect for the Object, and D.
Searching in sex like a great pantry for jars
Marked 'Plum and apple'; and the small, fell
Figure of Dorian ringing like a muffin-bell—
All indeed whom war or time threw up
On this littoral and tides could not move
Were objects for my study and my love.

And then turning where the last pale
Lighthouse, like a Samson blinded, stands
And turns its huge charred orbit on the sands
I think of you—indeed mostly of you,
In whom a writer would only name and lose
The dented boy's lip and the close
Archer's shoulders; but here to rediscover
By tides and faults of weather, by the rain
Which washes everything, the critic and the lover.

At the doors of Africa so many towns founded
Upon a parting could become Alexandria, like
The wife of Lot—a metaphor for tears;
And the queer student in his poky hot
Tenth floor room above the harbour hears
The sirens shaking the tree of his heart,
And shuts his books, while the most
Inexpressible longings like wounds unstitched
Stir in him some girl's unquiet ghost.

So we, learning to suffer and not condemn
Can only wish you this great pure wind
Condemned by Greece, and turning like a helm
Inland where it smokes the fires of men,
Spins weathercocks on farms or catches
The lovers at their quarrel in the sheets;
Or like a walker in the darkness might,
Knocks and disturbs the artist at his papers
Up there alone, upon the alps of night.

On First Looking into Loeb's Horace

I found your Horace with the writing in it;
Out of time and context came upon
This lover of vines and slave to quietness,
Walking like a figure of smoke here, musing
Among his high and lovely Tuscan pines.

All the small-holder's ambitions, the yield
Of wine-bearing grape, pruning and drainage
Laid out by laws, almost like the austere
Shell of his verses—a pattern of Latin thrift;
Waiting so patiently in a library for
Autumn and the drying of the apples;
The betraying hour-glass and its deathward drift.

Surely the hard blue winterset
Must have conveyed a message to him—

The premonitions that the garden heard
Shrunk in its shirt of hair beneath the stars,
How rude and feeble a tenant was the self,
An Empire, the body with its members dying—
And unwhistling now the vanished Roman bird?

The fruit-trees dropping apples; he counted them;
The soft bounding fruit on leafy terraces,
And turned to the consoling winter rooms
Where, facing south, began the great prayer,
With his reed laid upon the margins
Of the dead, his stainless authors,
Upright, severe on an uncomfortable chair.

Here, where your clear hand marked up
'The hated cypress' I added 'Because it grew
On tombs, revealed his fear of autumn and the urns',
Depicting a solitary at an upper window
Revising metaphors for the winter sea: 'O
Dark head of storm-tossed curls'; or silently
Watching the North Star which like a fever burns

Away the envy and neglect of the common,
Shining on this terrace, lifting up in recreation
The sad heart of Horace who must have seen it only
As a metaphor for the self and its perfection—
A burning heart quite constant in its station.

Easy to be patient in the summer,
The light running like fishes among the leaves,
Easy in August with its cones of blue
Sky uninvaded from the north; but winter
With its bareness pared his words to points
Like stars, leaving them pure but very few.

He will not know how we discerned him, disregarding
The pose of sufficiency, the landed man,
Found a suffering limb on the great Latin tree
Whose roots live in the barbarian grammar we

Use, yet based in him, his mason's tongue;
Describing clearly a bachelor, sedentary,
With a fond weakness for bronze-age conversation,
Disguising a sense of failure in a hatred for the young,

Who built in the Sabine hills this forgery
Of completeness, an orchard with a view of Rome;
Who studiously developed his sense of death
Till it was all around him, walking at the circus,
At the baths, playing dominoes in a shop—
The escape from self-knowledge with its tragic
Imperatives: *Seek, suffer, endure.* The Roman
In him feared the Law and told him where to stop.

So perfect a disguise for one who had
Exhausted death in art—yet who could guess
You would discern the liar by a line,
The suffering hidden under gentleness
And add upon the flyleaf in your tall
Clear hand: 'Fat, human and unloved,
And held from loving by a sort of wall,
Laid down his books and lovers one by one,
Indifference and success had crowned them all.'

The Lost Cities

For Paddy and Xan

One she floats as Venice might,
Bloated among her ambiguities:
What hebetude or carelessness shored up
Goths were not smart enough to capture.
The city, yes: the water: not the style.

Her dispossession now may seem to us
Idle and ridiculous, quivering
In the swollen woodwork of these
Floating carcases of the doges,

Dissolving into spires and cages of water:
Venice blown up, and turning green.

Another wears out humbly like a craft:
Red wells where the potter's thumb
Sealed his jars of guaranteed oil.
That fluent thumb which presses
On history's vibrating string,
Pressing here, there, in a wounded place.

Some have left names only: Carthage:
Where the traveller may squeeze out
A few drops of ink or salt,
On deserted promontories may think:
'No wonder. A river once turned over
In its sleep and all the cities fled.'

Now in Greece which is not yet Greece
The adversary was also strong.
Yet here the serfs have built their discontents
As spiders do their junctions, here,
This orchard, painted tables set outside
A whitewashed house,
And on a rusty nail the violin
Is hanging by one wrist, still ownerless:

Disowned by the devastator and as yet
Uncherished by its tenants in the old
Human smells of excrement and cooking:
Waiting till the spades press through to us,
To be discovered, standing in our lives,

Rhodes, death-mask of a Greek town.

The Critics

They never credit us
With being bad enough

The boys that come to edit us:
Of simply not caring when a prize,
Something for nothing, comes our way,
A wife, a mistress, or a holiday
From People living neckfast in their lies.

No: Shakespear's household bills
Could never be responsible, they say,
For all the heartbreak and the 1,000 ills
His work is heir to, poem, sonnet, play . . .
Emended readings give the real reason:
The times were out of joint, the loves, the season.

Man With A Message—how could you forget
To read your proofs, the heartache and the fret?
The copier or the printer
Must take the blame for it in all
The variants they will publish by the winter.

'By elision we quarter suffering.' Too true.
'From images and scansion can be learned.' . . .
Yet under it perhaps may be discerned
A something else afoot—a Thing
Lacking both precedent and name and gender:
An uncreated Weight which left its clue,
Making him run up bills,
Making him violent or distrait or tender:
Leaving for Stratford might have heard It say:
'Tell them I won't be back on Saturday.
My wife will understand I'm on a bender.'
And to himself muttering, muttering: 'Words
Added to words multiply the space
Between this feeling and my expressing It.
The wires get far too hot. Time smoulders
Like a burning rug. I *will* be free.' . . .

And all the time from the donkey's head
The lover is whispering: 'This is not

What I imagined as Reality.
If truth were needles surely eyes would see?

Song for Zarathustra

Le saltimbanque is coming with
His heels behind his head.
His smile is mortuary and
His whole expression dead.

The acrobat, the acrobat,
Demanding since the Fall
Little enough but hempen stuff
To climb and hang us all.

Mysterious inventions like
The trousers and the hat
Bewitched our real intentions:
We sewed the fig-leaves flat.

Man sewed his seven pockets
Upon his hairy clothes
But woman in her own white flesh
Has one she seldom shows.

An aperture on anguish,
A keyhole on disgrace:
The features stay grimacing
Upon the mossy face.

A cup without a handle
A staff without a crook,
The sawdust in the golly's head,
The teapot with the nook.

The Rib is slowly waking
Within the side of Man

And *le guignol* is making
Its faces while it can.

Compose us in the finder
Our organs upside down,
The parson in his widow's weeds,
The doctor in his gown.

What Yang and Yin divided
In one disastrous blunder
Must one day be united and
Let no man put asunder.

ROY FULLER

(1912–)

The Pure Poet

He spoke of poetry: his lips had shrunk
To lines across the gums: he also stank.
He said that since the Greeks few had the gifts,
That syphilis and lice were perquisites.
He brought a charnel breath and spotted cloths,
The swansdown shroud was fluttered when he coughed
His postulate of the sufficient word.
I felt viridian when he launched on blood,
Perceived the surgery behind the trance,
That his long travels in pursuit of tense
Were clearly all compelled by social syntax;
And but for his unpleasant human antics
I could have pitied him for being dead.
Still he sat on and told me how he made
His money, villa, servants, the model globe,
His regular habits and the seven-faced cube.
Further I could not follow him, among
The obscure allusions to important dung,
Nor as at length he tried a final scare
And vanished through the non-existent door.

Epitaph on a Bombing Victim

Reader, could his limbs be found
Here would lie a common man:
History inflicts no wound
But explodes what it began,
And with its enormous lust
For division splits the dust.
Do not ask his nation; that
Was History's confederate.

Y. M. C. A. Writing Room

A map of the world is on the wall: its lying
Order and compression shadow these bent heads.
Here we try to preserve communications;
The map mocks us with dangerous blues and reds.

Today my friends were drafted; they are about
To be exploded, to be scattered over
That coloured square which in reality
Is a series of scenes, is boredom, cover,

Nostalgia, labour, death. They will explore
Minutely particular deserts, seas and reefs,
Invest a thousand backcloths with their moods,
And all will carry, like a cancer, grief.

In England at this moment the skies contain
Ellipses of birds within their infinite planes,
At night the ragged patterns of the stars;
And distant trees are like the branching veins

Of an anatomical chart: as menacing
As pistols the levelled twigs present their buds.

They have exchanged for this illusion of danger
The ordeal of walking in the sacred wood.

The season cannot warm them nor art console.
These words are false as the returning Spring
From which this March history has made subtraction:
The spirit has gone and left the marble thing.

The Tribes

I think of the tribes: the women prized for fatness
Immovable, and by a sympathetic
   Magic sustaining the herds,
   On whose strange humps sit birds;

And those with long dung-stiffened capes of hair,
And those that ceremonially eat their dead;
   The ornamental gashes
   Festered and raised with ashes;

The captured and dishonoured king compelled
To straddle a vertical and sharpened stake,
   Until, his legs hauled at,
   The point burst from his throat;

And all the prohibitions and the cheapness
Of life so hardly got, where it is death
   Even to touch the palace
   And poison expresses malice.

Now in the white men's towns the tribes are gathered
Among the corrugated iron and
   The refuse bins where rats
   Dispute with them for scraps.

Truly, civilisation is for them
The most elemental struggle for bread and love;

For all the tabus have gone,
It is man against man alone.

On waste plots and in the decrepit shanties
They begin to discover the individual,
    And, with the sense in time
    Of Adam, perpetuate crime.

The most horrible things you can imagine are
Happening in the towns and the most senseless:
    There are no kings or poison,
    Are laws but no more reason.

Crustaceans

Upon the beach are thousands of crabs; they are
Small, with one foreclaw curiously developed.
Against the ashen sand I see a forest
Of waving, pink, in some way human, claws.
The crabs advance or, perhaps, retreat a step
And then like Hamlet's father slowly beckon
With that flesh-coloured, yes, obscene, incisor.
These actions in the mass take on a rhythm
—The sexual display of higher beasts,
The dance of the tribe, or the enthusiasm
Of a meeting.
                    If you go closer to the crabs
You see that with their normal claws they are making
Spheres from the sand, small perfect rounds, which they,
After a little preliminary twiddling,
Produce from beneath their bodies suddenly,
Like jugglers, and deposit by their holes.
While this goes on, that monstrous foreclaw, that
Button hole, is motionless. And all around
The shafts sunk by these creatures lie the eggs
Of sand, so patiently, endlessly evolved.
At last I stretch and wave my hand: the crabs
Instantly bolt down their holes and pull a sphere,

A trap door, after them, and in a second
The beach is still.
                    While I was watching them
My eyes unfocused with the effort, or
Maybe it was the whole activity
Which like an idea detached itself from its
Frame, background: and I thought, are these that I
Regard with such pity, disgust, absorption, crabs?

During a Bombardment by V-Weapons

The little noises of the house:
Drippings between the slates and ceiling;
From the electric fire's cooling,
Tickings; the dry feet of a mouse:

These at the ending of a war
Have power to alarm me more
Than the ridiculous detonations
Outside the gently coughing curtains.

And, love, I see your pallor bears
A far more pointed threat than steel.
Now all the permanent and real
Furies are settling in upstairs.

Rhetoric of a Journey

Train takes me away from the northern valleys
Where I lived my youth and where my youth lives on
In the person of my parent and the stone walls,
The dialect of love I understand
But scarcely speak, the mills and illnesses.

In Trollope's novel open on my knee
The characters are worried about money:
The action revolves round the right to a necklace.

I have only to bend my head and immediately
I am lost in this other reality, the world
Of art, where something is always missing.
In *The Eustace Diamonds* life is made tolerable
By standing away from time and refusing to write
Of the hours that link the official biography.

I think of the poem I wrote on another visit—
A list of the poet's hoarded perceptions:
The net of walls thrown over waves of green,
The valleys clogged with villages, the cattle
Pink against smoking mills—and only now
Experience what was delayed and omitted.
For those were rooms in which we dared not look
At each other's load of emotion: it was there
Our past had to die: and where we acknowledged
With pain and surprise our ties with the disregarded.
I would like to renounce the waking rational life,
The neat completed work, as being quite
Absurd and cowardly; and leave to posterity
The words on book-marks, enigmatic notes,
Thoughts before sleep, the vague unwritten verse
On people, on the city to which I travel.
I would like to resolve to live fully
In the barbarous world of sympathy and fear.

Says his life to the poet: 'Can you make verse of this?'
And the poet answers: 'Yes, it is your limitations
That enable me to get you down at all.'
The diamonds glitter on his paper and
His sons sail unloved to the Antipodes.
Those whom a lack of creativeness condemns
To truth see magazines in the hands of the patient
And realise that the serial will go on
After death; but the artist becomes ill himself.
For only the fully-committed participate
In the revolution of living, the coming to power
Of death: the others have always some excuse

To be absent from the shooting, to be at home
Curled up with a book or at the dentist's.

Sometimes I find it possible to feign
The accent of the past, the vulgar speech
Which snobbery and art have iced; but feel no longer
The compulsion of hills, the eternal interests
Which made my fathers understand each other.
That mockery of solidarity
Some of the civilised always experience,
Waiting half hopefully for the dreaded barbarians,
Sick of their culture, traitors to the division
Of toil and sensibility. Yet really
I can speak easily only to myself.
The tears meant for others are wept in front of the glass;
The confession is never posted; and the eye
Slides away from the proffered hand and discovers
An interesting view from the window.

The ridiculous mottled faces pass in stiff
Procession: relations, friends and chance encounters.
And the asinine minds that lie behind the gestures
Of goodness I can never reciprocate
Repel me with their inability
To escape from the grossest errors. Is it weakness
That sometimes imagines these shaped as heroes?
That cannot conceive of happiness as other
Than the apotheosis of the simple and kind?
That refuses to see how the century rises, pale,
From the death of its dream, ignoring the gains
Of the cruel, the different wishes of slaves?

The train removes me to another set
Of evasions. The valleys disappear. The train
Bolts through the central plain. I shall discover
Whether Lizzie Eustace retained her diamonds,
How far the hordes are from the city,
And my end will make significant for me
A casual place and date. My own child

Will grow from the generous warmth of his youth and perhaps
Discover, like me, that the solemn moments of life
Require their unbearable gaucheness translated to art.
For the guilt of being alive must be appeased
By the telling observation, and even feeling
Can only be borne retrospectively.
Bending over to kiss, the sensitive see with alarm
That their selves are still upright: the instant of death is announced
By a rattle of tin in the corridor. Meaning is given
These disparate happenings, our love is only
Revealed, by conventions: 'Dear Mother, I hope you are better.'
Or 'Lizzie resolved that she would have her revenge.'

The lilac will last a fortnight if the rain
Arrives, the sparrows will always turn to let
Their lime drop over the gutter, the gardener
Will lift the chickweed, and the clots of nests
In the elms disappear in the whirling green of summer.

At the end of the twilit road a figure is standing
Calling us to go in, while the far-off rumours
Of terrible facts which at last may destroy
Our happiness spoil our play. In the place we go to
The kettle boils on the fire, the brasses are polished,
But people are busy with pain in another room.
One night I shall watch the city and black sky meet
In the distance, the car lights stream on the heath like tracer,
And in such moments of lonely and mild exultation
This rhetoric will be forgotten, and the life of omission go on.
Behind me will lie the sad and convulsive events
As narrative art, and as fated, immortal and false.

The Image

A spider in the bath. The image noted:
Significant maybe but surely cryptic.
A creature motionless and rather bloated,
The barriers shining, vertical and white:
Passing concern, and pity mixed with spite.

Next day with some surprise one finds it there.
It seems to have moved an inch or two, perhaps.
It starts to take on that familiar air
Of prisoners for whom time is erratic:
The filthy aunt forgotten in the attic.

Quite obviously it came up through the waste,
Rejects through ignorance or apathy
That passage back. The problem must be faced;
And life go on though strange intruders stir
Among its ordinary furniture.

One jibs at murder, so a sheet of paper
Is slipped beneath the accommodating legs.
The bathroom window shows for the escaper
The lighted lanterns of laburnum hung
In copper beeches—on which scene it's flung.

We certainly would like thus easily
To cast out of the house all suffering things.
But sadness and responsibility
For our own kind lives in the image noted:
A half-loved creature, motionless and bloated.

On Reading a Soviet Novel

Will not the Local Party Secretary
Prove that his love of men's not innocent:
The heroine at last be blown off course
By some base, gusty, female element:
And the grave hero be eventually torn
By a disgraceful infantile event?

No, in this world the good works out its course
Unhindered by the real, irrelevant flaw.
Our guilty eyes glaze over with ennui
At so much honest purpose, rigid law.
This is not life, we say, who ask that art
Show mainly what the partial butler saw.

And yet with what disquiet we leave the tale!
The mere appearance of the descending Goth,
So frightful to a sedentary race,
Made him invincible. It is not wrath
That breaks up cultures but the virtues of
The stupid elephant, the piddling moth.

The threatened empire dreads its rival's arms
Less than the qualities at which it sneers—
The slave morality promoted to
A way of life: naïve, old-fashioned tears
Which once it shed itself by bucketsful
In nascent, optimistic, long-dead years.

The Day

At the time it seemed unimportant: he was lying
In bed, off work, with a sudden pain,
And she was haloed by the morning sun,
Enquiring if he'd like the daily paper.

So idle Byzantium scarcely felt at first
The presence in her remoter provinces
Of the destructive followers of the Crescent.

But in retrospect that day of moderate health
Stood fired in solid and delightful hues,
The last of joy, the first of something else—
An inconceivable time when sex could be
Grasped for the asking with gigantic limbs,
When interest still was keen in the disasters
Of others—accident, uprising, drouth—
And the sharp mind perceived the poignancy
Of the ridiculous thoughts of dissolution.

A day remembered by a shrivelled empire
Nursed by hermaphrodites and unsustained
By tepid fluids poured in its crying mouth.

Versions of Love

'My love for you has faded'—thus the Bad
Quarto, the earliest text, whose midget page
Derived from the imperfect memories
Of red-nosed, small-part actors
Or the atrocious shorthand of the age.

However, the far superior Folio had
'My love for you was fated'—thus implying
Illicit passion, a tragic final act.
And this was printed from the poet's own
Foul papers, it was reckoned;
Supported by the reading of the Second
Quarto, which had those sombre words exact.

Such evidence was shaken when collation
Showed that the Folio copied slavishly
The literals of that supposedly
Independent Quarto. Thus one had to go
Back to the first text of all.

'My love for you has faded'—quite impossible.
Scholars produced at last the emendation:
'My love for you fast endured.'
Our author's ancient hand that must have been
Ambiguous and intellectual
Foxed the compositors of a certainty.
And so the critical editions gave
Love the sound status that she ought to have
In poetry so revered.

But this conjecture cannot quite destroy
The question of what the poet really wrote
In the glum middle reaches of his life:
Too sage, too bald, too fearful of fiasco
To hope beyond his wife,
Yet aching almost as promptly as a boy.

GEORGE BARKER

(1913–)

Secular Elegies

I

My pig-faced kingdom with tongues of wrong
And an historical gait of trial and error,
Under whose bridges Time, faster than rivers,
Bears individual and event along
Into a past overloaded with souvenirs:

Now answer history with a marvellous golden Yes
As she steps up asking all future questions.
The historians in their tombs, sighing, will sleep
Deeper, and the sailors, who always had great visions,
Smile for the island that ceased to be an illusion.

The instinct of the bird governs its acts of war,
Who, titivating itself at crossroads, rises and rises
Singing from the destructive wheels that come roar-
ing towards it, and in the end, after the reverses,
Perches whistling on the shattered axles proudly.

The armies of Hohenzollern, brooding on loss,
Know best that the real enemy is never there
Pinned akimbo on the gun-sight, but in the cause.

O sheeted in their horoscopes like togas
Under red stars strut the catchpenny Caesars.

Heroes who ride your wishing horses over
The breakfast tables of the population,
Your beds are full of hands. And when you shiver
What stalks across your grave is a whole nation:
And when you close an eye your life is over.

But the conquerors, reddening their heels on us,
They will not ever really die, but continually
Thrash on the hotbed of their animus:
Not one of them shall die hopefully and finally,
For them the grave will also be full of us.

II

Where formerly he saw birds in bushes, now
The cyclist resting from his uphill labour
Observes the skull of Cromwell on a bough
Admonishing his half heart, and he shoulders
His way upward against the wind to the brow.

The political cartoonist in his bed
Hears voices break his sleep he does not know:
The morning papers show what the people said.
Librarians in their studies, the lights low,
Sense Milton breathing in his marble head.

The clerk hears Clive cheering in a darkness.
And from the ponds of commons, in broad day,
The effigies of great sailors rise in their starkness
With the *Hood* in their hands, and cry:
'Nevertheless we mourn also the *Bismarck!*'

There it is necessary to walk carefully
And swallows must dive wisely, for the air,
So full of poems and ghosts, is truly
Populated with more than meets the eye:
Some principles have become poltergeist there.

Where, in its sepulchres, the long past rests
Brocaded with daydreams, there the truth is known:
What makes the people happiest is best.
But the fish in its undersea caves and bird in its nest
Know that the shark and cuckoo never rest.

Sometimes the punts in summer on the rivers,
Gliding like dancers over the slovenly water
Saw as they traced their way among the shallows
Images under them pinned in a cage of shadows
Struggling to catch the eye. It was the future.

The quavering Chamberlain, trapped between disasters,
Hiding his head in an hour-glass: four kings and
The bicyclist Queen, like uprooted pilasters,
Flying across the sea: coiled in the ampersand
The hakencreutz accumulates but never masters.

And some, in silence, looking for their lives
In the lines of their hands, the merciless words saw
That turned Nebuchadnezzar into a cow:
Others, who came kissing and bringing olives,
Had a change of heart and are dead now.

Sad in his alcove of love Pascal lamented:
'My friend, my friend, you were born on the other side.'
Firstly we die because of places. O the demented
Alexander, who, eternally discontented,
Desires more, is us. Finally we die of pride.

III

Satan is on your tongue, sweet singer, with
Your eye on the income and the encomium:
Angels rhapsodise for and from their faith.
And in the studies of chromium
Lucifer seduces Orpheus with a myth.

But the principle of evil is not autonomous.
Like the Liberty Horse with a plume at a circus

136

Under the whipmaster it steps proud in its circles.
When I let slip one instant the whip of the will
All hell's scot free with fire at the nostril.

Thus if the crux and judgement never is
Left to our own to do with as we will,
But the decision, like a master key, lies
Wholly in the higher hands that hold all—
How can we be as innocent as this?

Everything that is profound loves the mask,
Said the Dionysian who never wore one.
Thus our damnation and our condemnation,
Wiser than Nietzsche, never taking a risk,
Wears the mask of a necessary satisfaction.

Not, Love, when we kiss do the archangels weep
For we are naked then wherever we are,
Like tigers in the night; but in our sleep
The masks go down, and the beast is bare:
It is not Love but double damnation there.

Marooned on the islands of pride, lonely
And mad on the pyramids of achievement,
Disillusioned in the cathedrals of doxology,
The sad man senses his continual bereavement:
God has just died, and now there is only

Us. The gold bull with its horns of finances
Over the sensual mountains goes gallivanting
In glory: all night and all day it dances,
Absurd and happy because nothing is wanting.
The sad man hides his grief in his five senses.

IV

Then from its labours I rest my hand on the table
And there where hitherto the poem had been,
Now, in its deadliness sleeping but capable,

Agent and gadget of destruction, the machine
Of actual damnation lies and is culpable.

Everything that we touch, sooner or later,—
The uprooted arbutus hung at the head of the bed,
The untouchable trophies in the arcanum of nature,
The dizzy stars, the testes, and the sacred
Dove—everything that we dissect for data
Dies as we finger for the heart of the matter.

O but the Doric arm tattooed with falsity
That riddles this embrace where worlds hide,
Larger than railways where they hold a country
Sleeping and waking in their iron anatomy,
Takes me to the breast where I am pacified

Under the frenzies of all sensual wonders.
What shall I say when, big at my mouth,
The Hesperidean with a worm in its splendours
Hangs like the bub of a whore? Or what truth
Find in the kiss that dazzles all my windows?

And so in circles over existential deserts
I and you wander, lost, and arm in arm;
Lost, lost. And the visions paying us visits
Lead us to mirages where, in a morning dream,
We forget the headaches and the lost Edens.

v

O Golden Fleece she is where she lies tonight
Trammelled in her sheets like midsummer on a bed,
Kisses like moths flitter over her bright
Mouth, and, as she turns her head,
All space moves over to give her beauty room.

Where her hand, like a bird on the branch of her arm,
Droops its wings over the bedside as she sleeps,
There the air perpetually stays warm

Since, nested, her hand rested there. And she keeps
Under her green thumb life like a growing poem.

My nine-tiered tigress in the cage of sex
I feed with meat that you tear from my side
Crowning your nine months with the paradox:
The love that kisses with a homicide
In robes of red generation resurrects.

The bride who rides the hymenæal waterfall
Spawning all possibles in her pools of surplus,
Whom the train rapes going into a tunnel,
The imperial multiplicator nothing can nonplus:
My mother Nature is the origin of it all.

At Pharaoh's Feast and in the family cupboard,
Gay corpse, bright skeleton, and the fly in amber,
She sits with her laws like antlers from her forehead
Enmeshing everyone, with flowers and thunder
Adorning the head that destiny never worried.

VI

Temper the whirlwind to the unborn lamb,
Mother of us all, lapped in your shawls of cause;
Large in your arms wrap our sad amalgam
That, spinning its tails among the other stars,
Mopes, lost and weeping, far, far from its home.

Cover with your pity the broken Pole
Where, like a rag, the pride of the human hangs
Dirty as dishcloths. And with summer console
Us for the equinox of our anguish.
Humour the arrogant ships that sail.

Too near the tooth of the truth and the weather,
The thinkers in their cockleshells, the captains
Sinking each other; and always permit neither
Wholly to find their ends, for they seek islands
Of Death and Truth that should always be further.

And in due season to their last bed take
The lovers who are the cause of all the trouble;
Let the manikin Adam successfully undertake
What Atlas only, bending an apish double,
Hitherto managed with the world on his back.

O temper the whirlwind to the unborn lamb!
And on the tongue of the young in its cradle
Lightly lay silver spoons. And the same
Love extend to those who groom your bridal
That they, mother of us all, suffer in your name.

Summer Song I

I looked into my heart to write
    And found a desert there.
But when I looked again I heard
Howling and proud in every word
    The hyena despair.

Great summer sun, great summer sun,
    All loss burns in trophies;
And in the cold sheet of the sky
Lifelong the fishlipped lovers lie
    Kissing catastrophes.

O loving garden where I lay
    When under the breasted tree
My son stood up behind my eyes
And groaned: Remember that the price
    Is vinegar for me.

Great summer sun, great summer sun,
    Turn back to the designer:
I would not be the one to start
The breaking day and the breaking heart
    For all the grief in China.

My one, my one, my only love,
  Hide, hide your face in a leaf,
And let the hot tear falling burn
The stupid heart that will not learn
  The everywhere of grief.

Great summer sun, great summer sun,
  Turn back to the never-never
Cloud-cuckoo, happy, far-off land
Where all the love is true love, and
  True love goes on for ever.

Summer Song II

Soft is the collied night, and cool
These regions where the dreamers rule,
As Summer, in her rose and robe,
Astride the horses of the globe,
Drags, fighting, from the midnight sky,
The mushroom at whose glance we die.

Channel Crossing

To John Lehmann

And just by crossing the short sea
To find the answer sitting there
Combing out its snaky hair
And with a smile regarding me
Because it knows only too well
That I shall never recognize
The axioms that I should prize
Or the lies that I should tell.

I saw the question in the sky
Ride like a gull to fool me, as
The squat boat butted at the seas

As grossly as through ultimates I
Churn up a frothy wake of verbs
Or stir a muddy residue
Looking for that answer who
Sanctifies where she perturbs.

The horror of the questionmark
I looked back and saw stand over
The white and open page of Dover
Huge as the horn of the scapegoat. Dark
It stood up in the English day
Interrogating Destiny
With the old lip of the sea:
"What can a dead nation say?"

As these words wailed in the air
I looked at Europe and I saw
The glittering instruments of war
Grow paler but not go from where
Like a Caesarian sunset on
The cold slab of the horizon
They lay foretelling for tomorrow
Another day of human sorrow.

But when I turned and looked into
The silent chambers of the sea
I saw the displaced fishes flee
From nowhere into nowhere through
Their continent of liberty.
O skipping porpoise of the tide
No longer shall the sailors ride
You cheering out to sea.

I thought of Britain in its cloud
Chained to the economic rocks
Dying behind me. I saw the flocks
Of great and grieving omens crowd
About the lion on the stone.

And I heard Milton's eagle mewing
Her desolation in the ruin
Of a great nation, alone.

That granite and gigantic sigh
Of the proud man beaten by
Those victories from which we die;
The gentle and defeated grief
Of the gale that groans among
Trees that are a day too strong
And, victorious by a leaf,
Show the winner he was wrong.

The continent of discontent
Rose up before me as I stood
Above the happy fish. Endued
With hotter and unhappier blood
Contented in my discontent,
I saw that every man's a soul
Caught in the glass wishing bowl:
To live at peace in discontent.

O somewhere in the seven leagues
That separate us from the stricken
Amphitheatre of the spirit,
O somewhere in that baleful sea
The answer of sad Europe lodges,
The clue that causes us to sicken
Because we cannot find and share it,
Or, finding, cannot see.

So in the sky the monstrous sun
Mocked like a punishment to be,
Extending, now, to you and me
The vision of what we have done:
And as the boat drew to the quay
I thought, by crossing the short water
I shall not find, in its place,
The answer with a silent face.

Stanzas on a Visit to Longleat House in Wiltshire, October 1953

To John Farrelly

Dead pomp sneering underground
Glares up at a horned foot of clay
Where the hog of multitude hangs around
Among these tremendous memories
That delegate to our day
The superannuated and damned glories.

A quidnunc with a shopping bag
Stops gossiping with another hag
And where immense conceptions were
Dragged shrieking from their cellars here
The ragged-arsed mechanics squat
Owning what they haven't got.

O rare rain of disinterest
Descend on this fouled public nest
And rout out all vulgarities
That, crowding through its majesties,
Gut to bare shell and bone
The grandeur of the dead and gone.

In car–park, garden and urinal
The free and ignorant, almost
As easy as at a Cup Final
Gawk through the stone-transparent ghost
Of this once noble house, now lost
In the gross error of survival.

"Come," said my proud and sulking friend,
"Four angels up to Heaven's Gate,
And looking down at Longleat
So far below, shall disappear
The human termite, leaving there
Stones and spectres hand in hand."

And from that aerial sweep of height
The valley fell through depths of pine
Down through green distances until
From glimmering water rising bright
Longleat, bird's-eyed in sunshine,
Smiled up from its own funeral.

I saw the heroic seizins fade
And hide in laurels of old trees
As brassbands of indignities
Exploded echoes to degrade
The splendours and the miseries
Of that cold illustrious shade.

A *Little Song in Assisi*

Sprightly the cockcrowing
sun from that stone bed
high in the hilly morning
where a saint lay down his head
steps gallivanting.

All small things including
bird lizard and beast
and the dayspring beginning
dance from the doors of the east
like lambs skedaddling.

There is such an alighting
tenderness in the air
like wings after hovering
that a dove might be here,
hidden but apprehending.

Peasant and priest toiling
over the patched hill side,
the acolyte at his hoeing,
see from that iron tressel
the saint's huge brother rising

until, like a lark, lifting
the valleyed Umbrian veils,
the heart of Francis, dazzling
bird in the air, reveals
the grace of that ragged man
transfiguring everywhere.

KARL SHAPIRO

(1913–)

Poet

Il arrive que l'esprit demande la poesie

Left leg flung out, head cocked to the right,
Tweed coat or army uniform, with book,
Beautiful eyes, who is this walking down?
Who, glancing at the pane of glass looks sharp
And thinks it is not he—as when a poet
Comes swiftly on some half-forgotten poem
And loosely holds the page, steady of mind,
　　　Thinking it is not his?

And when will *you* exist?—Oh, it is I,
Incredibly skinny, stooped, and neat as pie,
Ignorant as dirt, erotic as an ape,
Dreamy as puberty—with dirty hair!
Into the room like kangaroo he bounds,
Ears flopping like the most expensive hound's;
His chin receives all questions as he bows
　　　Mouthing a green bon-bon.

Has no more memory than rubber. Stands
Waist-deep in heavy mud of thought and broods
At his own wetness. When he would get out,

To his surprise he lifts in air a phrase
As whole and clean and silvery as a fish
Which jumps and dangles on his damned hooked grin,
But like a name-card on a man's lapel
    Calls him a conscious fool.

And child-like he remembers all his life
And cannily constructs it, fact by fact,
As boys paste postage stamps in careful books,
Denoting pence and legends and profiles,
Nothing more valuable.—And like a thief,
His eyes glassed over and congealed with guilt,
Fondles his secrets like a case of tools,
    And waits in empty doors.

By men despised for knowing what he is,
And by himself. But he exists for women.
As dolls to girls, as perfect wives to men,
So he to women. And to himself a thing,
All ages, epicene, without a trade.
To girls and wives always alive and fated;
To men and scholars always dead like Greek
    And always mistranslated.

Towards exile and towards shame he lures himself,
Tongue winding on his arm, and thinks like Eve
By biting apple will become most wise.
Sentio ergo sum: he feels his way
And words themselves stand up for him like Braille
And punch and perforate his parchment ear.
All language falls like Chinese on his soul,
    Image of song unsounded.

This is the coward's coward that in his dreams
Sees shapes of pain grow tall. Awake at night
He peers at sounds and stumbles at a breeze.
And none holds life less dear. For as a youth
Who by some accident observes his love
Naked and in some natural ugly act,

He turns with loathing and with flaming hands,
    Seared and betrayed by sight.

He is the business man, on beauty trades,
Dealer in arts and thoughts who, like the Jew,
Shall rise from slums and hated dialects
A tower of bitterness. Shall be always strange,
Hunted and then sought after. Shall be sat
Like an ambassador from another race
At tables rich with music. He shall eat flowers,
Chew honey and spit out gall. They shall all smile
    And love and pity him.

His death shall be by drowning. In that hour
When the last bubble of pure heaven's air
Hovers within his throat, safe on his bed,
A small eternal figurehead in terror,
He shall cry out and clutch his days of straw
Before the blackest wave. Lastly, his tomb
Shall list and founder in the troughs of grass
    And none shall speak his name.

Elegy for a Dead Soldier

I

A white sheet on the tail-gate of a truck
Becomes an altar; two small candlesticks
Sputter at each side of the crucifix
Laid round with flowers brighter than the blood,
Red as the red of our apocalypse,
Hibiscus that a marching man will pluck
To stick into his rifle or his hat,
And great blue morning-glories pale as lips
That shall no longer taste or kiss or swear.
The wind begins a low magnificat,
The chaplain chats, the palmtrees swirl their hair,
The columns come together through the mud.

II

We too are ashes as we watch and hear
The psalm, the sorrow, and the simple praise
Of one whose promised thoughts of other days
Were such as ours, but now wholly destroyed,
The service record of his youth wiped out,
His dream dispersed by shot, must disappear.
What can we feel but wonder at a loss
That seems to point at nothing but the doubt
Which flirts our sense of luck into the ditch?
Reader of Paul who prays beside this fosse,
Shall we believe our eyes or legends rich
With glory and rebirth beyond the void?

III

For this comrade is dead, dead in the war,
A young man out of millions yet to live,
One cut away from all that war can give,
Freedom of self and peace to wander free.
Who mourns in all this sober multitude
Who did not feel the bite of it before
The bullet found its aim? This worthy flesh,
This boy laid in a coffin and reviewed—
Who has not wrapped himself in this same flag,
Heard the light fall of dirt, his wound still fresh,
Felt his eyes closed, and heard the distant brag
Of the last volley of humanity?

IV

By chance I saw him die, stretched on the ground,
A tattooed arm lifted to take the blood
Of someone else sealed in a tin. I stood
During the last delirium that stays
The intelligence a tiny moment more,
And then the strangulation, the last sound.
The end was sudden, like a foolish play,
A stupid fool slamming a foolish door,
The absurd catastrophe, half-prearranged,

And all the decisive things still left to say.
So we disbanded, angrier and unchanged,
Sick with the utter silence of dispraise.

V

We ask for no statistics of the killed,
For nothing political impinges on
This single casualty, or all those gone,
Missing or healing, sinking or dispersed,
Hundreds of thousands counted, millions lost.
More than an accident and less than willed
Is every fall, and this one like the rest.
However others calculate the cost,
To us the final aggregate is *one*,
One with a name, one transferred to the blest;
And though another stoops and takes the gun,
We cannot add the second to the first.

VI

I would not speak for him who could not speak
Unless my fear were true: he was not wronged,
He knew to which decision he belonged
But let it choose itself. Ripe in instinct,
Neither the victim nor the volunteer,
He followed, and the leaders could not seek
Beyond the followers. Much of this he knew;
The journey was a detour that would steer
Into the Lincoln Highway of a land
Remorselessly improved, excited, new,
And that was what he wanted. He had planned
To earn and drive. He and the world had winked.

VII

No history deceived him, for he knew
Little of times and armies not his own;
He never felt that peace was but a loan,
Had never questioned the idea of gain.
Beyond the headlines once or twice he saw
The gathering of a power by the few

But could not tell their names; he cast his vote,
Distrusting all the elected but not law.
He laughed at socialism; *on mourrait*
Pour les industriels? He shed his coat
And not for brotherhood, but for his pay.
To him the red flag marked the sewer main.

VIII

Above all else he loathed the homily,
The slogan and the ad. He paid his bill
But not for Congressmen at Bunker Hill.
Ideals were few and those there were not made
For conversation. He belonged to church
But never spoke of God. The Christmas tree,
The Easter egg, baptism, he observed,
Never denied the preacher on his perch,
And would not sign Resolved That or Whereas.
Softness he had and hours and nights reserved
For thinking, dressing, dancing to the jazz.
His laugh was real, his manners were home made.

IX

Of all men poverty pursued him least;
He was ashamed of all the down and out,
Spurned the panhandler like an uneasy doubt,
And saw the unemployed as a vague mass
Incapable of hunger or revolt.
He hated other races, south or east,
And shoved them to the margin of his mind.
He could recall the justice of the Colt,
Take interest in a gang-war like a game.
His ancestry was somewhere far behind
And left him only his peculiar name.
Doors opened, and he recognized no class.

X

His children would have known a heritage,
Just or unjust, the richest in the world,

The quantum of all art and science curled
In the horn of plenty, bursting from the horn,
A people bathed in honey, Paris come,
Vienna transferred with the highest wage,
A World's Fair spread to Phoenix, Jacksonville,
Earth's capitol, the new Byzantium,
Kingdom of man—who knows? Hollow or firm,
No man can ever prophesy until
Out of our death some undiscovered germ,
Whole toleration or pure peace is born.

XI

The time to mourn is short that best becomes
The military dead. We lift and fold the flag,
Lay bare the coffin with its written tag,
And march away. Behind, four others wait
To lift the box, the heaviest of loads.
The anesthetic afternoon benumbs,
Sickens our senses, forces back our talk.
We know that others on tomorrow's roads
Will fall, ourselves perhaps, the man beside,
Over the world the threatened, all who walk:
And could we mark the grave of him who died
We would write this beneath his name and date:

EPITAPH

Underneath this wooden cross there lies
A Christian killed in battle. You who read,
Remember that this stranger died in pain;
And passing here, if you can lift your eyes
Upon a peace kept by a human creed,
Know that one soldier has not died in vain.

Jew

The name is immortal but only the name, for the rest
Is a nose that can change in the weathers of time or persist
Or die out in confusion or model itself on the best.

But the name is a language itself that is whispered and hissed
Through the houses of ages, and ever a language the same,
And ever and ever a blow on our heart like a fist.

And this last of our dream in the desert, O curse of our name,
Is immortal as Abraham's voice in our fragment of prayer
Adonai, Adonai, for our bondage of murder and shame!

And the word for the murder of God will cry out on the air
Though the race is no more and the temples are closed of our will
And the peace is made fast on the earth and the earth is made fair;

Our name is impaled in the heart of the world on a hill
Where we suffer to die by the hands of ourselves, and to kill.

Love for a Hand

Two hands lie still, the hairy and the white,
And soon down ladders of reflected light
The sleepers climb in silence. Gradually
They separate on paths of long ago,
Each winding on his arm the unpleasant clew
That leads, live as a nerve, to memory.

But often when too steep her dream descends,
Perhaps to the grotto where her father bends
To pick her up, the husband wakes as though
He had forgotten something in the house.
Motionless he eyes the room that glows
With the little animals of light that prowl

This way and that. Soft are the beasts of light
But softer still her hand that drifts so white
Upon the whiteness. How like a water-plant
It floats upon the black canal of sleep,
Suspended upward from the distant deep
In pure achievement of its lovely want!

154

Quietly then he plucks it and it folds
And is again a hand, small as a child's.
He would revive it but it barely stirs
And so he carries it off a little way
And breaks it open gently. Now he can see
The sweetness of the fruit, his hand eats hers.

The Potomac

The thin Potomac scarcely moves
But to divide Virginia from today;
　　Rider, whichever is your way
You go due south and neither South improves;
Not this, of fractured columns and queer rents
　　And rags that charm the nationalist,
Not that, the axle of the continents,
Nor the thin sky that flows unprejudiced
This side and that, cleansing the poisoned breath.

For Thomas died a Georgian death
And now the legion bones of Arlington
　　Laid out in marble alphabets
Stare on the great tombs of the capitol
　　Where heroes calcified and cool
　　Ponder the soldier named Unknown
Whose lips are guarded with live bayonets.

Yet he shall speak though sentries walk
And columns with their cold Corinthian stalk
　　Shed gold-dust pollen on Brazil
　　To turn the world to Roman chalk;
Yet he shall speak, yet he shall speak
　　Whose sulphur lit the flood-lit Dome,
　　Whose hands were never in the kill,
Whose will was furrows of Virginia loam.

But not like London blown apart by boys
Who learned the books of love in English schools,
His name shall strike the fluted columns down;
These shall lie buried deep as fifty Troys,
The money fade like leaves from green to brown,
And embassies dissolve to molecules.

from ADAM AND EVE

II

The Recognition of Eve

Whatever it was she had so fiercely fought
Had fled back to the sky, but still she lay
With arms outspread, awaiting its assault,
Staring up through the branches of the tree,
The fig tree. Then she drew a shuddering breath
And turned her head instinctively his way.
She had fought birth as dying men fight death.

Her sigh awakened him. He turned and saw
A body swollen, as though formed of fruits,
White as the flesh of fishes, soft and raw.
He hoped she was another of the brutes
So he crawled over and looked into her eyes,
The human wells that pool all absolutes.
It was like looking into double skies.

And when she spoke the first word (it was *thou*)
He was terror-stricken, but she raised her hand
And touched his wound where it was fading now,
For he must feel the place to understand.
Then he recalled the longing that had torn
His side, and while he watched it whitely mend,
He felt it stab him suddenly like a thorn.

156

He thought the woman had hurt him. Was it she
Or the same sickness seeking to return;
Or was there any difference, the pain set free
And she who seized him now as hard as iron?
Her fingers bit his body. She looked old
And involuted, like the newly-born.
He let her hurt him till she loosed her hold.

Then she forgot him and she wearily stood
And went in search of water through the grove.
Adam could see her wandering through the wood,
Studying her footsteps as her body wove
In light and out of light. She found a pool
And there he followed shyly to observe.
She was already turning beautiful.

[August Saturday Night on the Negro Street]

August Saturday night on the Negro street the trolleys clang and
break sweet dusty smoke. Cars hoot meaningless signals. The air is in
a sweat of Jim Crow gaiety, shopping, milling, rubbing of flesh, five
miles of laughter in white Baltimore. The second floor dance hall has
a famous trumpet. You can't move on the floor, which rolls like waves
and is in actual danger of giving way. The temperature adds to the
frenzy. There is a no pause in the jump and scream of the jazz, heat-
waves of laughter, untranslatable slang. The dancing is demotic, terp-
sichorean. It's like a war of pleasure. It's the joy of work. The fatigue
is its own reward.

Across the street in the corner drug store where whiskey is sold and
every blandishment of skin, a teeming Negress crowds at the perfume
counter, big arms like haunches and bosom practically bare. She
laughs with her friends above the cut-glass bottles with frenchified
names and recently invented colors. She purchases a sizeable vial of
some green scent, pays green dry money, unstoppers the bottle and
dumps the entire load between her breasts! O glorious act of laughter
in the half-serious bazaar of the Jew-store!

R. S. THOMAS

(1913–)

A *Labourer*

Who can tell his years, for the winds have stretched
So tight the skin on the bare racks of bone
That his face is smooth, inscrutable as stone?
And when he wades in the brown bilge of earth
Hour by hour, or stoops to pull
The reluctant swedes, who can read the look
In the colourless eye, as his back comes straight
Like an old tree lightened of the snow's weight?
Is there love there, or hope, or any thought
For the frail form broken beneath his tread,
And the sweet pregnancy that yields his bread?

A *Peasant*

Iago Prytherch his name, though, be it allowed,
Just an ordinary man of the bald Welsh hills,
Who pens a few sheep in a gap of cloud.
Docking mangels, chipping the green skin
From the yellow bones with a half-witted grin
Of satisfaction, or churning the crude earth
To a stiff sea of clods that glint in the wind—
So are his days spent, his spittled mirth

Rarer than the sun that cracks the cheeks
Of the gaunt sky perhaps once in a week.
And then at night see him fixed in his chair
Motionless, except when he leans to gob in the fire.
There is something frightening in the vacancy of his
    mind.
His clothes, sour with years of sweat
And animal contact, shock the refined,
But affected, sense with their stark naturalness.
Yet this is your prototype, who, season by season
Against siege of rain and the wind's attrition,
Preserves his stock, an impregnable fortress
Not to be stormed even in death's confusion.
Remember him, then, for he, too, is a winner of wars,
Enduring like a tree under the curious stars.

Song

We, who are men, how shall we know
Earth's ecstasy, who feels the plough
Probing her womb,
And after, the sweet gestation
And the year's care for her condition?
We, who have forgotten, so long ago
It happened, our own orgasm,
When the wind mixed with our limbs
And the sun had suck at our bosom;
We, who have affected the livery
Of the times' prudery,
How shall we quicken again
To the lust and thrust of the sun
And the seedling rain?

The Airy Tomb

Twm was a dunce at school, and was whipped and shaken
More than I care to say, but without avail,

159

For where one man can lead a horse to the pail
Twenty can't make him drink what is not to his mind,
And books and sums were poison to Tomos, he was stone
    blind
To the printer's magic; yet his grass-green eye
Missed neither swoop nor swerve of the hawk's wing
Past the high window, and the breeze could bring,
Above the babble of the room's uproar,
Songs to his ear from the sun-dusted moor,
The grey curlew's whistle and the shrill, far cry
Of circling buzzard . . . This was Twm at school,
Subject to nothing but the sky and the wind's rule.
And then at fourteen term ended and the lad was free.
Scatheless as when he entered, he could write and spell
No more than the clouds could or the dribbling rain,
That scrawled vague messages on the window pane.

And so he returned to the Bwlch to help his father
With the rough work of the farm, to ditch, and gather
The slick ewes from the hill; to milk the cow,
And coax the mare that dragged the discordant plough.
Stepping with one stride thus from boy to man,
His school books finished with, he now began
Learning what none could teach but the hill people
In that cold country, where grass and tree
Are a green heritage more rich and rare
Than a queen's emerald or an untouched maid.
It were as well to bring the tup to the wild mare,
Or put the heron and the hen to couple,
As mate a stranger from the fat plain
With that gaunt wilderness, where snow is laid
Deadly as leprosy till the first of May,
And a man counts himself lucky if All Saints' Day
Finds his oats hived in the tottering barn.
But Tomos took to the life like a hillman born;
His work was play after the dull school, and hands,
Shamed by the pen's awkwardness, toyed with the fleece
Of ewe and wether; eyes found a new peace
Tracing the poems, which the rooks wrote in the sky.

So his shadow lengthened, and the years sped by
With the wind's quickness; Twm had turned nineteen,
When his father sickened and at the week's end died,
Leaving him heir to the lean patch of land,
Pinned to the hill-top, and the cloudy acres,
Kept as a sheep-walk. At his mother's side
He stood in the graveyard, where the undertaker
Sprinkled earth rubble with a loud tattoo
On the cheap coffin; but his heart was hurt
By the gash in the ground, and too few, too few,
Were the tears that he dropped for that lonely man
Beginning his journey to annihilation.
He had seen sheep rotting in the wind and sun,
And a hawk floating in a bubbling pool,
Its weedy entrails mocking the breast
Laced with bright water; but the dead and living
Moved hand in hand on the mountain crest
In the calm circle of taking and giving.
A wide sepulchre of brisk, blue air
Was the beast's portion, but a mortal's lot
The board's strictness, and an ugly scar
On the earth's surface, till the deliberate sod
Sealed off for ever the green land he trod.

But the swift grass, that covered the unsightly wound
In the prim churchyard, healed Tomos' mind
Of its grave-sickness, and December shadows
Dwindled to nothingness in the spring meadows,
That were blowsy with orchis and the loose bog-cotton.
Then the sun strengthened and the hush of June
Settled like lichen on the thick-timbered house,
Where Twm and his mother ate face to face
At the bare table, and each tick of the clock
Was a nail knocked in the lid of the coffin
Of that pale, spent woman, who sat with death
Jogging her elbow through the hot, still days
Of July and August, or passed like a ghost
By the scurrying poultry—it was ever her boast
Not to stay one winter with the goodman cold

161

In his callous bed. Twm was bumpkin blind
To the vain hysteria of a woman's mind,
And prated of sheep fairs, but the first frost came
To prove how ungarnished was the truth she told.

Can you picture Tomos now in the house alone,
The room silent, and the last mourner gone
Down the hill pathway? Did he sit by the flame
Of his turf fire and watch till dawn
The slow crumbling of the world he had known?
Did he rebuild out of the ragged embers
A new life, tempered to the sting of sorrow?
Twm went to bed and woke on the grey morrow
To the usual jobbery in sty and stable;
Cleaned out the cow-house, harnessed the mare,
And went prospecting with the keen ploughshare.
Yet sometimes the day was dark, and the clouds remembered,
Herded in the bare lanes of sky, the funeral rite,
And Tomos about the house or set at table
Was aware of something for which he had no name,
Though the one tree, which dripped through the winter
        night
With a clock's constancy, tried hard to tell
The insensitive mind what the heart knew well.

But March squalls, making the windows rattle,
Blew great gaps in his thoughts, till April followed
With a new sweetness, that set the streams gossiping.
On Easter Day he heard the first warbler sing
In the quick ash by the door, and the snow made room
On the sharp turf for the first fumbling lamb.
Docking and grading now until after dark
In the green field or fold, there was too much work
For the mind to wander, though the robin wove
In the young hazel a sweet tale of love.
And what is love to an uncultured youth
In the desolate pastures, but the itch of cattle
At set times and seasons? Twm rarely went down

With his gay neighbours to the petticoat town
In a crook of the valley, and his mind was free
Of the dream pictures which lead to romance.
Hearts and arrows, scribbled at the lane's entrance,
Were a meaningless symbol, as esoteric
As his school fractions; the one language he knew
Was the shrill scream in the dark, the shadow within the
    shadow,
The glimmer of flesh, deadly as mistletoe.

Of course there was talk in the parish, girls stood at their
    doors
In November evenings, their glances busy as moths
Round that far window; and some, whom passion made
    bolder
As the buds opened, lagged in the bottom meadow
And coughed and called. But never a voice replied
From that grim house, nailed to the mountain side,
For Tomos was up with the lambs, or stealthily hoarding
The last light from the sky in his soul's crannies.
So the tongues still wagged, and Tomos became a story
To please a neighbour with, or raise the laughter
In the lewd tavern, for folk cannot abide
The inscrutable riddle, posed by their own kin.
And you, hypocrite reader, at ease in your chair,
Do not mock their conduct, for are you not also weary
Of this odd tale, preferring the usual climax?
He was not well-favoured, you think, nor gay, nor rich,
But surely it happened that one of those supple bitches
With the sly haunches angled him into her net
At the male season, or, what is perhaps more romantic,
Some lily-white maid, a clerk or a minister's daughter,
With delicate hands, and eyes brittle as flowers
Or curved sea-shells, taught him the tender airs
Of a true gallant?
           No, no, you must face the fact
Of his long life alone in that crumbling house
With winds rending the joints, and the grey rain's claws

Sharp in the thatch; of his work up on the moors
With the moon for candle, and the shrill rabble of stars
Crowding his shoulders. For Twm was true to his fate,
That wound solitary as a brook through the crimson heather,
Trodden only by sheep, where youth and age
Met in the circle of a buzzard's flight
Round the blue axle of heaven; and a fortnight gone
Was the shy soul from the festering flesh and bone
When they found him there, entombed in the lucid weather.

Saint Antony

Saint Antony in the sand saw shapes rising,
Formed by the wind, sinuous, lewd
As snakes dancing; their bitter poison
Entered the soul through his pale eyes.

Sleep came; the dances were renewed
Upon the retina, the lids not proof
Against the orgy of the spheres.
Night long he ranged the Bacchanalian dark,
Himself the prey, the hunter and the wood.

In a Country Church

To one kneeling down no word came,
Only the wind's song, saddening the lips
Of the grave saints, rigid in glass;
Or the dry whisper of unseen wings,
Bats not angels, in the high roof.

Was he balked by silence? He kneeled long,
And saw love in a dark crown
Of thorns blazing, and a winter tree
Golden with fruit of a man's body.

Chapel Deacon

Who put that crease in your soul,
Davies, ready this fine morning
For the staid chapel, where the Book's frown
Sobers the sunlight? Who taught you to pray
And scheme at once, your eyes turning
Skyward, while your swift mind weighs
Your heifer's chances in the next town's
Fair on Thursday? Are your heart's coals
Kindled for God, or is the burning
Of your lean cheeks because you sit
Too near that girl's smouldering gaze?
Tell me, Davies, for the faint breeze
From heaven freshens and I roll in it,
Who taught you your deft poise?

Age

Farmer, you were young once.
And she was there, waiting, the unique flower
That only you could find in the wild moor
Of your experience.
Gathered, she grew to the warm woman
Your hands had imagined
Fondling soil in the spring fields.

And she was fertile; four strong sons
Stood up like corn in June about you.
But, farmer, did you cherish, tend her
As your own flesh, this dry stalk
Where the past murmurs its sad tune?
Is this the harvest of your blithe sowing?

If you had spared from your long store
Of days lavished upon the land

But one for her where she lay fallow,
Drying, hardening, withering to waste.
But now—too late! You're an old tree,
Your roots groping in her in vain.

Poetry for Supper

'Listen, now, verse should be as natural
As the small tuber that feeds on muck
And grows slowly from obtuse soil
To the white flower of immortal beauty.'

'Natural, hell! What was it Chaucer
Said once about the long toil
That goes like blood to the poem's making?
Leave it to nature and the verse sprawls,
Limp as bindweed, if it break at all
Life's iron crust. Man, you must sweat
And rhyme your guts taut, if you'd build
Your verse a ladder.'
                              'You speak as though
No sunlight ever surprised the mind
Groping on its cloudy path.'

'Sunlight's a thing that needs a window
Before it enter a dark room.
Windows don't happen.'
                              So two old poets,
Hunched at their beer in the low haze
Of an inn parlour, while the talk ran
Noisily by them, glib with prose.

Anniversary

Nineteen years now
Under the same roof

166

Eating our bread,
Using the same air;
Sighing, if one sighs,
Meeting the other's
Words with a look
That thaws suspicion.

Nineteen years now
Sharing life's table,
And not to be first
To call the meal long
We balance it thoughtfully
On the tip of the tongue,
Careful to maintain
The strict palate.

Nineteen years now
Keeping simple house,
Opening the door
To friend and stranger;
Opening the womb
Softly to let enter
The one child
With his huge hunger.

A Welsh Testament

All right, I was Welsh. Does it matter?
I spoke the tongue that was passed on
To me in the place I happened to be,
A place huddled between grey walls
Of cloud for at least half the year.
My word for heaven was not yours.
The word for hell had a sharp edge
Put on it by the hand of the wind
Honing, honing with a shrill sound
Day and night. Nothing that Glyn Dwr

Knew was armour against the rain's
Missiles. What was descent from him?

Even God had a Welsh name:
We spoke to him in the old language;
He was to have a peculiar care
For the Welsh people. History showed us
He was too big to be nailed to the wall
Of a stone chapel, yet still we crammed him
Between the boards of a black book.

Yet men sought us despite this.
My high cheek-bones, my length of skull
Drew them as to a rare portrait
By a dead master. I saw them stare
From their long cars, as I passed knee-deep
In ewes and wethers. I saw them stand
By the thorn hedges, watching me string
The far flocks on a shrill whistle.

And always there was their eyes' strong
Pressure on me: You are Welsh, they said;
Speak to us so; keep your fields free
Of the smell of petrol, the loud roar
Of hot tractors; we must have peace
And quietness.
                                Is a museum
Peace? I asked. Am I the keeper
Of the heart's relics, blowing the dust
In my own eyes? I am a man;
I never wanted the drab rôle
Life assigned me, an actor playing
To the past's audience upon a stage
Of earth and stone; the absurd label
Of birth, of race hanging askew
About my shoulders. I was in prison
Until you came; your voice was a key
Turning in the enormous lock
Of hopelessness. Did the door open
To let me out or yourselves in?

LAURIE LEE

(1914–)

The Long War

Less passionate the long war throws
its burning thorn about all men,
caught in one grief, we share one wound,
and cry one dialect of pain.

We have forgot who fired the house,
whose easy mischief spilt first blood,
under one raging roof we lie
the fault no longer understood.

But as our twisted arms embrace
the desert where our cities stood,
death's family likeness in each face
must show, at last, our brotherhood.

First Love

That was her beginning, an apparition
of rose in the unbreathed airs of his love,
her heart revealed by the wash of summer
sprung from her childhood's shallow stream.

Then it was that she put up her hair,
inscribed her eyes with a look of grief,
while her limbs grew as curious as coral branches,
her breast full of secrets.

But the boy, confused in his day's desire,
was searching for herons, his fingers bathed
in the green of walnuts, or watching at night
the Great Bear spin from the maypole star.

It was then that he paused in the death of a game,
felt the hook of her hair on his swimming throat,
saw her mouth at large in the dark river
flushed like a salmon.

But he covered his face and hid his joy
in a wild-goose web of false directions,
and hunted the woods for eggs and glow-worms,
for rabbits tasteless as moss.

And she walked in fields where the crocuses
branded her feet, and mares' tails sprang
from the prancing lake, and the salty grasses
surged round her stranded body.

Field of Autumn

Slow moves the acid breath of noon
over the copper-coated hill,
slow from the wild crab's bearded breast
the palsied apples fall.

Like coloured smoke the day hangs fire,
taking the village without sound;
the vulture-headed sun lies low
chained to the violet ground.

The horse upon the rocky height
rolls all the valley in his eye,
but dares not raise his foot or move
his shoulder from the fly.

The sheep, snail-backed against the wall,
lifts her blind face but does not know
the cry her blackened tongue gives forth
is the first bleat of snow.

Each bird and stone, each roof and well,
feels the gold foot of autumn pass;
each spider binds with glittering snare
the splintered bones of grass.

Slow moves the hour that sucks our life,
slow drops the late wasp from the pear,
the rose tree's thread of scent draws thin—
and snaps upon the air.

Bombay Arrival

Slow-hooved across the carrion sea,
Smeared by the betel-spitting sun,
Like cows the Bombay islands come
Dragging the mainland into view.

The loose flank loops the rocky bone,
The light beats thin on horn and hill;
Still breeds the flesh for hawks, and still
The Hindu heart drips on a stone.

Around the wide dawn-ridden bay
The waters move their daggered wings;
The dhow upon its shadow clings—
A dark moth pinioned to the day.

False in the morning, screened with silk,
Neat as an egg the Town draws near,
False as a map her streets appear
Ambling, and odourless as milk.

Until she holds us face to face—
A crumbling mask with bullet pores,
A nakedness of jewels and sores
Clutched with our guilt in her embrace.

The Edge of Day

The dawn's precise pronouncement waits
With breath of light indrawn,
Then forms with smoky, smut-red lips
The great O of the sun.

The mouldering atoms of the dark
Blaze into morning air;
The birdlike stars droop down and die,
The starlike birds catch fire.

The thrush's tinder throat strikes up,
The sparrow chips hot sparks
From flinty tongue, and all the sky
Showers with electric larks.

And my huge eye a chaos is
Where molten worlds are born;
Where floats the eagle's flaming moon,
And crows, like clinkers, burn;

Where blackbirds scream with comet tails,
And flaring finches fall,
And starlings, aimed like meteors,
Bounce from the garden wall;

Where, from the edge of day I spring
Alive for mortal flight,
Lit by the heart's exploding sun
Bursting from night to night.

Sunken Evening

The green light floods the city square—
  A sea of fowl and feathered fish,
    Where squalls of rainbirds dive and splash
And gusty sparrows chop the air.

Submerged, the prawn-blue pigeons feed
  In sandy grottoes round the Mall,
    And crusted lobster-buses crawl
Among the fountains' silver weed.

There, like a wreck, with mast and bell,
  The torn church settles by the bow,
    While phosphorescent starlings stow
Their mussel shells along the hull.

The oyster-poet, drowned but dry,
  Rolls a black pearl between his bones;
    The typist, trapped by telephones,
Gazes in bubbles at the sky.

Till, with the dark, the shallows run,
  And homeward surges tides and fret—
    The slow night trawls its heavy net
And hauls the clerk to Surbiton.

Home from Abroad

Far-fetched with tales of other worlds and ways,
My skin well-oiled with wines of the Levant,

I set my face into a filial smile
To greet the pale, domestic kiss of Kent.

But shall I never learn? That gawky girl,
Recalled so primly in my foreign thoughts,
Becomes again the green-haired queen of love
Whose wanton form dilates as it delights.

Her rolling tidal landscape floods the eye
And drowns Chianti in a dusky stream;
The flower-flecked grasses swim with simple horses,
The hedges choke with roses fat as cream.

So do I breathe the hayblown airs of home,
And watch the sea-green elms drip birds and shadows,
And as the twilight nets the plunging sun
My heart's keel slides to rest among the meadows.

Town Owl

On eves of cold, when slow coal fires,
rooted in basements, burn and branch,
brushing with smoke the city air;

When quartered moons pale in the sky,
and neons glow along the dark
like deadly nightshade on a briar;

Above the muffled traffic then
I hear the owl, and at his note
I shudder in my private chair.

For like an augur he has come
to roost among our crumbling walls,
his blooded talons sheathed in fur.

Some secret lure of time it seems
has called him from his country wastes
to hunt a newer wasteland here.

And where the candelabra swung
bright with the dancers' thousand eyes,
now his black, hooded pupils stare,

And where the silk-shoed lovers ran
with dust of diamonds in their hair,
he opens now his silent wing,

And, like a stroke of doom, drops down,
and swoops across the empty hall,
and plucks a quick mouse off the stair . . .

Scot in the Desert

All day the sand, like golden chains,
The desert distance binds;
All day the crouching camels groan,
Whipped by the gritty winds.

The mountain, flayed by sun, reveals
Red muscles, wounds of stone,
While on its face the black goats swarm
And bite it to the bone.

Here light is death; on every rock
It stretches like a cry,
Its fever burns up every bush,
It drinks each river dry.

It cracks with thirst the creviced lip,
It fattens black the tongue,
It turns the storm cloud into dust,
The morning dew to dung.

Men were not made to flourish here,
They shroud their heads and fly—
Save one, who stares into the sun
With sky-blue British eye.

Who stares into the zenith sun
And smiles and feels no pain,
Blood-cooled by Calvin, mist and bog,
And summers in the rain.

Long Summer

Gold as an infant's humming dream,
Stamped with its timeless, tropic blush,
The steady sun stands in the air
And burns like Moses' holy bush.

And burns while nothing it consumes;
The smoking branch but greener grows,
The crackling briar, from budded lips,
A floating stream of blossom blows.

A daze of hours, a blaze of noons,
Licks my cold shadow from the ground;
A flaming trident rears each dawn
To stir the blood of earth around.

Unsinged beneath the furnace sky
The frenzied beetle runs reborn,
The ant his antic mountain moves,
The rampant ram rewinds his horn.

I see the crazy bees drop fat
From tulips ten times gorged and dry;
I see the sated swallow plunge
To drink the dazzled waterfly.

A halo flares around my head,
A sunflower flares across the sun,
While down the summer's seamless haze
Such feasts of milk and honey run

That lying with my orchid love,
Whose kiss no frost of age can sever,
I cannot doubt the cold is dead,
The gold earth turned to good—forever.

HOWARD SERGEANT

(1914-)

High Kingdom

PART I

Climbing the beanstalk of your mind, I reach
a star, the private country you inhabit,
where no adult proprieties encroach
upon the candleflame that is your spirit.

A myriad landscapes lie within your eyes.
Here Hamelin shadows caper to piping light;
castles rise and crumble with miraculous ease
but leave no hurt perceptions in the heart.

Wind sings its crazy swallows over lake
and shallow river, or thoughtfully carves
a symphony in stone: wind your broomstick,
you mark the intimations of the leaves.

And here the wild white horses of your will—
so fallible gods to fellow your footsteps—
leap, as my hand leaps, or this eager wall,
when you balance my world on fingertips.

No time no seasons urging, you salvage
every idle minute with your child-true

faculty for indiscriminate coinage;
importunate twig, absorb the whole tree.

Names have no meaning; eyes mean what they say
(later, perhaps, you'll learn to parry truth
with words). Each day an adventure, you see
parents as mountains moving by your faith.

PART II

And I recall that unconquerable land
where morning tiptoes the foothills, the sly
vision breaking through rocks, and vagabond
druids in the cromlechs of childhood, cautiously

hoarding their miracles from man. So, ghost
of my own unreason, I mourn the fallen
dream; and heart awaits the fabulous guest
whose gift of laughter will deliver Merlin.

You are the stranger rapping on my window,
sowing me messages of love and pain;
the looting angel at my side, whose oneday
fingers hold the nails, the healing crown of thorn.

Years fall like petals. You too must emigrate
and, O my darling, I pray that you, aloof
from the high kingdom, may yet hold passport;
may never lose this poem, starpoise to life.

The Inland Sea

Here and near as the hands of the sea
  Where the sea holds the land
Till the climbing dark and all time are dying,
  Where the walls are down, and the sand
  Is a building-ground for the flair
Of a poet or lover, or the boy highflying,

And the dunes of the heart are free,
Is the country we know. Wholly days and night
Are trapped in the sea's green hair
And this half-darkness here is half our light.

Fair and far from the prayers of the kind
And their wiles who'd have you sleep
Safe and sound in the boisterous shires of land
And surf, is the country we keep
Reclaimed in the bay of the mind,
Where the smooth white gulls rise over the sand
And the nodding heads of the blind.
Walk firmly that shore, whatever the wise ones
Devise for your footsteps, and find
In yourself the unknown, the only horizons.

Morning Song for a Lover

Now you are nearer than my heart
. . . and yet inexorably far.
Sleeping, you rift my world apart;
I cannot climb to where you are.
Behind those eyelashes, my Love,
lies dormant all your womanhood—
gentle tigress and savage dove,
the witches of each broomstick mood,
pagan and pilgrim, yield their place
to this one child who, like a ghost,
assumes your lovely form and face.
Eurydice was not more lost
in darkness when her prince forgot
hell's terms (*I shall invoke you with
my kiss*). Eurydice was not
more loved, and she a minor myth
beside your mystery (*can I
then hold you by my faith?*). For in
your flesh two separate legends lie,

two spirits share the discipline
that sleep and waking, birth and death
and time and being you impose—
the woman who, with every breath,
adopts the appropriate mask and poise
(*yet have I torn the masks aside*),
and treads my future as a stair
lightly, politely, in her pride;
or in her passion makes it flare
beyond the planets with her name:
and then the child transcending all
her beauty, arrogance and flame.
So in my morning presence fall
the attributes I deified,
leaving the unknown, this shy grave
enigma sleeping at my side.
Desire is stilled beneath the wave
and cannot now be reconciled
with a reverence such as this.
But dream, my Darling, in the child
and I shall call you with a kiss.

from ''THE LEAVES OF EUROPE''

v

Man Meeting Himself

They are moving inwards, the circle is closing.
Tonight I have heard them again among
the houses, a million voices rising as one
in the darkness, hounding our lives with their
pitiless tongues, the voices of leaves and children
crying, as children cry, for light—where is
no light; for love, where there is only silence:

and under my feet stars like dead leaves falling
under my feet the bloodless faces staring . . .

There is one hand, five-barbed with innocence,
can start a conflagration in the breast.
There is one force can find a man his likeness
in a stone, and we have buried it with lies;
but not for ever—we have not earth enough
nor words to turn the wind back from our hearts.
Come day the rocks will open and ourselves
walk out in freedom to startle the world as men.

Look into their eyes and faces if you dare
and, if you dare, describe a victory.
Not history, not hate, flows over them.

> And this is guilt—
> man meeting himself in the night,
> and hating himself and the wind
> and the lips of the wind; the swivelling
> eye and the lies most known
> by the light, the beast in the man
> and the man in the beast and himself;
> but hating most deeply and deadly
> his hatred of self—
> to answer
> *I do not know their language!*

V I

The Inundation

> Moon at the full. Europe has burst its banks
> and the first floodwaters rising reach our doors.
> Look down, you lovers, now, from your high towers;
> your stone cannot long withstand their violent fingers
> *who were no enemies*

> And you who kept the willows bright by summer
> or by winter conjured aprils from the flesh,
> look to your trophies now—desire is withered
> at their cold breath, the born and the unborn riding
> *who were no enemies*

And you who dreamt of islands winking in the sun,
horizons like stepping-stones beneath your heels,
but feared too much the faring—they know well
your shallow harbours, the dead and the half-dead rising
who were no enemies

Soldiers and civilians, all you who shouted
in the streets, first for a saviour, but louder
for the killer, your catchwords will not appease
them now, the dispossessing and the dispossessed
who were no enemies

Not even you whose hands were clean, the mass-
observers perched upon the skull-shaped hill,
can hold them with all your monumental tears:
the graves are open and they have taken the cities
who were no enemies

VII

Autumn again, the leopardlike and burning
season, but with it no discovery in sky
or feather, no flicker in the lantern eyes
of berries. The word we learnt has lost its meaning.

Today the sun is impotent, either to salve
our consciousness with the touch of hands or strike
for us a fountain from the voiceless rock;
our only light an evanescence clipped
through the folds of cloud by the wild geese flying
homewards to the saltings, to the uninhibited land.
The stone lies heavy on the heart and is not now
to be moved by time or the snow-bright angel's shoulder.

Autumn again and I have seen the cold
grey fingers of death at work among the trees,
a traffic in limbs and faces, star following
fading star to the beaten grass like infants
racing out of school—but these are children

without joy or gesture, without the anarchy
of childhood:
                        their lips will be remembered by
the hungry breasts of Europe when the soft
wind-voices speak, and small ghosts lift their faces
in the darkness for kisses that cannot be given.
The twigs that wear the horse-shoe scars for grief
will never know their soft green flesh again.

Autumn again, and I have seen the labourers
gather on a frosty morning at the wood's bare fringes
where the furrows, rich with a memory of summer,
the bearded corn, lie easy as a woman after
travail and stretch their fingertips under
the briars, under the rough warm blankets of soil.
I have seen them burning leaves, the smoke curling
above the meadows, a flock of bewildered lambs
bursting upon the hedges and the pastures of wind.
A *shepherd would know these lambs—their ears are notched
with a cross—would know the pitchmarks on their backs*

Sparks aim for the heart on the crimpled air
but the leafburners have instructions, hirelings
accustomed to obey. The old men, slow-moving
and cautious, keep always to windward and lean
upon their long broomhandles when the tongues
of flame stammer into speech over the branches,
absorbing the language into their cold bones.
Now more than leaves are heaped on the smouldering fires.
Somewhere in the distance the lost music rises,
the autumn songs of children, for whom the wind
is a voice in the trees and the berries douse their light.

        This is the chosen darkness,
        this is the myth our fathers
        and their fathers knew, and choosing
        closed their eyes and ears, and gave
        their willing hands to any cause

that named them heroes, that promised
no responsibility—
to plead
I am absolved; I was commanded

And this is false
to murmur
I was not there.

DYLAN THOMAS

(1914–53)

The Force that Through the Green Fuse Drives the Flower

The force that through the green fuse drives the flower
Drives my green age; that blasts the roots of trees
Is my destroyer.
And I am dumb to tell the crooked rose
My youth is bent by the same wintry fever.

The force that drives the water through the rocks
Drives my red blood; that dries the mouthing streams
Turns mine to wax.
And I am dumb to mouth unto my veins
How at the mountain spring the same mouth sucks.

The hand that whirls the water in the pool
Stirs the quicksand; that ropes the blowing wind
Hauls my shroud sail.
And I am dumb to tell the hanging man
How of my clay is made the hangman's lime.

The lips of time leech to the fountain head;
Love drips and gathers, but the fallen blood
Shall calm her sores.

And I am dumb to tell a weather's wind
How time has ticked a heaven round the stars.

And I am dumb to tell the lover's tomb
How at my sheet goes the same crooked worm.

Especially When the October Wind

Especially when the October wind
With frosty fingers punishes my hair,
Caught by the crabbing sun I walk on fire
And cast a shadow crab upon the land,
By the sea's side, hearing the noise of birds,
Hearing the raven cough in winter sticks,
My busy heart who shudders as she talks
Sheds the syllabic blood and drains her words.

Shut, too, in a tower of words, I mark
On the horizon walking like the trees
The wordy shapes of women, and the rows
Of the star-gestured children in the park.
Some let me make you of the vowelled beeches,
Some of the oaken voices, from the roots
Of many a thorny shire tell you notes,
Some let me make you of the water's speeches.

Behind a pot of ferns the wagging clock
Tells me the hour's word, the neural meaning
Flies on the shafted disk, declaims the morning
And tells the windy weather in the cock.
Some let me make you of the meadow's signs;
The signal grass that tells me all I know
Breaks with the wormy winter through the eye.
Some let me tell you of the raven's sins.

Especially when the October wind
(Some let me make you of autumnal spells,

The spider-tongued, and the loud hill of Wales)
With fists of turnips punishes the land,
Some let me make you of the heartless words.
The heart is drained that, spelling in the scurry
Of chemic blood, warned of the coming fury.
By the sea's side hear the dark-vowelled birds.

Incarnate Devil

Incarnate devil in a talking snake,
The central plains of Asia in his garden,
In shaping-time the circle stung awake,
In shapes of sin forked out the bearded apple,
And God walked there who was a fiddling warden
And played down pardon from the heavens' hill.

When we were strangers to the guided seas,
A handmade moon half holy in a cloud,
The wisemen tell me that the garden gods
Twined good and evil on an eastern tree;
And when the moon rose windily it was
Black as the beast and paler than the cross.

We in our Eden knew the secret guardian
In sacred waters that no frost could harden,
And in the mighty mornings of the earth;
Hell in a horn of sulphur and the cloven myth,
All heaven in a midnight of the sun,
A serpent fiddled in the shaping-time.

Do You Not Father Me

Do you not father me, nor the erected arm
For my tall tower's sake cast in her stone?
Do you not mother me, nor, as I am,
The lovers' house, lie suffering my stain?

Do you not sister me, nor the erected crime
For my tall turrets carry as your sin?
Do you not brother me, nor, as you climb,
Adore my windows for their summer scene?

Am I not father, too, and the ascending boy,
The boy of woman and the wanton starer
Marking the flesh and summer in the bay?
Am I not sister, too, who is my saviour?
Am I not all of you by the directed sea
Where bird and shell are babbling in my tower?
Am I not you who front the tidy shore,
Nor roof of sand, nor yet the towering tiler?

You are all these, said she who gave me the long suck,
All these, he said who sacked the children's town,
Up rose the Abraham-man, mad for my sake,
They said, who hacked and humoured, they were mine.
I am, the tower told, felled by a timeless stroke,
Who razed my wooden folly stands aghast,
For man-begetters in the dry-as-paste,
The ringed-sea ghost, rise grimly from the wrack.

Do you not father me on the destroying sand?
You are your sisters' sire, said seaweedy,
The salt sucked dam and darlings of the land
Who play the proper gentleman and lady.
Shall I still be love's house on the widdershin earth,
Woe to the windy masons at my shelter?
Love's house, they answer, and the tower death
Lie all unknowing of the grave sin-eater.

And Death Shall Have No Dominion

And death shall have no dominion.
Dead men naked they shall be one
With the man in the wind and the west moon;

When their bones are picked clean and the clean bones gone,
They shall have stars at elbow and foot;
Though they go mad they shall be sane,
Though they sink through the sea they shall rise again;
Though lovers be lost love shall not;
And death shall have no dominion.

And death shall have no dominion.
Under the windings of the sea
They lying long shall not die windily;
Twisting on racks when sinews give way,
Strapped to a wheel, yet they shall not break;
Faith in their hands shall snap in two,
And the unicorn evils run them through;
Split all ends up they shan't crack;
And death shall have no dominion.

And death shall have no dominion.
No more may gulls cry at their ears
Or waves break loud on the seashores;
Where blew a flower may a flower no more
Lift its head to the blows of the rain;
Though they be mad and dead as nails,
Heads of the characters hammer through daisies;
Break in the sun till the sun breaks down,
And death shall have no dominion.

Altarwise by Owl-Light

I

Altarwise by owl-light in the half-way house
The gentleman lay graveward with his furies;
Abaddon in the hangnail cracked from Adam,
And, from his fork, a dog among the fairies,
The atlas-eater with a jaw for news,
Bit out the mandrake with to-morrow's scream.
Then, penny-eyed, that gentleman of wounds,

Old cock from nowheres and the heaven's egg,
With bones unbuttoned to the half-way winds,
Hatched from the windy salvage on one leg,
Scraped at my cradle in a walking word
That night of time under the Christward shelter:
I am the long world's gentleman, he said,
And share my bed with Capricorn and Cancer.

II

Death is all metaphors, shape in one history;
The child that sucketh long is shooting up,
The planet-ducted pelican of circles
Weans on an artery the gender's strip;
Child of the short spark in a shapeless country
Soon sets alight a long stick from the cradle;
The horizontal cross-bones of Abaddon,
You by the cavern over the black stairs,
Rung bone and blade, the verticals of Adam,
And, manned by midnight, Jacob to the stars.
Hairs of your head, then said the hollow agent,
Are but the roots of nettles and of feathers
Over these groundworks thrusting through a pavement
And hemlock-headed in the wood of weathers.

III

First there was the lamb on knocking knees
And three dead seasons on a climbing grave
That Adam's wether in the flock of horns,
Butt of the tree-tailed worm that mounted Eve,
Horned down with skullfoot and the skull of toes
On thunderous pavements in the garden time;
Rip of the vaults, I took my marrow-ladle
Out of the wrinkled undertaker's van,
And, Rip Van Winkle from a timeless cradle,
Dipped me breast-deep in the descended bone;
The black ram, shuffling of the year, old winter,
Alone alive among his mutton fold,
We rung our weathering changes on the ladder,
Said the antipodes, and twice spring chimed.

IV

What is the metre of the dictionary?
The size of genesis? the short spark's gender?
Shade without shape? the shape of Pharaoh's echo?
(My shape of age nagging the wounded whisper).
Which sixth of wind blew out the burning gentry?
(Questions are hunchbacks to the poker marrow).
What of a bamboo man among your acres?
Corset the boneyards for a crooked boy?
Button your bodice on a hump of splinters,
My camel's eyes will needle through the shrowd.
Love's reflection of the mushroom features,
Stills snapped by night in the bread-sided field,
Once close-up smiling in the wall of pictures,
Arc-lamped thrown back upon the cutting flood.

V

And from the windy West came two-gunned Gabriel,
From Jesu's sleeve trumped up the king of spots,
The sheath-decked jacks, queen with a shuffled heart;
Said the fake gentleman in suit of spades,
Black-tongued and tipsy from salvation's bottle.
Rose my Byzantine Adam in the night.
For loss of blood I fell on Ishmael's plain,
Under the milky mushrooms slew my hunger,
A climbing sea from Asia had me down
And Jonah's Moby snatched me by the hair,
Cross-stroked salt Adam to the frozen angel
Pin-legged on pole-hills with a black medusa
By waste seas where the white bear quoted Virgil
And sirens singing from our lady's sea-straw.

VI

Cartoon of slashes on the tide-traced crater,
He in a book of water tallow-eyed
By lava's light split through the oyster vowels
And burned sea silence on a wick of words.

Pluck, cock, my sea eye, said medusa's scripture,
Lop, love, my fork tongue, said the pin-hilled nettle;
And love plucked out the stinging siren's eye,
Old cock from nowheres lopped the minstrel tongue
Till tallow I blew from the wax's tower
The fats of midnight when the salt was singing;
Adam, time's joker, on a witch of cardboard
Spelt out the seven seas, an evil index,
The bagpipe-breasted ladies in the deadweed
Blew out the blood gauze through the wound of manwax.

VII

Now stamp the Lord's Prayer on a grain of rice,
A Bible-leaved of all the written woods
Strip to this tree: a rocking alphabet,
Genesis in the root, the scarecrow word,
And one light's language in the book of trees.
Doom on deniers at the wind-turned statement.
Time's tune my ladies with the teats of music,
The scaled sea-sawers, fix in a naked sponge
Who sucks the bell-voiced Adam out of magic,
Time, milk, and magic, from the world beginning.
Time is the tune my ladies lend their heartbreak,
From bald pavilions and the house of bread
Time tracks the sound of shape on man and cloud,
On rose and icicle the ringing handprint.

VIII

This was the crucifixion on the mountain,
Time's nerve in vinegar, the gallow grave
As tarred with blood as the bright thorns I wept;
The world's my wound, God's Mary in her grief,
Bent like three trees and bird-papped through her shift,
With pins for teardrops is the long wound's woman.
This was the sky, Jack Christ, each minstrel angle
Drove in the heaven-driven of the nails
Till the three-coloured rainbow from my nipples
From pole to pole leapt round the snail-waked world.

I by the tree of thieves, all glory's sawbones,
Unsex the skeleton this mountain minute,
And by this blowclock witness of the sun
Suffer the heaven's children through my heartbeat.

IX

From the oracular archives and the parchment,
Prophets and fibre kings in oil and letter,
The lamped calligrapher, the queen in splints,
Buckle to lint and cloth their natron footsteps,
Draw on the glove of prints, dead Cairo's henna
Pour like a halo on the caps and serpents.
This was the resurrection in the desert,
Death from a bandage, rants the mask of scholars
Gold on such features, and the linen spirit
Weds my long gentleman to dusts and furies;
With priest and pharaoh bed my gentle wound,
World in the sand, on the triangle landscape,
With stones of odyssey for ash and garland
And rivers of the dead around my neck.

X

Let the tale's sailor from a Christian voyage
Atlaswise hold half-way off the dummy bay
Time's ship-racked gospel on the globe I balance:
So shall winged harbours through the rockbirds' eyes
Spot the blown word, and on the seas I image
December's thorn screwed in a brow of holly.
Let the first Peter from a rainbow's quayrail
Ask the tall fish swept from the bible east,
What rhubarb man peeled in her foam-blue channel
Has sown a flying garden round that sea-ghost?
Green as beginning, let the garden diving
Soar, with its two bark towers, to that Day
When the worm builds with the gold straws of venom
My nest of mercies in the rude, red tree.

When All My Five and Country Senses See

When all my five and country senses see,
The fingers will forget green thumbs and mark
How, through the halfmoon's vegetable eye,
Husk of young stars and handfull zodiac,
Love in the frost is pared and wintered by,
The whispering ears will watch love drummed away
Down breeze and shell to a discordant beach,
And, lashed to syllables, the lynx tongue cry
That her fond wounds are mended bitterly.
My nostrils see her breath burn like a bush.

My one and noble heart has witnesses
In all love's countries, that will grope awake;
And when blind sleep drops on the spying senses,
The heart is sensual, though five eyes break.

After the Funeral

(*In memory of Ann Jones*)

After the funeral, mule praises, brays,
Windshake of sailshaped ears, muffle-toed tap
Tap happily of one peg in the thick
Grave's foot, blinds down the lids, the teeth in black,
The spittled eyes, the salt ponds in the sleeves,
Morning smack of the spade that wakes up sleep,
Shakes a desolate boy who slits his throat
In the dark of the coffin and sheds dry leaves,
That breaks one bone to light with a judgment clout,
After the feast of tear-stuffed time and thistles
In a room with a stuffed fox and a stale fern,
I stand, for this memorial's sake, alone
In the snivelling hours with dead, humped Ann
Whose hooded, fountain heart once fell in puddles

Round the parched worlds of Wales and drowned each sun
(Though this for her is a monstrous image blindly
Magnified out of praise; her death was a still drop;
She would not have me sinking in the holy
Flood of her heart's fame; she would lie dumb and deep
And need no druid of her broken body).
But I, Ann's bard on a raised hearth, call all
The seas to service that her wood-tongued virtue
Babble like a bellbuoy over the hymning heads,
Bow down the walls of the ferned and foxy woods
That her love sing and swing through a brown chapel,
Bless her bent spirit with four, crossing birds.
Her flesh was meek as milk, but this skyward statue
With the wild breast and blessed and giant skull
Is carved from her in a room with a wet window
In a fiercely mourning house in a crooked year.
I know her scrubbed and sour humble hands
Lie with religion in their cramp, her threadbare
Whisper in a damp word, her wits drilled hollow,
Her fist of a face died clenched on a round pain;
And sculptured Ann is seventy years of stone.
These cloud-sopped, marble hands, this monumental
Argument of the hewn voice, gesture and psalm,
Storm me forever over her grave until
The stuffed lung of the fox twitch and cry Love
And the strutting fern lay seeds on the black sill.

Twenty-Four Years

Twenty-four years remind the tears of my eyes.
(Bury the dead for fear that they walk to the grave in labour.)
In the groin of the natural doorway I crouched like a tailor
Sewing a shroud for a journey
By the light of the meat-eating sun.
Dressed to die, the sensual strut begun,
With my red veins full of money,
In the final direction of the elementary town
I advance for as long as forever is.

A Refusal to Mourn the Death, by Fire, of a Child in London

Never until the mankind making
Bird beast and flower
Fathering and all humbling darkness
Tells with silence the last light breaking
And the still hour
Is come of the sea tumbling in harness

And I must enter again the round
Zion of the water bead
And the synagogue of the ear of corn
Shall I let pray the shadow of a sound
Or sow my salt seed
In the least valley of sackcloth to mourn

The majesty and burning of the child's death.
I shall not murder
The mankind of her going with a grave truth
Nor blaspheme down the stations of the breath
With any further
Elegy of innocence and youth.

Deep with the first dead lies London's daughter,
Robed in the long friends,
The grains beyond age, the dark veins of her mother,
Secret by the unmourning water
Of the riding Thames.
After the first death, there is no other.

Poem in October

It was my thirtieth year to heaven
Woke to my hearing from harbour and neighbour wood
And the mussel pooled and the heron

197

Priested shore
The morning beckon
With water praying and call of seagull and rook
And the knock of sailing boats on the net webbed wall
Myself to set foot
That second
In the still sleeping town and set forth.

My birthday began with the water-
Birds and the birds of the winged trees flying my name
Above the farms and the white horses
And I rose
In rainy autumn
And walked abroad in a shower of all my days.
High tide and the heron dived when I took the road
Over the border
And the gates
Of the town closed as the town awoke.

A springful of larks in a rolling
Cloud and the roadside bushes brimming with whistling
Blackbirds and the sun of October
Summery
On the hill's shoulder,
Here were fond climates and sweet singers suddenly
Come in the morning where I wandered and listened
To the rain wringing
Wind blow cold
In the wood faraway under me.

Pale rain over the dwindling harbour
And over the sea wet church the size of a snail
With its horns through mist and the castle
Brown as owls
But all the gardens
Of spring and summer were blooming in the tall tales
Beyond the border and under the lark full cloud.

There could I marvel
My birthday
Away but the weather turned around.

It turned away from the blithe country
And down the other air and the blue altered sky
Streamed again a wonder of summer
With apples
Pears and red currants
And I saw in the turning so clearly a child's
Forgotten mornings when he walked with his mother
Through the parables
Of sun light
And the legends of the green chapels

And the twice told fields of infancy
That his tears burned my cheeks and his heart moved in mine.
These were the woods the river and sea
Where a boy
In the listening
Summertime of the dead whispered the truth of his joy
To the trees and the stones and the fish in the tide.
And the mystery
Sang alive
Still in the water and singingbirds.

And there could I marvel my birthday
Away but the weather turned around. And the true
Joy of the long dead child sang burning
In the sun.
It was my thirtieth
Year to heaven stood there then in the summer noon
Though the town below lay leaved with October blood.
O may my heart's truth
Still be sung
On this high hill in a year's turning.

The Hunchback in the Park

The hunchback in the park
A solitary mister
Propped between trees and water
From the opening of the garden lock
That lets the trees and water enter
Until the Sunday sombre bell at dark

Eating bread from a newspaper
Drinking water from the chained cup
That the children filled with gravel
In the fountain basin where I sailed my ship
Slept at night in a dog kennel
But nobody chained him up.

Like the park birds he came early
Like the water he sat down
And Mister they called Hey mister
The truant boys from the town
Running when he had heard them clearly
On out of sound

Past lake and rockery
Laughing when he shook his paper
Hunchbacked in mockery
Through the loud zoo of the willow groves
Dodging the park keeper
With his stick that picked up leaves.

And the old dog sleeper
Alone between nurses and swans
While the boys among willows
Made the tigers jump out of their eyes
To roar on the rockery stones
And the groves were blue with sailors

Made all day until bell time
A woman figure without fault
Straight as a young elm
Straight and tall from his crooked bones
That she might stand in the night
After the locks and chains

All night in the unmade park
After the railings and shrubberies
The birds the grass the trees the lake
And the wild boys innocent as strawberries
Had followed the hunchback
To his kennel in the dark.

Do Not Go Gentle into that Good Night

Do not go gentle into that good night,
Old age should burn and rave at close of day;
Rage, rage against the dying of the light.

Though wise men at their end know dark is right,
Because their words had forked no lightning they
Do not go gentle into that good night.

Good men, the last wave by, crying how bright
Their frail deeds might have danced in a green bay,
Rage, rage against the dying of the light.

Wild men who caught and sang the sun in flight,
And learn, too late, they grieved it on its way,
Do not go gentle into that good night.

Grave men, near death, who see with blinding sight
Blind eyes could blaze like meteors and be gay,
Rage, rage against the dying of the light.

And you, my father, there on the sad height,
Curse, bless, me now with your fierce tears, I pray.
Do not go gentle into that good night.
Rage, rage against the dying of the light.

Fern Hill

Now as I was young and easy under the apple boughs
About the lilting house and happy as the grass was green,
    The night above the dingle starry,
        Time let me hail and climb
      Golden in the heydays of his eyes,
And honoured among wagons I was prince of the apple towns
And once below a time I lordly had the trees and leaves
        Trail with daisies and barley
      Down the rivers of the windfall light.

And as I was green and carefree, famous among the barns
About the happy yard and singing as the farm was home,
      In the sun that is young once only,
        Time let me play and be
      Golden in the mercy of his means,
And green and golden I was huntsman and herdsman, the
           calves
Sang to my horn, the foxes on the hills barked clear and cold,
        And the sabbath rang slowly
      In the pebbles of the holy streams.

All the sun long it was running, it was lovely, the hay
Fields high as the house, the tunes from the chimneys, it
          was air
      And playing, lovely and watery
        And fire green as grass.
      And nightly under the simple stars
As I rode to sleep the owls were bearing the farm away,
All the moon long I heard, blessed among stables, the nightjars
      Flying with the ricks, and the horses
        Flashing into the dark.

And then to awake, and the farm, like a wanderer white
With the dew, come back, the cock on his shoulder: it was all
    Shining, it was Adam and maiden,
        The sky gathered again
    And the sun grew round that very day.
So it must have been after the birth of the simple light
In the first, spinning place, the spellbound horses walking
            warm
    Out of the whinnying green stable
      On to the fields of praise.

And honoured among foxes and pheasants by the gay house
Under the new made clouds and happy as the heart was long
    In the sun born over and over,
      I ran my heedless ways,
    My wishes raced through the house high hay
And nothing I cared, at my sky blue trades, that time allows
In all his tuneful turning so few and such morning songs
    Before the children green and golden
      Follow him out of grace,

Nothing I cared, in the lamb white days, that time would
        take me
Up to the swallow thronged loft by the shadow of my hand,
    In the moon that is always rising,
      Nor that riding to sleep
    I should hear him fly with the high fields
And wake to the farm forever fled from the childless land.
Oh as I was young and easy in the mercy of his means,
      Time held me green and dying
    Though I sang in my chains like the sea.

In the White Giant's Thigh

    Through throats where many rivers meet, the curlews cry,
    Under the conceiving moon, on the high chalk hill,

And there this night I walk in the white giant's thigh
Where barren as boulders women lie longing still

To labour and love though they lay down long ago.

Through throats where many rivers meet, the women pray,
Pleading in the waded bay for the seed to flow
Though the names on their weed grown stones are rained away,

And alone in the night's eternal, curving act
They yearn with tongues of curlews for the unconceived
And immemorial sons of the cudgelling, hacked

Hill. Who once in gooseskin winter loved all ice leaved
In the courters' lanes, or twined in the ox roasting sun
In the wains tonned so high that the wisps of the hay
Clung to the pitching clouds, or gay with any one
Young as they in the after milking moonlight lay

Under the lighted shapes of faith and their moonshade
Petticoats galed high, or shy with the rough riding boys,
Now clasp me to their grains in the gigantic glade,

Who once, green countries since, were a hedgerow of joys.
Time by, their dust was flesh the swineherd rooted sly,
Flared in the reek of the wiving sty with the rush
Light of his thighs, spreadeagle to the dunghill sky,
Or with their orchard man in the core of the sun's bush
Rough as cows' tongues and thrashed with brambles their buttermilk
Manes, under his quenchless summer barbed gold to the bone,

Or rippling soft in the spinney moon as the silk
And ducked and draked white lake that harps to a hail stone.

Who once were a bloom of wayside brides in the hawed house
And heard the lewd, wooed field flow to the coming frost,
The scurrying, furred small friars squeal, in the dowse
Of day, in the thistle aisles, till the white owl crossed

Their breast, the vaulting does roister, the horned bucks climb
Quick in the wood at love, where a torch of foxes foams,
All birds and beasts of the linked night uproar and chime

And the mole snout blunt under his pilgrimage of domes,
Or, butter fat goosegirls, bounced in a gambo bed,
Their breasts full of honey, under their gander king
Trounced by his wings in the hissing shippen, long dead
And gone that barley dark where their clogs danced in the spring,
And their firefly hairpins flew, and the ricks ran round—

(But nothing bore, no mouthing babe to the veined hives
Hugged, and barren and bare on Mother Goose's ground
They with the simple Jacks were a boulder of wives)—

Now curlew cry me down to kiss the mouths of their dust.

The dust of their kettles and clocks swings to and fro
Where the hay rides now or the bracken kitchens rust
As the arc of the billhooks that flashed the hedges low
And cut the birds' boughs that the minstrel sap ran red.
They from houses where the harvest kneels, hold me hard,
Who heard the tall bell sail down the Sundays of the dead
And the rain wring out its tongues on the faded yard,
Teach me the love that is evergreen after the fall leaved
Grave, after Belovéd on the grass gulfed cross is scrubbed
Off by the sun and Daughters no longer grieved
Save by their long desirers in the fox cubbed
Streets or hungering in the crumbled wood: to these
Hale dead and deathless do the women of the hill
Love for ever meridian through the courters' trees

And the daughters of darkness flame like Fawkes fires still.

JOHN CIARDI
(1916–)

Elegy

My father was born with a spade in his hand and traded it
for a needle's eye to sit his days cross-legged on tables
till he could sit no more, then sold insurance, reading
the ten-cent-a-week lives like logarithms from
the Tables of Metropolitan to their prepaid tombstones.

Years of the little dimes twinkling on kitchen tables
at Mrs. Fauci's at Mrs. Locatelli's at Mrs. Cataldo's
(*Arrividerla, signora. A la settimana prossima. Mi saluta,
la prego, il marito, Ciao, Anna. Bye-bye.*)
—known as a Debit. And with his ten-year button

he opened a long dream like a piggy bank, spilling the dimes
like mountain water into the moss of himself, and bought
ten piney lots in Wilmington. Sunday by Sunday
he took the train to his woods and walked under the trees
to leave his print on his own land, a patron of seasons.

I have done nothing as perfect as my father's Sundays
on his useless lots. Gardens he dreamed from briar tangle
and the swampy back slope of his ridge rose over him
more flowering than Brazil. Maples transformed to figs,
and briar to blood-blue grapes in his look around

when he sat on a stone with his wine-jug and cheese beside him,
his collar and coat on a branch, his shirt open,
his derby back on his head like a standing turtle. A big
man he was. When he sang *Celeste Aida* the woods
filled as if a breeze were swelling through them.

When he stopped, I thought I could hear the sound still moving.
—Well, I have lied. Not so much lied as dreamed it.
I was three when he died. It was someone else—my sister—
went with him under the trees. But if it was her
memory then, it became mine so long since

I will owe nothing on it, having dreamed it from all
the nights I was growing, the wet-pants man of the family.
I have done nothing as perfect as I have dreamed him
from old-wives tales and the running of my blood.
God knows what queer long darks I had no eyes for

followed his stairwell weeks to his Sunday breezeways.
But I will swear the world is not well made that rips
such gardens from the week. Or I should have walked
a saint's way to the cross and nail by nail
hymned out my blood to glory, for one good reason.

from "FRAGMENTS FROM ITALY"

I

Nona Domenica Garnaro sits in the sun
    on the step of her house in Calabria.
      There are seven men and four women in the village
      who call her *Mama*, and the orange trees
      fountain their blooms down all the hill and valley.
      No one can see more memory from this step

    than Nona Domenica. When she folds her hands
      in her lap they fall together

like two Christs fallen from a driftwood shrine.
All their weathers are twisted into them.
There is that art in them that will not be carved
but can only be waited for. These hands are not

sad nor happy nor tired nor strong. They are simply
complete. They lie still in her lap
and she sits waiting quietly in the sun
for what will happen, as for example, a petal
may blow down on the wind and lie across
both of her thumbs, and she look down at it.

To Judith Asleep

My dear, darkened in sleep, turned from the moon
that riots on curtain-stir with every breeze,
leaping in moths of light across your back . . .
far off, then soft and sudden as petals shower
down from wired roses—silently, all at once—
you turn, abandoned and naked, all let down
in ferny streams of sleep and petaled thighs
rippling into my flesh's buzzing garden.

Far and familiar your body's myth-map lights,
traveled by moon and dapple. Sagas were curved
like scimitars to your hips. The raiders' ships
all sailed to your one port. And watchfires burned
your image on the hills. Sweetly you drown
male centuries in your chiaroscuro tide
of breast and breath. And all my memory's shores
you frighten perfectly, washed familiar and far.

Ritual wars have climbed your shadowed flank
where bravos dreaming of fair women tore
rock out of rock to have your cities down
in loot of hearths and trophies of desire.
And desert monks have fought your image back

in a hysteria of mad skeletons.
Bravo and monk (the heads and tails of love)
I stand, a spinning coin of wish and dread,

counting our life, our chairs, our books and walls,
our clock whose radium eye and insect voice
owns all our light and shade, and your white shell
spiraled in moonlight on the bed's white beach;
thinking, I might press you to my ear
and all your coils fall out in sounds of surf
washing a mystery sudden as you are
a light on light in light beyond the light.

Child, child, and making legend of my wish
fastened alive into your naked sprawl—
stir once to stop my fear and miser's panic
that time shall have you last and legendry
undress to old bones from its moon brocade.
Yet sleep and keep our prime of time alive
before that death of legend. My dear of all

saga and century, sleep in familiar-far.
Time still must tick *this is, I am, we are.*

A *Thanks That Flesh Is Sad*

The sad soft scars, childbitten
        from the rose-dust once of flesh,
        I kiss unhailed in my arms and sigh for.
        A thanks all lovers come to when they dare.

That you were sunblush lit as the writhen
        sprays of orchards in the rush of Spring,
        and swelled and softened as ever peach on its bough,
        an allegory of plenty on stilled air;

and that I laid my last tears in your breast
        like worms' eyes from the long sods of my death,

and sang that sadness over in your arms
till I outlived the white bone in its grave—

I rise past pity in a lust of praise
for every loss that stores us. Scar by scar
the dearest flesh is sad, and spins in man
his rose of fire, the raging of his joys.

In Ego with Us All

In ego with us all, behind the world and Mother,
in the woods behind the house, where the old well is
for everyone to remember, I remember
the stone-green water's far-down breathing over
the lead-gold-emerald frog that shines there
when the light goes high enough to find him.

It was the Secret Place. Jesse James came there,
Babe Ruth, Charlie Chaplin, Captain Nemo.
And when the light fell deepest, Pa came smiling:
"See, I'm not dead: show me what's in the well."
Then how the frog sang up from the stones and water,
sweet as canaries, and golden in our look!

Till a bell clanged it to lead. "All right, I'm coming!"
It was The Lonely Place, bell-emptied in a wink,
even the Frog gone, which was again only
the round stone I had dropped, both arms extended
over the center to aim it true and forever.
And counted all my nights to the sound of the splash.

And never heard it. In ego with us all
I think there is no hearing it. It is dropped,
it lies there, it changes when the light lets it.
But no one hears it hit. Is it forever
the bell clangs just at that instant?
Are the clang and the splash one sound neither

Father nor Mother, but both? I do not know
what there is of us in that well that dreamed me
through light and dark. The thought is years from the thought,
and our lives are not a thing chosen but a thing
that happens to us. Out of that well, perhaps.
Out of it or another impossibility, certainly.

I have let go my tears for less than this.
Even at movies, damning myself for a fool,
I have leaked sentiment for dead dolls.
Who are you? Have you a drier eye?—
In ego with us all, I confess all:
there is no world but what falls in that well,

sings out when the light goes high enough, sinks off
to slime and stone between. And the thought
lies years from the thought. The Lonely Place
is the ruins of The Secret Place. The True is quiet:
leaves nudge it, grasshoppers fizz in it, water laps it,
the singing comes up from the well—the voice of Quiet.

And years from all, in ego with us all, as I have shed
with all of us, damning for all of us, the wrong
tears for not-enough reason, I will sit tending
the silence coldly told of what tears are true
in ego with us all, in the secret place
a noise can shatter, and a life not mend.

Palaver's No Prayer

PALAVER'S no prayer.
There's a nice-ninny priest
at tea in everyone,
all cosy and chatty as auntie,
but a saint comes
and throws rocks through the window.

In Place of a Curse

At the next vacancy for God, if I am elected,
I shall forgive last the delicately wounded
who, having been slugged no harder than anyone else,
never got up again, neither to fight back,
nor to finger their jaws in painful admiration.

They who are wholly broken, and they in whom
mercy is understanding, I shall embrace at once
and lead to pillows in heaven. But they who are
the meek by trade, baiting the best of their betters
with extortions of a mock-helplessness

I shall take last to love, and never wholly.
Let them all into Heaven—I abolish Hell—
but let it be read over them as they enter:
"Beware the calculations of the meek, who gambled nothing,
gave nothing, and could never receive enough."

After Sunday Dinner We Uncles Snooze

Banana-stuffed, the ape behind the brain
scratches his crotch in nature and lies back,
one arm across his eyes, one on his belly.
Thanksgiving afternoon in Africa,
the jungle couches heaped with hairy uncles
between a belch and a snore. All's well that yawns.

Seas in the belly lap a high tide home.
A kind of breathing flip-flop, all arrival,
souses the world full in the sog of time,
lifting slopped apes and uncles from their couches
for the long drift of self to self. Goodbye:
I'm off to idiot heaven in a drowse.

This is a man. This blubbermouth at air
sucking its flaps of breath, grimacing, blowing,

212

rasping, whistling. Walked through by a zoo
of his own reveries, he changes to it.
His palm's huge dabble over his broken face
rubs out the carnivores. His pixie pout

diddles a butterfly across his lip.
His yeasty smile drools Edens at a spring
where girls from Bali, kneeling to their bath,
cup palms of golden water to their breasts.
His lower lip thrusts back the angry chiefs:
he snarls and clicks his teeth: "Stand back, by God!"

And so, by God, they do, while he descends
to rape those knobs of glory with a sigh,
then clouds, surceased, and drifts away or melts
into another weather of himself
where only a drowned mumble far away
sounds in his throat the frog-pond under time.

O apes and hairy uncles of us all,
I hear the gibberish of a mother tongue
inside this throat. (A prattle from the sea.
A hum in the locked egg. A blather of bloods.)
O angels and attendants past the world,
what shall the sleeps of heaven dream but time?

A Thousandth Poem for Dylan Thomas

Waking outside his Babylonian binge
    in the wet and cramp of morningstone, the sot
begins his daily death. A first stiff wince
    numbers his bones, each like a tooth of God.

Where did night end? Girlies in a red flame
    squeal through his broken memory like pigs:
Hell's barnyard burning or the zoo of days,
    stampeded shapes exploded from their skins.

He tastes again the ooze of a first sigh
    dead in his throat; his mouth, a rotten fig;
his sex, a broken glue-pot in the thighs;
    his breath, a shudder from below the will.

Sooner or later he must break an eye
    to look at what he sees of what he is.
An angel beating at the trap of time?
    A bird-heart pulsing in an idiot's fist?

Both. Either. Floated open from its muds,
    that moment in the clear, the sot's eye sees
as much as saints could bear of the fireblood
    God's heart pumps in its seizure of the skies.

Then how the man could sing his ghost to tears,
    there in God's eye and blood, for that lost place
where he was innocent, before his need
    changed to a thirst inside the worm of waste.

He pours his celebrations of regret,
    tormented joyous from the throat of mud,
hawk-hearted as Augustine in his sweat,
    dove-eyed as Francis' bridal with the wood.

It is the age of sots. Our holiness
    wakens outside the minareted fronts
of a jazzy, airless, and expensive hell.
    He sings our wish. He drinks his death for us

who have no throats to die of or to sing.
    He is Saint Binge at death in his own meat,
the blaze meant in the char we make of things,
    our addict, and our angel of defeat.

The Dolls

Night after night forever the dolls lay stiff
by the children's dreams. On the goose-feathers of the rich,

on the straw of the poor, on the gypsy ground—
wherever the children slept, dolls have been found
in the subsoil of the small loves stirred again
by the Finders After Everything. Down lay
the children by their hanks and twists. Night after night
grew over imagination. The fuzzies shed, the bright
buttons fell out of the heads, arms ripped, and down
through goose-feathers, straw, and the gypsy ground
the dolls sank, and some—the fuzziest and most loved—
changed back to string and dust, and the dust moved
dream-puffs round the Finders' boots as they dug,
sieved, brushed, and came on a little clay dog,
and a little stone man, and a little bone girl, that had kept
their eyes wide open forever, while all the children slept.

An Island Galaxy

Once on Saipan at the end of the rains
I came on a flooded tire rut in a field
and found it boiling with a galaxy
of pollywogs, each millionth micro-dot
avid and home in an original swarm.

For twenty yards between the sodden tents
and a coral cliff, a universe ran on
in a forgotten dent of someone's passing.
Clusters and nebulae of whirligigs
whorled and maddened, a burst gas of life

from the night hop of unholdable energy.
Did one frog squatting heavy at the full
of its dark let out this light, these black rapids
inside the heart of light in the light-struck dent
of the accidental and awakened waters?

There on the island of our burning, in man's place
in the fire-swarm of war, and in a sunburst
lens, I stood asking—what? Nothing.

Universes happen. Happen and are come upon.
I stood in the happening of an imagination.

Ten days later, having crossed two seas,
I passed that rut again. The sun had burned
the waters back to order. The rut lay baked.
Twenty upthrust shoreline yards of time
slept in the noon of a finished imagination.

And the bed and the raised faces of the world
lay stippled with the dry seals of the dead,
black wafers with black ribbons, as if affixed
to a last writ, but with such waste of law,
I could not read its reasons for its proofs.

Credibility

Who could believe an ant in theory?
a giraffe in blueprint?
Ten thousand doctors of what's possible
could reason half the jungle out of being.
I speak of love, and something more,
to say we are the thing that proves itself
not against reason, but impossibly true,
and therefore to teach reason reason.

Vodka

Vodka, I hope you will note, is
upwind from all other essences.
Drink it all night and all day
and your aunt's minister could
not track you to perdition, not
even with his nose for it. Vodka
has no breath. Call it the dead-
man's drink. But praise it. As
long as he can stand, a vodka-

drinker is sober, and when he
falls down he is merely sleepy.
Like poetry, vodka informs anything with which it is diluted,
and like poetry, alas, it must be
diluted. Only a Russian can take
it straight, and only after long
conditioning, and just see what
seems to be coming of that!

English A

No paraphrase does
between understanding
and understanding.

You are either
that noun beyond
qualification into

whose round fact
I pass unparsed
and into whose eyes

I speak idioms
beyond construction;
or else get up,

fasten your suffixes
and your hyphenations,
buckle your articles,

spray modifiers
and moods
behind your ears

and take the whole
developed discourse
of your thighs to

any damned grammarian
you whatsoever
wish. Period.

Suburban Homecoming

As far as most of what you call people, my darling, are
concerned, I don't care who or what gets into the phone. I
am not home and not expected and I even, considerably,
    doubt I live here.

I mean this town and its everlasting katzenjammer whenever whoever dials again, is going to hell, or to some other
perpetual buffet, in a wheelbarrowful of bad martinis: and
    you, my

legal sweet, forever in the act of putting your hat on
as I come in the door to be told I have exactly five—
or, on good days, ten—minutes to change in because here we
    go

again to some collection of never-quite-the-same-but-
always-no-different faces; you, my moth-brained flutter
from bright cup to cup, no matter what nothing is in them;
    you, my own

brand-named, laboratory-tested, fair-trade-priced, wedded
(as advertised in *Life*) feather-duster, may go jump into
twenty fathoms of Advice to the Lovelorn and pull it in after
    you—

but I have not arrived, am not it, the phone did not ring
and was not answered, we have not really, I believe, met, and
if we do and if I stay to be (I doubt it) introduced, I'm still
    not going.

ROBERT LOWELL

(1917–)

The Holy Innocents

Listen, the hay-bells tinkle as the cart
Wavers on rubber tires along the tar
And cindered ice below the burlap mill
And ale-wife run. The oxen drool and start
In wonder at the fenders of a car,
And blunder hugely up St. Peter's hill.
These are the undefiled by woman—their
Sorrow is not the sorrow of this world:
King Herod shrieking vengeance at the curled
Up knees of Jesus choking in the air,

A king of speechless clods and infants. Still
The world out-Herods Herod; and the year,
The nineteen-hundred forty-fifth of grace,
Lumbers with losses up the clinkered hill
Of our purgation; and the oxen near
The worn foundations of their resting-place,
The holy manger where their bed is corn
And holly torn for Christmas. If they die,
As Jesus, in the harness, who will mourn?
Lamb of the shepherds, Child, how still you lie.

Christmas in Black Rock

Christ God's red shadow hangs upon the wall
The dead leaf's echo on these hours
Whose burden spindles to no breath at all;
Hard at our heels the huntress moonlight towers
And the green needles bristle at the glass
Tiers of defense-plants where the treadmill night
Churns up Long Island Sound with piston-fist.
Tonight, my child, the lifeless leaves will mass,
Heaving and heaping, as the swivelled light
Burns on the bell-spar in the fruitless mist.

Christ Child, your lips are lean and evergreen
Tonight in Black Rock, and the moon
Sidles outside into the needle-screen
And strikes the hand that feeds you with a spoon
Tonight, as drunken Polish night-shifts walk
Over the causeway and their juke-box booms
Hosannah in excelsis Domino.
Tonight, my child, the foot-loose hallows stalk
Us down in the blind alleys of our rooms;
By the mined root the leaves will overflow.

December, old leech, has leafed through Autumn's store
Where Poland has unleashed its dogs
To bay the moon upon the Black Rock shore:
Under our windows, on the rotten logs
The moonbeam, bobbing like an apple, snags
The undertow. O Christ, the spiralling years
Slither with child and manger to a ball
Of ice; and what is man? We tear our rags
To hang the Furies by their itching ears,
And the green needles nail us to the wall.

ROBERT LOWELL

The Quaker Graveyard in Nantucket

For Warren Winslow, dead at sea

> *Let man have dominion over the fishes of the sea and the fowls of the air and the beasts and the whole earth, and every creeping creature that moveth upon the earth.*

I

A brackish reach of shoal off Madaket,—
The sea was still breaking violently and night
Had steamed into our North Atlantic Fleet,
When the drowned sailor clutched the drag-net. Light
Flashed from his matted head and marble feet,
He grappled at the net
With the coiled, hurdling muscles of his thighs:
The corpse was bloodless, a botch of reds and whites,
Its open, staring eyes
Were lustreless dead-lights
Or cabin-windows on a stranded hulk
Heavy with sand. We weight the body, close
Its eyes and heave it seaward whence it came,
Where the heel-headed dogfish barks its nose
On Ahab's void and forehead; and the name
Is blocked in yellow chalk.
Sailors, who pitch this portent at the sea
Where dreadnaughts shall confess
Its hell-bent deity,
When you are powerless
To sand-bag this Atlantic bulwark, faced
By the earth-shaker, green, unwearied, chaste
In his steel scales: ask for no Orphean lute
To pluck life back. The guns of the steeled fleet
Recoil and then repeat
The hoarse salute.

II

Whenever winds are moving and their breath
Heaves at the roped-in bulwarks of this pier,

The terns and sea-gulls tremble at your death
In these home waters. Sailor, can you hear
The Pequod's sea wings, beating landward, fall
Headlong and break on our Atlantic wall
Off 'Sconset, where the yawing S-boats splash
The bellbuoy, with ballooning spinnakers,
As the entangled, screeching mainsheet clears
The blocks: off Madaket, where lubbers lash
The heavy surf and throw their long lead squids
For blue-fish? Sea-gulls blink their heavy lids
Seaward. The winds' wings beat upon the stones,
Cousin, and scream for you and the claws rush
At the sea's throat and wring it in the slush
Of this old Quaker graveyard where the bones
Cry out in the long night for the hurt beast
Bobbing by Ahab's whaleboats in the East.

III

All you recovered from Poseidon died
With you, my cousin, and the harrowed brine
Is fruitless on the blue beard of the god,
Stretching beyond us to the castles in Spain,
Nantucket's westward haven. To Cape Cod
Guns, cradled on the tide,
Blast the eelgrass about a waterclock
Of bilge and backwash, roil the salt and sand
Lashing earth's scaffold, rock
Our warships in the hand
Of the great God, where time's contrition blues
Whatever it was these Quaker sailors lost
In the mad scramble of their lives. They died
When time was open-eyed,
Wooden and childish; only bones abide
There, in the nowhere, where their boats were tossed
Sky-high, where mariners had fabled news
Of IS, the whited monster. What it cost
Them is their secret. In the sperm-whale's slick
I see the Quakers drown and hear their cry:
"If God himself had not been on our side,

If God himself had not been on our side,
When the Atlantic rose against us, why,
Then it had swallowed us up quick."

IV

This is the end of the whaleroad and the whale
Who spewed Nantucket bones on the thrashed swell
And stirred the troubled waters to whirlpools
To send the Pequod packing off to hell:
This is the end of them, three-quarters fools,
Snatching at straws to sail
Seaward and seaward on the turntail whale,
Spouting out blood and water as it rolls,
Sick as a dog to these Atlantic shoals:
Clamavimus, O depths. Let the sea-gulls wail

For water, for the deep where the high tide
Mutters to its hurt self, mutters and ebbs.
Waves wallow in their wash, go out and out,
Leave only the death-rattle of the crabs,
The beach increasing, its enormous snout
Sucking the ocean's side.
This is the end of running on the waves;
We are poured out like water. Who will dance
The mast-lashed master of Leviathans
Up from this field of Quakers in their unstoned graves?

V

When the whale's viscera go and the roll
Of its corruption overruns this world
Beyond tree-swept Nantucket and Wood's Hole
And Martha's Vineyard, Sailor, will your sword
Whistle and fall and sink into the fat?
In the great ash-pit of Jehoshaphat
The bones cry for the blood of the white whale,
The fat flukes arch and whack about its ears,
The death-lance churns into the sanctuary, tears
The gun-blue swingle, heaving like a flail,

And hacks the coiling life out: it works and drags
And rips the sperm-whale's midriff into rags,
Gobbets of blubber spill to wind and weather,
Sailor, and gulls go round the stoven timbers
Where the morning stars sing out together
And thunder shakes the white surf and dismembers
The red flag hammered in the mast-head. Hide,
Our steel, Jonas Messias, in Thy side.

Winter in Dunbarton

Time smiling on this sundial of a world
Sweltered about the snowman and the worm,
Sacker of painted idols and the peers
Of Europe; but my cat is cold, is curled
Tight as a boulder: she no longer smears
Her catnip mouse from Christmas, for the germ—
Mindless and ice, a world against our world—
Has tamped her round of brains into her ears.

This winter all the snowmen turn to stone,
Or, sick of the long hurly-burly, rise
Like butterflies into Jehovah's eyes
And shift until their crystals must atone

In water. Belle, the cat that used to rat
About my father's books, is dead. All day
The wastes of snow about my house stare in
Through idle windows at the brainless cat;
The coke-barrel in the corner whimpers. May
The snow recede and red clay furrows set
In the grim grin of their erosion, in
The caterpillar tents and roadslides, fat

With muck and winter dropsy, where the tall
Snow-monster wipes the coke-fumes from his eyes
And scatters his corruption and it lies
Gaping until the fungus-eyeballs fall

Into this eldest of the seasons. Cold
Snaps the bronze toes and fingers of the Christ
My father fetched from Florence, and the dead
Chatters to nothing in the thankless ground
His father screwed from Charlie Stark and sold
To the selectmen. Cold has cramped his head
Against his heart: my father's stone is crowned
With snowflakes and the bronze-age shards of Christ.

Salem

In Salem seasick spindrift drifts or skips
To the canvas flapping on the seaward panes
Until the knitting sailor stabs at ships
Nosing like sheep of Morpheus through his brain's
Asylum. Seaman, seaman, how the draft
Lashes the oily slick about your head,
Beating up whitecaps! Seaman, Charon's raft
Dumps its damned goods into the harbor-bed,—
There sewage sickens the rebellious seas.
Remember, seaman, Salem fishermen
Once hung their nimble fleets on the Great Banks.
Where was it that New England bred the men
Who quartered the Leviathan's fat flanks
And fought the British Lion to his knees?

Children of Light

Our fathers wrung their bread from stocks and stones
And fenced their gardens with the Redman's bones;
Embarking from the Nether Land of Holland,
Pilgrims unhoused by Geneva's night,
They planted here the Serpent's seeds of light;
And here the pivoting searchlights probe to shock
The riotous glass houses built on rock,
And candles gutter by an empty altar,

And light is where the landless blood of Cain
Is burning, burning the unburied grain.

Mr. Edwards and the Spider

I saw the spiders marching through the air,
Swimming from tree to tree that mildewed day
   In latter August when the hay
   Came creaking to the barn. But where
      The wind is westerly,
Where gnarled November makes the spiders fly
Into the apparitions of the sky,
   They purpose nothing but their ease and die
Urgently beating east to sunrise and the sea;

What are we in the hands of the great God?
It was in vain you set up thorn and briar
   In battle array against the fire
   And treason crackling in your blood;
      For the wild thorns grow tame
And will do nothing to oppose the flame;
Your lacerations tell the losing game
   You play against a sickness past your cure.
How will the hands be strong? How will the heart endure?

A very little thing, a little worm,
Or hourglass-blazoned spider, it is said,
   Can kill a tiger. Will the dead
   Hold up his mirror and affirm
      To the four winds the smell
And flash of his authority? It's well
If God who holds you to the pit of hell,
   Much as one holds a spider, will destroy,
Baffle and dissipate your soul. As a small boy

On Windsor Marsh, I saw the spider die
When thrown into the bowels of fierce fire:

There's no long struggle, no desire
To get up on its feet and fly—
    It stretches out its feet
And dies. This is the sinner's last retreat;
Yes, and no strength exerted on the heat
Then sinews the abolished will, when sick
And full of burning, it will whistle on a brick.

But who can plumb the sinking of that soul?
Josiah Hawley, picture yourself cast
    Into a brick-kiln where the blast
    Fans your quick vitals to a coal—
        If measured by a glass,
How long would it seem burning! Let there pass
A minute, ten, ten trillion; but the blaze
Is infinite, eternal: this is death,
To die and know it. This is the Black Widow, death.

The Dead in Europe

After the planes unloaded, we fell down
Buried together, unmarried men and women;
Not crown of thorns, not iron, not Lombard crown,
Not grilled and spindle spires pointing to heaven
Could save us. Raise us, Mother, we fell down
Here hugger-mugger in the jellied fire:
Our sacred earth in our day was our curse.

Our Mother, shall we rise on Mary's day
In Maryland, wherever corpses married
Under the rubble, bundled together? Pray
For us whom the blockbusters marred and buried;
When Satan scatters us on Rising-day,
O Mother, snatch our bodies from the fire:
Our sacred earth in our day was our curse.

Mother, my bones are trembling and I hear
The earth's reverberations and the trumpet

Bleating into my shambles. Shall I bear,
(O Mary!) unmarried man and powder-puppet,
Witness to the Devil? Mary, hear,
O Mary, marry earth, sea, air and fire;
Our sacred earth in our day is our curse.

Falling Asleep over the Aeneid

An old man in Concord forgets to go to morning service. He falls asleep,
while reading Vergil, and dreams that he is Aeneas at the funeral of Pallas,
an Italian prince.

The sun is blue and scarlet on my page,
And *yuck-a, yuck-a, yuck-a, yuck-a,* rage
The yellowhammers mating. Yellow fire
Blankets the captives dancing on their pyre,
And the scorched lictor screams and drops his rod.
Trojans are singing to their drunken God,
Ares. Their helmets catch on fire. Their files
Clank by the body of my comrade—miles
Of filings! Now the scythe-wheeled chariot rolls
Before their lances long as vaulting poles,
And I stand up and heil the thousand men,
Who carry Pallas to the bird-priest. Then
The bird-priest groans, and as his birds foretold,
I greet the body, lip to lip. I hold
The sword that Dido used. It tries to speak,
A bird with Dido's sworded breast. Its beak
Clangs and ejaculates the Punic word
I hear the bird-priest chirping like a bird.
I groan a little. "Who am I, and why?"
It asks, a boy's face, though its arrow-eye
Is working from its socket. "Brother, try,
O Child of Aphrodite, try to die:
To die is life." His harlots hang his bed
With feathers of his long-tailed birds. His head
Is yawning like a person. The plumes blow;
The beard and eyebrows ruffle. Face of snow,

You are the flower that country girls have caught,
A wild bee-pillaged honey-suckle brought
To the returning bridegroom—the design
Has not yet left it, and the petals shine;
The earth, its mother, has, at last, no help:
It is itself. The broken-winded yelp
Of my Phoenician hounds, that fills the brush
With snapping twigs and flying, cannot flush
The ghost of Pallas. But I take his pall,
Stiff with its gold and purple, and recall
How Dido hugged it to her, while she toiled,
Laughing—her golden threads, a serpent coiled
In cypress. Now I lay it like a sheet;
It clinks and settles down upon his feet,
The careless yellow hair that seemed to burn
Beforehand. Left foot, right foot—as they turn,
More pyres are rising: armed horses, bronze,
And gagged Italians, who must file by ones
Across the bitter river, when my thumb
Tightens into their wind-pipes. The beaks drum;
Their headman's cow-horned death's-head bites its tongue,
And stiffens, as it eyes the hero slung
Inside his feathered hammock on the crossed
Staves of the eagles that we winged. Our cost
Is nothing to the lovers, whoring Mars
And Venus, father's lover. Now his car's
Plumage is ready, and my marshals fetch
His squire, Acoetes, white with age, to hitch
Aethon, the hero's charger, and its ears
Prick, and it steps and steps, and stately tears
Lather its teeth; and then the harlots bring
The hero's charms and baton—but the King,
Vain-glorious Turnus, carried off the rest.
"I was myself, but Ares thought it best
The way it happened." At the end of time,
He sets his spear, as my descendants climb
The knees of Father Time, his beard of scalps,
His scythe, the arc of steel that crowns the Alps.
The elephants of Carthage hold those snows,

Turms of Numidian horse unsling their bows,
The flaming turkey-feathered arrows swarm
Beyond the Alps. "Pallas," I raise my arm
And shout, "Brother, eternal health. Farewell
Forever." Church is over, and its bell
Frightens the yellowhammers, as I wake
And watch the whitecaps wrinkle up the lake.
Mother's great-aunt, who died when I was eight,
Stands by our parlor sabre. "Boy, it's late.
Vergil must keep the Sabbath." Eighty years!
It all comes back. My Uncle Charles appears.
Blue-capped and bird-like. Phillips Brooks and Grant
Are frowning at his coffin, and my aunt,
Hearing his colored volunteers parade
Through Concord, laughs, and tells her English maid
To clip his yellow nostril hairs, and fold
His colors on him. . . . It is I, I hold
His sword to keep from falling, for the dust
On the stuffed birds is breathless, for the bust
Of young Augustus weighs on Vergil's shelf:
It scowls into my glasses at itself.

Inauguration Day: January 1953

The snow had buried Stuyvesant.
The subways drummed the vaults. I heard
the El's green girders charge on Third,
Manhattan's truss of adamant,
that groaned in ermine, slummed on want. . . .
Cyclonic zero of the word,
God of our armies, who interred
Cold Harbor's blue immortals, Grant!
Horseman, your sword is in the groove!

Ice, ice. Our wheels no longer move.
Look, the fixed stars, all just alike
as lack-land atoms, split apart,

and the Republic summons Ike,
the mausoleum in her heart.

Grandparents

They're altogether otherworldly now,
those adults champing for their ritual Friday spin
to pharmacist and five-and-ten in Brockton.
Back in my throw-away and shaggy span
of adolescence, Grandpa still waves his stick
like a policeman;
Grandmother, like a Mohammedan, still wears her thick
lavender mourning and touring veil;
the Pierce Arrow clears its throat in a horse-stall.
Then the dry road dust rises to whiten
the fatigued elm leaves—
the nineteenth century, tired of children, is gone.
They're all gone into a world of light; the farm's my own.

The farm's my own!
Back there alone,
I keep indoors, and spoil another season.
I hear the rattley little country gramophone
racking its five foot horn:
"O Summer Time!"
Even at noon here the formidable
Ancien Régime still keeps nature at a distance. Five
green shaded light bulbs spider the billiards-table;
no field is greener than its cloth,
where Grandpa, dipping sugar for us both,
once spilled his demitasse.
His favorite ball, the number three,
still hides the coffee stain.

Never again
to walk there, chalk our cues,
insist on shooting for us both.
Grandpa! Have me, hold me, cherish me!

Tears smut my fingers. There
half my life-lease later,
I hold an *Illustrated London News*—;
disloyal still,
I doodle handlebar
mustaches on the last Russian Czar.

Memories of West Street and Lepke

Only teaching on Tuesdays, book-worming
in pajamas fresh from the washer each morning,
I hog a whole house on Boston's
"hardly passionate Marlborough Street,"
where even the man
scavenging filth in the back alley trash cans,
has two children, a beach wagon, a helpmate,
and is a "young Republican."
I have a nine months' daughter,
young enough to be my granddaughter.
Like the sun she rises in her flame-flamingo infants' wear.

These are the tranquillized *Fifties*,
and I am forty. Ought I to regret my seedtime?
I was a fire-breathing Catholic C.O.,
and made my manic statement,
telling off the state and president, and then
sat waiting sentence in the bull pen
beside a Negro boy with curlicues
of marijuana in his hair.

Given a year,
I walked on the roof of the West Street Jail, a short
enclosure like my school soccer court,
and saw the Hudson River once a day
through sooty clothesline entanglements
and bleaching khaki tenements.

Strolling, I yammered metaphysics with Abramowitz,
a jaundice-yellow ("it's really tan")
and fly-weight pacifist,
so vegetarian,
he wore rope shoes and preferred fallen fruit.
He tried to convert Bioff and Brown,
the Hollywood pimps, to his diet.
Hairy, muscular, suburban,
wearing chocolate double-breasted suits,
they blew their tops and beat him black and blue.

I was so out of things, I'd never heard
of the Jehovah's Witnesses.
"Are you a C.O.?" I asked a fellow jailbird.
"No," he answered, "I'm a J.W."
He taught me the "hospital tuck,"
and pointed out the T shirted back
of *Murder Incorporated's* Czar Lepke,
there piling towels on a rack,
or dawdling off to his little segregated cell full
of things forbidden the common man:
a portable radio, a dresser, two toy American
flags tied together with a ribbon of Easter palm.
Flabby, bald, lobotomized,
he drifted in a sheepish calm,
where no agonizing reappraisal
jarred his concentration on the electric chair—
hanging like an oasis in his air
of lost connections. . . .

GIL ORLOVITZ
(1918–)

The Rooster

the rooster crows in my belly
an old hangout for the billiard cues of the morning
and table-hopping hail hail the ganglias all here
after sunset like a mouthwash last yesterlight
and the white tails of the gorillas on television
and that liberal politician stumping for twilight
       supremacy
down by that old
          shill
          stream
As I buttonholed the Ancient Auctioneer
how goes America going
            going

after the thunderbird pooped out over the canyon
when he clovered her cleavage
and she pleaded like an electric organ in the rain
the moon greased out of the ten commandments a make-
      up too late
what about the negative feedback of death
what about magnetism striking as a poisonous snake
or a hoop of jazzedup wire
snarling up communications over the Morse Pole

after the statesmen belched ionized yeast
and the physics convention approved the musical
        selection
        Quartet
        For
        Four
        Mesons

in an expanding economy they do not matter

the rooster will take us on a guided missile tour
we are knellbent for automation
the minister prays Our Lord Who Art in Heaven judge
        us not by our actions
but fractions
the skullskinner intones judge us not by our trans-
        gressions
but analytic sessions
the physicist says christ anybody can have a halo
        wheres the hesitance
when we can boast electronic resonance

you think anybodyll look for the pinprick in an
        expanding economy

look easy and you will see
a cad and a ford in every nebulae
that no comettail you lost
but gods custombuilt Buicks exhaust
Americas producing for the Infinite
Holy Ghost Mongerers for the Universe
Export or Die
theres a report we got a parimutuel for the flying angels
constipation
will be solved by
                automation

Miss Wall Street does a dance of the seven ticker-
        tapes

mathematicians enter the bullring to lock equations
in the circus the economists show off their
        Trained Graphs
the specialists hide from the specialists
the whores organize their first Vertical Union
to which madames
        pimps and
        cops must belong
waddya mean youre contemptuous of the Middle Class
      theyre the
         National
         Compromise
         going
         going

(its like some sort of abdominal bell)
the historians yang and yin
says its not too late to get out
and not too late to get in
hole hole the gongs all here
like some sort of abdominal bell
shes a Supermarket Baby with all the skimmings
mate doth look for automate
male finds femalleable
we dont die we reincarnate
this goes for everybody but the lower animal orders
those down-at-the-heel aristocrats who simply wont
      take in boarders

its already noon and I'm still expanding
I'm a Paul Bunyan Giveaway
schizophrenia for lonely dolts
manic nuts for shy bolts
paranoia for those who say nobody has followed them
telescopes by god for those who say we've hollowed
      them
hail to the architects whove eliminated the five-
      oclock shadow

we function beardless from the cradle to the nave
free sexual irrigation for the ascetic
and thorns to bower the apoplectic
the cardiacs will look like roses
in this Promised Land without a Moses

hail to the farmers and their cows
in swimmingpools of milk and honey
hail to parity granaries of money
the worker with his fake-home pay
and the sociological gangster parentally rejected
steals his fathers in property quite protected

alls fair in an expanding economy

alls fair in love and boredom
the heavyweight champ
is still damp
                behind his fears
the opera star endorses beers
the homerun king belts one into the stratofears
rich as a churchmouse the saying goes
the deacon leaves cheese between the foes
the cathedral is built in stunted gothic
this is america
        their very own
I'm going to the bank to get a loan
get a loan
        little dogie
        get a loan
        going
        going

get a loan to
            integrate the negro in the south
            with white hoof-&-mouth
            a new perfume
            for the bladderroom
            pouting purses

for wetnurses
democratic steel
for teething kings
david-slings
for the delinquent
juvenile
and giant breweries
spiking castoroil with luminal
waddya mean whats the international policy
we got an expanding economy

we're counting cosmic rays in the bank
crow
rooster
crow
we got cocacola in labrador
thats what you call getting your mouth in the door
crow
rooster
crow
we'll have skyscrapers in the ionosfear
every suicide'll live a charged particle here
crow
rooster
crow
we're putting extra-sensory-production on the
perception line
get rid of that goose
our economys on the loose
we'll advertise a hermit for snob-appeal
we'll get every hunchbacked shoulder behind the
commonweal
crow
rooster
crow
pile all your energies into the new Golden Calf
THE ELECTRONOLAUGH
THE COMPUTER
WITH THE SMILING TOMORROW

all the great comics willed their bodies to it
the graveyard with the future in it
WHEN IT LAUGHS IT DISPLAYS URANIUM-FILLED
      TOMBSTONES
the bones
    of contemporary saints
CROW
   ROOSTER
   CROW

                                    going

             going
Forest Lawn?
     NO!
            ELECTRONOLAUGH!

Lyric

      when I am gone and green
      who will winter the scene
      what shadows storm the sheen
      and who the icicle hear scold
      the spring for what it had seen
      when I am gone and green

      when I am gone and green
      who shall turn the eye out on the world
      like flocks of sailing sheep
      who graze the shearer and who wind the keep
      and quiet the bleating visions in the sleep
      against the sleepers eyelids fold
      when I am gone and green

      when I am gone and green
      who will tell them how to live and die
      in stern summer and sensual cold
      and who tell them I am gone

239

and green when I shall be blue as the sky
when I am gone and green

Art of the Sonnet: XXXIII

If I could rise and see my father young,
with horse and Torah in the Russian town,
sugar might tremble on my tongue,
and Jehovah roar as I tumble Him down.
If I could rise and see my father sweet
and stern, as boys endure a boyhood dream
only to surrender secretly,
love's espionage I could memorize
knowing I have his youth before he dies.
I could at last allow the man his age
without the stupefying lamentations
that must have him obsolete before assuage,
that this sweet epitaph dissolve upon my tongue:
Thus my father—Living old, died young.

Art of the Sonnet: XXIX—For Lynn

Such folly of margins that may retaliate
against my separation of man and state,
to deify the one, the other castigate,
my wife in sleep will annotate
by dreaming I leaped down one sheer unconscious
cliff at bottom to await my own fall consciously.
Let us have wives, then, before we rush
into folly, lest we become abandoned quarry
and no dichotomies ever marry.
Whatever the men of state, whatever the state of men,
I shall walk untroubled the baffled battlements
and gaze with loving astonishment upon
her impossible breathing that rises like a mist
from wherever last we slept and kissed.

Art of the Sonnet: IX

Bowed negress, who aghast but the light
nailed by its own decimal points?
We seem computed, and dare not shift;
we go handcuffed by shadows, and despite
our fingers' skeleton-keys, and the simple lifting
of the head
above the dead.
You have said that someone touching you would be cheating;
but not many would grope about within a human dark,
fearful that its hidden snowstorm might put them all asleep.
I know you are weary as a wrestler at last in love with the long hold,
and that children dance about you as about some inanimate object.
It is time, then, that your hands bless someone taller than yourself;
and your eyes, like moths of snowflakes, float to the white winepress.

Index (8)

from the island aquamarine
her eyelashes the combers the sunburnt breakers

I am deaf to the seashell at his ear
blind to the knives of noon between his teeth
but who shall walk with me when the truth comes
in without love's familiar infamies

the wind hollowed her cheekbones
shook bronze bracelet breast and breast
beneath her belly the sacrificial network caught
thoughts of children their heads on chins

shuddering at the planets those coldcream jars
the fauna these perfume bottles drinking
at the mirror's edge
and the flower Beget-me-not from the diaphragm moon
he shall not have me anymore

but then who can
I have not said anymore to him but that women
took Christs down
oh God how they prefer their arms about the cross and thieves
let me laugh
let me laugh at their mistletoe martyrdoms

naked she bit the sea's green apples
plunging at the white salt fruit

naked her horses on the foaming vines

Lyric

Angora anger who art in heaven,
hunger be thy name.
Show the marvel-mean
in the foamgrass down for green.
Threaten us with marine mosque
up the terrace sail.
Condemn us softly, softly condemn
the man timing his shadow
drying unto heaven.
Angora anger, purr under the heart
of all hungering for thy last name.

Masterindex: 23

I hear the night hanging down in white holes
barbecuing my fathers morning face
on the golden vending poles of the sun
I hear the aluminum slicer of the sea
sailing up the deafening nerve narrows
at night the phosphorescence harpooning
hummingbird spines my fathers face
hovering over nectars vaportrails
the aluminum slicer of the sea spinning

cyclones around my eyes hurtling at
hangman velocities I hear storms
grazing like cattle at night over
my black grasses through which my
fathers face crawls on its bellybrain
I hear my native boys beating my bush
so I can pose him through oceanic
lenses discovering the golden vending
poles of the sun barbecuing white
glacier steaks sheared from the aluminum
slicer of the sea I hear the night

Homage to Charles Laughton

As Quasimodo in the scene of the drinking of water brought by Esmeralda
after he has been whipped

I have tied my humpback behind my mother,
I have a hunchbacked tongue:
if I drink water, it must go uphill;
if I drink water, I must lean back
and to one side, around my mother who leans forward from the watch-
      ing crowd
who saw me whipped within an inch of my birth
for wanting a girl
who brings me water from a gargoyle's tongue,
at whose bucking I was conceived.
She may have been God, to have left
me a foundling on a human doorstep.
She may have been God,
so that we do not see each other; not I, from a turning pillory,
nor she, from a crowd.
I am a humpback between myself and God;
and here comes a girl
to peer over the fathomless foundling of punishment.
I must lean down to one side to hear the bucking bells above,
ashamed that for a moment I am shorn of a hump,
whose clapper is in my mouth,

a naked lamb.
I am thirsty for stone.
She will have me with water.
I will go down into her more easily.
I am a dry thing, and cause pain.
"But," she says, "drink the water and the guilt will go down;"
and my mother is tied behind my hump.
Against my mother's will, she pours water into my mouth,
so that at least I can lean forward toward the crowd,
for there is nothing more than a stone wants from its life
but water.

LAWRENCE FERLINGHETTI
(1919–)

from ''PICTURES OF THE GONE WORLD''

2

        Just as I used to say
             love comes harder to the aged
because they've been running
           on the same old rails too long
  and then when the sly switch comes along
               they miss the turn
   and burn up the wrong rail while
          the gay caboose goes flying
    and the steamengine driver don't recognize
            them new electric horns
and the aged run out on the rusty spur
          which ends up in
       the dead grass where
  the rusty tincans and bedsprings and old razor
      blades and moldy mattresses
         lie
   and the rail breaks off dead
        right there
    though the ties go on awhile
        and the aged

say to themselves
        Well
             this must be the place
           we were supposed to lie down

  And they do

           while the bright saloon careens along away
    on a high
        hilltop
            its windows full of bluesky and lovers
      with flowers
           their long hair streaming
               and all of them laughing
       and waving and
             whispering to each other
    and looking out and
          wondering what that graveyard
     where the rails end
           is

from ''A CONEY ISLAND OF THE MIND''
8

  In Golden Gate Park that day
          a man and his wife were coming along
    thru the enormous meadow
         which was the meadow of the world
He was wearing green suspenders
        and carrying an old beat-up flute
             in one hand
  while his wife had a bunch of grapes
        which she kept handing out
             individually
       to various squirrels
            as if each
       were a little joke

And then the two of them came on
                thru the enormous meadow
which was the meadow of the world
            and then
     at a very still spot where the trees dreamed
     and seemed to have been waiting thru all time
                for them
    they sat down together on the grass
             without looking at each other
      and ate oranges
          without looking at each other
             and put the peels
   in a basket which they seemed
           to have brought for that purpose
   without looking at each other

And then
     he took his shirt and undershirt off
   but kept his hat on
        sideways
         and without saying anything
   fell asleep under it
         And his wife just sat there looking
at the birds which flew about
   calling to each other
       in the stilly air
  as if they were questioning existence
       or trying to recall something forgotten

But then finally
     she too lay down flat
        and just lay there looking up
           at nothing
    yet fingering the old flute
        which nobody played
    and finally looking over
       at him
without any particular expression

                              except a certain awful look
            of terrible depression

15

        Constantly risking absurdity
                                and death
                whenever he performs
                            above the heads
                                        of his audience
            the poet like an acrobat
                        climbs on rime
                            to a high wire of his own making
        and balancing on eyebeams
                            above a sea of faces
                paces his way
                            to the other side of day
            performing entrechats
                        and sleight-of-foot tricks
        and other high theatrics
                        and all without mistaking
                any thing
                            for what it may not be

            For he's the super realist
                            who must perforce perceive
                taut truth
                            before the taking of each stance or step
        in his supposed advance
                            toward that still higher perch
        where Beauty stands and waits
                            with gravity
                                to start her death-defying leap

            And he
                a little charleychaplin man
                            who may or may not catch

          her fair eternal form
                    spreadeagled in the empty air
          of existence

28

                         Dove sta amore
                         Where lies love
                         Dove sta amore
                         Here lies love
                         The ring dove love
                         In lyrical delight
                         Hear love's hillsong
                         Love's true willsong
                         Love's low plainsong
                         Too sweet painsong
                         In passages of night
                         Dove sta amore
                         Here lies love
                         The ring dove love
                         Dove sta amore
                         Here lies love

from ''ORAL MESSAGES''

Dog *

     The dog trots freely in the street
     and sees reality
     and the things he sees
     are bigger than himself
     and the things he sees

     * "Dog" is one of a group of poems that were "conceived specifically for
jazz accompaniment and as such should be considered as spontaneously spoken
'oral messages' rather than as poems written for the printed page. As a result of
continued experimental reading with jazz, they are still in a state of change."—
Author's note.

are his reality
Drunks in doorways
Moons on trees
The dog trots freely thru the street
and the things he sees
are smaller than himself
Fish on newsprint
Ants in holes
Chickens in Chinatown windows
their heads a block away
The dog trots freely in the street
and the things he smells
smell something like himself
The dog trots freely in the street
past puddles and babies
cats and cigars
poolrooms and policemen
He doesn't hate cops
He merely has no use for them
and he goes past them
and past the dead cows hung up whole
in front of the San Francisco Meat Market
He would rather eat a tender cow
than a tough policeman
though either might do
And he goes past the Romeo Ravioli Factory
and past Coit's Tower
and past Congressman Doyle
He's afraid of Coit's Tower
but he's not afraid of Congressman Doyle
although what he hears is very discouraging
very depressing
very absurd
to a sad young dog like himself
to a serious dog like himself
But he has his own free world to live in
His own fleas to eat
He will not be muzzled

Congressman Doyle is just another
fire hydrant
to him
The dog trots freely in the street
and has his own dog's life to live
and to think about
and to reflect upon
touching and tasting and testing everything
investigating everything
without benefit of perjury
a real realist
with a real tale to tell
and a real tail to tell it with
a real live
   barking
     democratic dog
engaged in real
     free enterprise
with something to say
      about ontology
something to say
    about reality
      and how to see it
        and how to hear it
with his head cocked sideways
     at streetcorners
as if he is just about to have
     his picture taken
       for Victor Records
    listening for
      His Master's Voice
   and looking
     like a living questionmark
      into the
      great gramaphone
      of puzzling existence
with its wondrous hollow horn
  which always seems

> just about to spout forth
> > some Victorious answer
> > to everything

The Great Chinese Dragon

The great Chinese dragon which is the greatest dragon in all the
world and which once upon a time was towed across
the Pacific by a crew of coolies rowing in an open boat
—was the first real live dragon ever actually to reach
these shores
And the great Chinese dragon passing thru the Golden Gate spouting
streams of water like a string of fireboats then broke
loose somewhere near China Camp gulped down a
hundred Chinese seamen and forthwith ate up all the
shrimp in San Francisco Bay
And the great Chinese dragon was therefore forever after confined in
a Chinatown basement and ever since allowed out only
for Chinese New Year's parades and other Unamerican
demonstrations paternally watched-over by those be-
nevolent men in blue who represent our more advanced
civilization which has reached such a high state of democracy as to allow even a few barbarians to carry on
their quaint native customs in our midst
And thus the great Chinese dragon which is the greatest dragon in all
the world now can only be seen creeping out of an Adler
Alley cellar like a worm out of a hole sometime during
the second week in February every year when it sorties
out of hibernation in its Chinese storeroom pushed
from behind by a band of fortythree Chinese elec-
tricians and technicians who stuff its peristaltic ac-
cordion-body up thru a sidewalk delivery entrance
And first the swaying snout appears and then the eyes at ground level
feeling along the curb and then the head itself casting
about and swaying and heaving finally up to the corner
of Grant Avenue itself where a huge paper sign proclaims the *World's Largest Chinatown*

And the great Chinese dragon's jaws wired permanently agape as if
by a demented dentist to display the Cadmium teeth
as the hungry head heaves out into Grant Avenue right
under the sign and raising itself with a great snort of
fire suddenly proclaims the official firecracker start of
the Chinese New Year

And the lightbulb eyes lighting up and popping out on coiled wire
springs and the body stretching and rocking further and
further around the corner and down Grant Avenue like
a caterpillar roller-coaster with the eyes sprung out and
waving in the air like the blind feelers of some me-
chanical preying mantis and the eyes blinking on and
off with Chinese red pupils and tiny bamboo-blind eyelids going up and down

And still the tail of the dragon in the Adler Alley cellar uncoiling and
unwinding out into the street with the fortythree Chi-
nese technicians still stuffing the dragon out the hole
in the sidewalk and the head of the dragon now three
blocks away in the middle of the parade of fancy floats
presided over by Chinese virgins

And here comes the St. Mary's Chinese Girls' Drum Corps and here
come sixteen white men in pith helmets beating big
bass drums representing the Order of the Moose and
here comes a gang of happy car salesmen disguised as
Islam Shriners and here comes a chapter of the Order
of Improved Red Men and here comes a cordon of
motorcycle cops in crash helmets with radios going followed by a small papier-mâché lion fed with Nekko
wafers and run by two guys left over from a Ten-Ten
festival which in turn is followed by the great Chinese
dragon itself gooking over balconies as it comes

And the great Chinese dragon has eaten a hundred humans and their
legs pop out of his underside and are his walking legs
which are not mentioned in the official printed program
in which he is written up as the Great Golden Dragon
made in Hong Kong to the specifications of the Chinese
Chamber of Commerce and he represents the force and
mystery of life and his head sways in the sky between the
balconies as he comes followed by six Chinese boy

253

scouts wearing Keds and carrying strings of batteries
that light up the dragon like a nighttime freeway
And he has lain all winter among a heap of collapsed paper lanterns
and green rubber lizards and ivory backscratchers with
the iron sidewalk doors closed over his head but he has
now sprung up with the first sign of Spring like the
force of life itself and his head sways in the sky and
gooks in green windows as he comes
And he is a monster with the head of a dog and the body of a serpent
risen yearly out of the sea to devour a virgin thrown
from a cliff to appease him and he is a young man handsome and drunk ogling the girls and he has high ideals
and a hundred sport shoes and he says No to Mother
and he is a big red table the world will never tilt and
he has big eyes everywhere thru which he sees all
womankind milkwhite and dove-breasted and he will
eat their waterflowers for he is the cat with future feet
wearing Keds and he eats cake out of pastry windows
and is hungrier and more potent and more powerful
and more omniverous than the papier-mâché lion run
by two guys and he is the great earthworm of lucky life
filled with flowing Chinese semen and he considers his
own and our existence in its most profound sense as he
comes and he has no Christian answer to the existential
question even as he sees the spiritual everywhere trans-
lucent in the material world and he does not want to
escape the responsibility of being a dragon or the consequences of his long horny tail still buried in the basement but the blue citizens on their talking cycles think
that he wants to escape and at all costs he must not be
allowed to escape because the great Chinese dragon is
the greatest potential dragon in all the world and if allowed to escape from Chinatown might gallop away up
their new freeway at the Broadway entrance mistaking
it for a Great Wall of China or some other barbarian
barrier and so go careening along it chewing up stan-
chions and signposts and belching forth some strange
disintegrating medium which might melt down the
great concrete walls of America and they are afraid of

how far the great Chinese dragon might really go starting from San Francisco and so they have secretly and
securely tied down the very end of his tail in its hole
                    so that
                            this great pulsing phallus of
life at the very end of its parade at the very end of
Chinatown gives one wild orgasm of a shudder and rolls
over fainting in the bright night street since even for a
dragon every orgasm is a little death
And then the great Chinese dragon starts silently shrinking and
shriveling up and drawing back and back and back to its
first cave and the soft silk skin wrinkles up and shrinks
and shrinks on its sprung bamboo bones and the handsome dejected head hangs down like a defeated prize-
fighter's and so is stuffed down again at last into its
private place and the cellar sidewalk doors press down
again over the great wilted head with one small hole of
an eye blinking still thru the gratings of the metal doors
as the great Chinese dragon gives one last convulsive
earthquake shake and rolls over dead-dog to wait another white year for the final coming and the final
sowing of his oats and teeth

HOWARD NEMEROV

(1920–)

Brainstorm

The house was shaken by a rising wind
That rattled window and door. He sat alone
In an upstairs room and heard these things: a blind
Ran up with a bang, a door slammed, a groan
Came from some hidden joist, a leaky tap,
At any silence of the wind walked like
A blind man through the house. Timber and sap
Revolt, he thought, from washer, baulk and spike.
Bent to his book, continued unafraid
Until the crows came down from their loud flight
To walk along the rooftree overhead.
Their horny feet, so near but out of sight,
Scratched on the slate; when they were blown away
He heard their wings beat till they came again,
While the wind rose, and the house seemed to sway,
And window panes began to blind with rain.
The house was talking, not to him, he thought,
But to the crows; the crows were talking back
In their black voices. The secret might be out:
Houses are only trees stretched on the rack.
And once the crows knew, all nature would know.
Fur, leaf and feather would invade the form,
Nail rust with rain and shingle warp with snow,

Vine tear the wall, till any straw-borne storm
Could rip both roof and rooftree off and show
Naked to nature what they had kept warm.

He came to feel the crows walk on his head
As if he were the house, their crooked feet
Scratched, through the hair, his scalp. He might be dead,
It seemed, and all the noises underneath
Be but the cooling of the sinews, veins,
Juices, and sodden sacks suddenly let go;
While in his ruins of wiring, his burst mains,
The rainy wind had been set free to blow
Until the green uprising and mob rule
That ran the world had taken over him,
Split him like seed, and set him in the school
Where any crutch can learn to be a limb.

Inside his head he heard the stormy crows.

Runes

"... insaniebam salubriter et moriebar vitaliter."

ST. AUGUSTINE

I

This is about the stillness in moving things,
In running water, also in the sleep
Of winter seeds, where time to come has tensed
Itself, enciphering a script so fine
Only the hourglass can magnify it, only
The years unfold its sentence from the root.
I have considered such things often, but
I cannot say I have thought deeply of them:
That is my theme, of thought and the defeat
Of thought before its object, where it turns
As from a mirror, and returns to be
The thought of something and the thought of thought,

A trader doubly burdened, commercing
Out of one stillness and into another.

11

About Ulysses, the learned have reached two
Distinct conclusions. In one, he secretly
Returns to Ithaca, is recognized
By Euryclea, destroys the insolent suitors,
And makes himself known to Penelope,
Describing the bed he built; then, at the last
Dissolve, we see him with Telemachus
Leaving the palace, planning to steal sheep:
The country squire resumes a normal life.
But in the other, out beyond the gates
Of Hercules, gabbling persuasively
About virtue and knowledge, he sails south
To disappear from sight behind the sun;
Drowning near blessed shores he flames in hell.
I do not know which ending is the right one.

111

Sunflowers, traders rounding the horn of time
Into deep afternoons, sleepy with gain,
The fall of silence has begun to storm
Around you where you nod your heavy heads
Whose bare poles, raking out of true, will crack,
Driving your wreckage on the world's lee shore.
Your faces no more will follow the sun,
But bow down to the ground with a heavy truth
That dereliction learns, how charity
Is strangled out of selfishness at last;
When, golden misers in the courts of summer,
You are stripped of gain for coining images
And broken on this quarter of the wheel,
It is on savage ground you spill yourselves,
And spend the tarnished silver of your change.

IV

The seed sleeps in the furnaces of death,
A cock's egg slept till hatching by a serpent
Wound in his wintry coil, a spring so tight
In his radical presence that every tense
Is now. Out of this head the terms of kind,
Distributed in syntax, come to judgment,
Are basilisks who write our sentences
Deep at the scripture's pith, in rooted tongues,
How one shall marry while another dies.
Give us our ignorance, the family tree
Grows upside down and shakes its heavy fruit,
Whose buried stones philosophers have sought.
For each stone bears the living word, each word
Will be made flesh, and all flesh fall to seed:
Such stones from the tree; and from the stones, such blood.

V

The fat time of the year is also time
Of the Atonement; birds to the berry bushes,
Men to the harvest; a time to answer for
Both present plenty and emptiness to come.
When the slain legal deer is salted down,
When apples smell like goodness, cold in the cellar,
You hear the ram's horn sounded in the high
Mount of the Lord, and you lift up your eyes
As though by this observance you might hide
The dry husk of an eaten heart which brings
Nothing to offer up, no sacrifice
Acceptable but the canceled-out desires
And satisfactions of another year's
Abscess, whose zero in His winter's mercy
Still hides the undecipherable seed.

VI

White water now in the snowflake's prison,
A mad king in a skullcap thinks these thoughts

259

In regular hexagons, each one unlike
Each of the others. The atoms of memory,
Like those that Democritus knew, have hooks
At either end, but these? Insane tycoon,
These are the riches of order snowed without end
In this distracted globe, where is no state
To fingerprint the flakes or number these
Moments melting in flight, seeds mirroring
Substance without position or a speed
And course unsubstanced. What may the spring be,
Deep in the atom, among galactic snows,
But the substance of things hoped for, argument
Of things unseen? White water, fall and fall.

VII

Unstable as water, thou shalt not excel
—Said to the firstborn, the dignity and strength,
And the defiler of his father's bed.
Fit motto for a dehydrated age
Nervously watering whisky and stock,
Quick-freezing dreams into realities.
Brain-surgeons have produced the proustian syndrome,
But patients dunk their tasteless madeleines
In vain, those papers that the Japanese
Amused themselves by watering until
They flowered and became Combray, flower
No more. The plastic and cosmetic arts
Unbreakably record the last word and
The least word, till sometimes even the Muse,
In her transparent raincoat, resembles a condom.

VIII

To go low, to be as nothing, to die,
To sleep in the dark water threading through
The fields of ice, the soapy, frothing water
That slithers under the culvert below the road,
Water of dirt, water of death, dark water,
And through the tangle of the sleeping roots

Under the coppery cold beech woods, the green
Pinewoods, and past the buried hulls of things
To come, and humbly through the breathing dreams
Of all small creatures sleeping in the earth;
To fall with the weight of things down on the one
Still ebbing stream, to go on to the end
With the convict hunted through the swamp all night.
The dog's corpse in the ditch, to come at last
Into the pit where zero's eye is closed.

IX

In this dehydrated time of digests, pills
And condensations, the most expensive presents
Are thought to come in the smallest packages:
In atoms, for example. There are still
To be found, at carnivals, men who engrave
The Lord's Prayer on a grain of wheat for pennies,
But they are a dying race, unlike the men
Now fortunate, who bottle holy water
In plastic tears, and bury mustard seeds
In lucite lockets, and for safety sell
To be planted on the dashboard of your car
The statues, in durable celluloid,
Of Mary and St. Christopher, who both
With humble power in the world's floodwaters
Carried their heavy Savior and their Lord.

X

White water, white water, feather of a form
Between the stones, is the race run to stay
Or pass away? Your utterance is riddled,
Rainbowed and clear and cold, tasting of stone,
Its brilliance blinds me. But still I have seen,
White water, at the breaking of the ice,
When the high places render up the new
Children of water and their tumbling light
Laughter runs down the hills, and the small fist
Of the seed unclenches in the day's dazzle,

How happiness is helpless before your fall,
White water, and history is no more than
The shadows thrown by clouds on mountainsides,
A distant chill, when all is brought to pass
By rain and birth and rising of the dead.

XI

A holy man said to me, "Split the stick
And there is Jesus." When I split the stick
To the dark marrow and the splintery grain
I saw nothing that was not wood, nothing
That was not God, and I began to dream
How from the tree that stood between the rivers
Came Aaron's rod that crawled in front of Pharaoh,
And came the rod of Jesse flowering
In all the generations of the Kings,
And came the timbers of the second tree,
The sticks and yardarms of the holy three-
masted vessel whereon the Son of Man
Hung between thieves, and came the crown of thorns,
The lance and ladder, when was shed that blood
Streamed in the grain of Adam's tainted seed.

XII

Consider how the seed lost by a bird
Will harbor in its branches most remote
Descendants of the bird; while everywhere
And unobserved, the soft green stalks and tubes
Of water are hardening into wood, whose hide,
Gnarled, knotted, flowing, and its hidden grain,
Remember how the water is streaming still.
Now does the seed asleep, as in a dream
Where time is compacted under pressures of
Another order, crack open like stone
From whose division pours a stream, between
The raindrop and the sea, running in one
Direction, down, and gathering in its course
That bitter salt which spices us the food
We sweat for, and the blood and tears we shed.

XIII

There sailed out on the river, Conrad saw,
The dreams of men, the seeds of commonwealths,
The germs of Empire. To the ends of the earth
One many-veined bloodstream swayed the hulls
Of darkness gone, of darkness still to come,
And sent its tendrils steeping through the roots
Of wasted continents. That echoing pulse
Carried the ground swell of all sea-returns
Muttering under history, and its taste,
Saline and cold, was as a mirror of
The taste of human blood. The sailor leaned
To lick the mirror clean, the somber and
Immense mirror that Conrad saw, and saw
The other self, the sacred Cain of blood
Who would seed a commonwealth in the Land of Nod.

XIV

There is a threshold, that meniscus where
The strider walks on drowning waters, or
That tense, curved membrane of the camera's lens
Which darkness holds against the battering light
And the distracted drumming of the world's
Importunate plenty.—Now that threshold,
The water of the eye where the world walks
Delicately, is as a needle threaded
From the reel of a raveling stream, to stitch
Dissolving figures in a watered cloth,
A damask either-sided as the shroud
Of the lord of Ithaca, labored at in light,
Destroyed in darkness, while the spidery oars
Carry his keel across deep mysteries
To harbor in unfathomable mercies.

XV

To watch water, to watch running water
Is to know a secret, seeing the twisted rope

Of runnels on the hillside, the small freshets
Leaping and limping down the tilted field
In April's light, the green, grave and opaque
Swirl in the millpond where the current slides
To be combed and carded silver at the fall;
It is a secret. Or it is not to know
The secret, but to have it in your keeping,
A locked box, Bluebeard's room, the deathless thing
Which it is death to open. Knowing the secret,
Keeping the secret—herringbones of light
Ebbing on beaches, the huge artillery
Of tides—it is not knowing, it is not keeping,
But being the secret hidden from yourself.

A *Spell before Winter*

After the red leaf and the gold have gone,
Brought down by the wind, then by hammering rain
Bruised and discolored, when October's flame
Goes blue to guttering in the cusp, this land
Sinks deeper into silence, darker into shade.
There is a knowledge in the look of things,
The old hills hunch before the north wind blows.

Now I can see certain simplicities
In the darkening rust and tarnish of the time,
And say over the certain simplicities,
The running water and the standing stone,
The yellow haze of the willow and the black
Smoke of the elm, the silver, silent light
Where suddenly, readying toward nightfall,
The sumac's candelabrum darkly flames.
And I speak to you now with the land's voice,
It is the cold, wild land that says to you
A knowledge glimmers in the sleep of things:
The old hills hunch before the north wind blows.

Human Things

When the sun gets low, in winter,
The lapstreaked side of a red barn
Can put so flat a stop to its light
You'd think everything was finished.

Each dent, fray, scratch, or splinter,
Any gray weathering where the paint
Has scaled off, is a healed scar
Grown harder with the wounds of light.

Only a tree's trembling shadow
Crosses that ruined composure; even
Nail holes look deep enough to swallow
Whatever light has left to give.

And after sundown, when the wall
Slowly surrenders its color, the rest
Remains, its high, obstinate
Hulk more shadowy than the night.

De Anima

Now it is night, now in the brilliant room
A girl stands at the window looking out,
But sees, in the darkness of the frame,
Only her own image.

And there is a young man across the street
Who looks at the girl and into the brilliant room.
They might be in love, might be about to meet,
If this were a romance.

In looking at herself, she tries to look
Beyond herself, and half become another,

Admiring and resenting, maybe dreaming
Her lover might see her so.

The other, the stranger standing in cold and dark,
Looks at the young girl in her crystalline room.
He sees clearly, and hopelessly desires,
A life that is not his.

Given the blindness of her self-possession,
The luminous vision revealed to his despair,
We look to both sides of the glass at once
And see no future in it.

These pure divisions hurt us in some realm
Of parable beyond belief, beyond
The temporal mind. Why is it sorrowful?
Why do we want them together?

Is it the spirit, ransacking through the earth
After its image, its being, its begetting?
The spirit sorrows, for what lovers bring
Into the world is death,

The most exclusive romance, after all,
The sort that lords and ladies listen to
With selfish tears, when she draws down the shade,
When he has turned away,

When the blind embryo with his bow of bees,
His candied arrows tipped with flower heads,
Turns from them too, for mercy or for grief
Refusing to be, refusing to die.

The Dial Tone

A moment of silence, first, then there it is.
But not as though it only now began

Because of my attention; rather, this,
That I begin at one point on its span
Brief kinship with its endless going on.

Between society and self it poses
Neutrality perceptible to sense,
Being a no man's land the lawyer uses
Much as the lover does: charged innocence,
It sits on its own electrified fence,

Is neither pleased nor hurt by race results
Or by the nasty thing John said to Jane;
Is merely interrupted by insults,
Devotions, lecheries; after the sane
And mad hang up at once, it will remain.

Suppose that in God a black bumblebee
Or colorless hummingbird buzzed all night,
Divided the abyss up equally;
And carried its neither sweetness nor its light
Across impossible eternity.

Now take this hummingbird, this bee, away;
And like the Cheshire smile without its cat
The remnant hum continues on its way,
Unwinged, able at once to move and wait,
An endless freight train on an endless flat.

Something like that, some loneliest of powers
That never has confessed its secret name.
I do not doubt that if you gave it hours
And then lost patience, it would be the same
After you left that it was before you came.

RICHARD WILBUR
(1921–)

The Pardon

My dog lay dead five days without a grave
In the thick of summer, hid in a clump of pine
And a jungle of grass and honeysuckle-vine.
I who had loved him while he kept alive

Went only close enough to where he was
To sniff the heavy honeysuckle-smell
Twined with another odor heavier still
And hear the flies' intolerable buzz.

Well, I was ten and very much afraid.
In my kind world the dead were out of range
And I could not forgive the sad or strange
In beast or man. My father took the spade

And buried him. Last night I saw the grass
Slowly divide (it was the same scene
But now it glowed a fierce and mortal green)
And saw the dog emerging. I confess

I felt afraid again, but still he came
In the carnal sun, clothed in a hymn of flies,

And death was breeding in his lively eyes.
I started in to cry and call his name,

Asking forgiveness of his tongueless head.
. . . I dreamt the past was never past redeeming:
But whether this was false or honest dreaming
I beg death's pardon now. And mourn the dead.

Still, Citizen Sparrow

Still, citizen sparrow, this vulture which you call
Unnatural, let him but lumber again to air
Over the rotten office, let him bear
The carrion ballast up, and at the tall

Tip of the sky lie cruising. Then you'll see
That no more beautiful bird is in heaven's height,
No wider more placid wings, no watchfuller flight;
He shoulders nature there, the frightfully free,

The naked-headed one. Pardon him, you
Who dart in the orchard aisles, for it is he
Devours death, mocks mutability,
Has heart to make an end, keeps nature new.

Thinking of Noah, childheart, try to forget
How for so many bedlam hours his saw
Soured the song of birds with its wheezy gnaw,
And the slam of his hammer all the day beset

The people's ears. Forget that he could bear
To see the towns like coral under the keel,
And the fields so dismal deep. Try rather to feel
How high and weary it was, on the waters where

He rocked his only world, and everyone's.
Forgive the hero, you who would have died

Gladly with all you knew; he rode that tide
To Ararat; all men are Noah's sons.

Love Calls Us to the Things of This World

The eyes open to a cry of pulleys,
And spirited from sleep, the astounded soul
Hangs for a moment bodiless and simple
As false dawn.
                  Outside the open window
The morning air is all awash with angels.

Some are in bed-sheets, some are in blouses,
Some are in smocks: but truly there they are.
Now they are rising together in calm swells
Of halcyon feeling, filling whatever they wear
With the deep joy of their impersonal breathing;

Now they are flying in place, conveying
The terrible speed of their omnipresence, moving
And staying like white water; and now of a sudden
They swoon down into so rapt a quiet
That nobody seems to be there.
                      The soul shrinks

From all that it is about to remember,
From the punctual rape of every blessèd day,
And cries,
            "Oh, let there be nothing on earth but laundry,
Nothing but rosy hands in the rising steam
And clear dances done in the sight of heaven."

Yet, as the sun acknowledges
With a warm look the world's hunks and colors,
The soul descends once more in bitter love
To accept the waking body, saying now
In a changed voice as the man yawns and rises,

> "Bring them down from their ruddy gallows;
> Let there be clean linen for the backs of thieves;
> Let lovers go fresh and sweet to be undone,
> And the heaviest nuns walk in a pure floating
> Of dark habits,
>   keeping their difficult balance."

A Voice from under the Table

To Robert and Jane Brooks

How shall the wine be drunk, or the woman known?
I take this world for better or for worse,
But seeing rose carafes conceive the sun
My thirst conceives a fierier universe:
And then I toast the birds in the burning trees
That chant their holy lucid drunkenness;
I swallowed all the phosphorus of the seas
Before I fell into this low distress.

You upright people all remember how
Love drove you first to the woods, and there you heard
The loose-mouthed wind complaining *Thou* and *Thou*;
My gawky limbs were shuddered by the word.
Most of it since was nothing but charades
To spell that hankering out and make an end,
But the softest hands against my shoulder-blades
Only increased the crying of the wind.

For this the goddess rose from the midland sea
And stood above the famous wine-dark wave,
To ease our drouth with clearer mystery
And be a South to all our flights of love.
And down by the selfsame water I have seen
A blazing girl with skin like polished stone
Splashing until a far-out breast of green
Arose and with a rose contagion shone.

"A myrtle-shoot in hand, she danced; her hair
Cast on her back and shoulders a moving shade."
Was it some hovering light that showed her fair?
Was it of chafing dark that light was made?
Perhaps it was Archilochus' fantasy,
Or that his saying sublimed the thing he said.
All true enough; and true as well that she
Was beautiful, and danced, and is now dead.

Helen was no such high discarnate thought
As men in dry symposia pursue,
But was as bitterly fugitive, not to be caught
By what men's arms in love or fight could do.
Groan in your cell; rape Troy with sword and flame;
The end of thirst exceeds experience.
A devil told me it was all the same
Whether to fail by spirit or by sense.

God keep me a damned fool, nor charitably
Receive me into his shapely resignations.
I am a sort of martyr, as you see,
A horizontal monument to patience.
The calves of waitresses parade about
My helpless head upon this sodden floor.
Well, I am down again, but not yet out.
O sweet frustrations, I shall be back for more.

Beasts

Beasts in their major freedom
Slumber in peace tonight. The gull on his ledge
Dreams in the guts of himself the moon-plucked waves below,
And the sunfish leans on a stone, slept
By the lyric water,

In which the spotless feet
Of deer make dulcet splashes, and to which
The ripped mouse, safe in the owl's talon, cries

Concordance. Here there is no such harm
And no such darkness

As the selfsame moon observes
Where, warped in window-glass, it sponsors now
The werewolf's painful change. Turning his head away
On the sweaty bolster, he tries to remember
The mood of manhood,

But lies at last, as always,
Letting it happen, the fierce fur soft to his face,
Hearing with sharper ears the wind's exciting minors,
The leaves' panic, and the degradation
Of the heavy streams.

Meantime, at high windows
Far from thicket and pad-fall, suitors of excellence
Sigh and turn from their work to construe again the painful
Beauty of heaven, the lucid moon
And the risen hunter,

Making such dreams for men
As told will break their hearts as always, bringing
Monsters into the city, crows on the public statues,
Navies fed to the fish in the dark
Unbridled waters.

A Baroque Wall-Fountain in the Villa Sciarra

For Dore and Adja

Under the bronze crown
Too big for the head of the stone cherub whose feet
A serpent has begun to eat,
Sweet water brims a cockle and braids down

Past spattered mosses, breaks
On the tipped edge of a second shell, and fills

The massive third below. It spills
In threads then from the scalloped rim, and makes

A scrim or summery tent
For a faun-ménage and their familiar goose.
Happy in all that ragged, loose
Collapse of water, its effortless descent

And flatteries of spray,
The stocky god upholds the shell with ease,
Watching, about his shaggy knees,
The goatish innocence of his babes at play;

His fauness all the while
Leans forward, slightly, into a clambering mesh
Of water-lights, her sparkling flesh
In a saecular ecstasy, her blinded smile

Bent on the sand floor
Of the trefoil pool, where ripple-shadows come
And go in swift reticulum,
More addling to the eye than wine, and more

Interminable to thought
Than pleasure's calculus. Yet since this all
Is pleasure, flash, and waterfall,
Must it not be too simple? Are we not

More intricately expressed
In the plain fountains that Maderna set
Before St. Peter's—the main jet
Struggling aloft until it seems at rest

In the act of rising, until
The very wish of water is reversed,
That heaviness borne up to burst
In a clear, high, cavorting head, to fill

With blaze, and then in gauze
Delays, in a gnatlike shimmering, in a fine
    Illumined version of itself, decline,
And patter on the stones its own applause?

    If that is what men are
Or should be, if those water-saints display
    The pattern of our areté,[1]
What of these showered fauns in their bizarre,

    Spangled, and plunging house?
They are at rest in fulness of desire
    For what is given, they do not tire
Of the smart of the sun, the pleasant water-douse

    And riddled pool below,
Reproving our disgust and our ennui
    With humble insatiety.
Francis, perhaps, who lay in sister snow

    Before the wealthy gate
Freezing and praising, might have seen in this
    No trifle, but a shade of bliss—
That land of tolerable flowers, that state

    As near and far as grass
Where eyes become the sunlight, and the hand
    Is worthy of water: the dreamt land
Toward which all hungers leap, all pleasures pass.

Advice to a Prophet *

When you come, as you soon must, to the streets of our city,
    Mad-eyed from stating the obvious,

[1] Note: *areté*, a Greek word meaning roughly "virtue."—Author.
* Hephaestus, invoked by Achilles, scalded the river Xanthus (Scamander)
in *Iliad* xxi.—Author's note.

Not proclaiming our fall but begging us
In God's name to have self-pity,

Spare us all word of the weapons, their force and range,
The long numbers that rocket the mind;
Our slow, unreckoning hearts will be left behind,
Unable to fear what is too strange.

Nor shall you scare us with talk of the death of the race.
How should we dream of this place without us?—
The sun mere fire, the leaves untroubled about us,
A stone look on the stone's face?

Speak of the world's own change. Though we cannot conceive
Of an undreamt thing, we know to our cost
How the dreamt cloud crumbles, the vines are blackened by frost,
How the view alters. We could believe,

If you told us so, that the white-tailed deer will slip
Into perfect shade, grown perfectly shy,
The lark avoid the reaches of our eye,
The jack-pine lose its knuckled grip

On the cold ledge, and every torrent burn
As Xanthus once, its gliding trout
Stunned in a twinkling. What should we be without
The dolphin's arc, the dove's return,

These things in which we have seen ourselves and spoken?
Ask us, prophet, how we shall call
Our natures forth when that live tongue is all
Dispelled, that glass obscured or broken

In which we have said the rose of our love and the clean
Horse of our courage, in which beheld
The singing locust of the soul unshelled,
And all we mean or wish to mean.

Ask us, ask us whether with the worldless rose
Our hearts shall fail us; come demanding
Whether there shall be lofty or long standing
When the bronze annals of the oak-tree close.

She

What was her beauty in our first estate
When Adam's will was whole, and the least thing
Appeared the gift and creature of his king,
How should we guess? Resemblance had to wait

For separation, and in such a place
She so partook of water, light, and trees
As not to look like any one of these.
He woke and gazed into her naked face.

But then she changed, and coming down amid
The flocks of Abel and the fields of Cain,
Clothed in their wish, her Eden graces hid,
A shape of plenty with a mop of grain,

She broke upon the world, in time took on
The look of every labor and its fruits.
Columnar in a robe of pleated lawn
She cupped her patient hand for attributes,

Was radiant captive of the farthest tower
And shed her honor on the fields of war,
Walked in her garden at the evening hour,
Her shadow like a dark ogival door,

Breasted the seas for all the westward ships
And, come to virgin country, changed again—
A moonlike being truest in eclipse,
And subject goddess of the dreams of men.

Tree, temple, valley, prow, gazelle, machine,
More named and nameless than the morning star,
Lovely in every shape, in all unseen,
We dare not wish to find you as you are,

Whose apparition, biding time until
Desire decay and bring the latter age,
Shall flourish in the ruins of our will
And deck the broken stones like saxifrage.

In the Smoking-Car

The eyelids meet. He'll catch a little nap.
The grizzled, crew-cut head drops to his chest.
It shakes above the briefcase on his lap.
Close voices breathe, "Poor sweet, he did his best."

"Poor sweet, poor sweet," the bird-hushed glades repeat,
Through which in quiet pomp his litter goes,
Carried by native girls with naked feet.
A sighing stream concurs in his repose.

Could he but think, he might recall to mind
The righteous mutiny or sudden gale
That beached him here; the dear ones left behind . . .
So near the ending, he forgets the tale.

Were he to lift his eyelids now, he might
Behold his maiden porters, brown and bare.
But even here he has no appetite.
It is enough to know that they are there.

Enough that now a honeyed music swells,
The gentle, mossed declivities begin,
And the whole air is full of flower-smells.
Failure, the longed-for valley, takes him in.

PHILIP LARKIN

(1922–)

[One Man Walking a Deserted Platform]

One man walking a deserted platform;
Dawn coming, and rain
Driving across a darkening autumn;
One man restlessly waiting a train
While round the streets the wind runs wild,
Beating each shuttered house, that seems
Folded full of the dark silk of dreams,
A shell of sleep cradling a wife or child.

Who can this ambition trace,
To be each dawn perpetually journeying?
To trick this hour when lovers re-embrace
With the unguessed-at heart riding
The winds as gulls do? What lips said
Starset and cockcrow call the dispossessed
On to the next desert, lest
Love sink a grave round the still-sleeping head?

[Heaviest of Flowers, the Head]

Heaviest of flowers, the head
Forever hangs above a stormless bed;

Hands that the heart can govern
Shall be at last by darker hands unwoven;
Every exultant sense
Unstrung to silence—
The sun drift away.

And all the memories that best
Run back beyond this season of unrest
Shall lie upon the earth
That gave them birth.
Like fallen apples, they will lose
Their sweetness at the bruise,
And then decay.

Lines on a Young Lady's Photograph Album

At last you yielded up the album, which,
Once open, sent me distracted. All your ages
Matt and glossy on the thick black pages!
Too much confectionery, too rich:
I choke on such nutritious images.

My swivel eye hungers from pose to pose—
In pigtails, clutching a reluctant cat;
Or furred yourself, a sweet girl-graduate;
Or lifting a heavy-headed rose
Beneath a trellis, or in a trilby hat

(Faintly disturbing, that, in several ways)—
From every side you strike at my control,
Not least through these disquieting chaps who loll
At ease about your earlier days:
Not quite your class, I'd say, dear, on the whole.

But o, photography! as no art is,
Faithful and disappointing! that records
Dull days as dull, and hold-it smiles as frauds,

And will not censor blemishes
Like washing-lines, and Hall's-Distemper boards,

But shows the cat as disinclined, and shades
A chin as doubled when it is, what grace
Your candour thus confers upon her face!
How overwhelmingly persuades
That this is a real girl in a real place,

In every sense empirically true!
Or is it just *the past?* Those flowers, that gate,
These misty parks and motors, lacerate
Simply by being over; you
Contract my heart by looking out of date.

Yes, true; but in the end, surely, we cry
Not only at exclusion, but because
It leaves us free to cry. We know *what was*
Won't call on us to justify
Our grief, however hard we yowl across

The gap from eye to page. So I am left
To mourn (without a chance of consequence)
You, balanced on a bike against a fence;
To wonder if you'd spot the theft
Of this one of you bathing; to condense,

In short, a past that no one now can share,
No matter whose your future; calm and dry,
It holds you like a heaven, and you lie
Unvariably lovely there,
Smaller and clearer as the years go by.

Wedding-Wind

The wind blew all my wedding-day,
And my wedding-night was the night of the high wind;

And a stable door was banging, again and again,
That he must go and shut it, leaving me
Stupid in candlelight, hearing rain,
Seeing my face in the twisted candlestick,
Yet seeing nothing. When he came back
He said the horses were restless, and I was sad
That any man or beast that night should lack
The happiness I had.

              Now in the day
All's ravelled under the sun by the wind's blowing.
He has gone to look at the floods, and I
Carry a chipped pail to the chicken-run,
Set it down, and stare. All is the wind
Hunting through clouds and forests, thrashing
My apron and the hanging cloths on the line.
Can it be borne, this bodying-forth by wind
Of joy my actions turn on, like a thread
Carrying beads? Shall I be let to sleep
Now this perpetual morning shares my bed?
Can even death dry up
These new delighted lakes, conclude
Our kneeling as cattle by all-generous waters?

Reasons for Attendance

The trumpet's voice, loud and authoritative,
Draws me a moment to the lighted glass
To watch the dancers—all under twenty-five—
Shifting intently, face to flushed face,
Solemnly on the beat of happiness.

—Or so I fancy, sensing the smoke and sweat,
The wonderful feel of girls. Why be out here?
But then, why be in there? Sex, yes, but what
Is sex? Surely, to think the lion's share
Of happiness is found by couples—sheer

Inaccuracy, as far as I'm concerned.
What calls me is that lifted, rough-tongued bell
(Art, if you like) whose individual sound
Insists I too am individual.
It speaks; I hear; others may hear as well,

But not for me, nor I for them; and so
With happiness. Therefore I stay outside,
Believing this; and they maul to and fro,
Believing that; and both are satisfied,
If no one has misjudged himself. Or lied.

Going

There is an evening coming in
Across the fields, one never seen before,
That lights no lamps.

Silken it seems at a distance, yet
When it is drawn up over the knees and breast
It brings no comfort.

Where has the tree gone, that locked
Earth to the sky? What is under my hands,
That I cannot feel?

What loads my hands down?

Maiden Name

Marrying left your maiden name disused.
Its five light sounds no longer mean your face,
Your voice, and all your variants of grace;
For since you were so thankfully confused
By law with someone else, you cannot be
Semantically the same as that young beauty:
It was of her that these two words were used.

283

Now it's a phrase applicable to no one,
Lying just where you left it, scattered through
Old lists, old programmes, a school prize or two,
Packets of letters tied with tartan ribbon—
Then is it scentless, weightless, strengthless, wholly
Untruthful? Try whispering it slowly.
No, it means you. Or, since you're past and gone,

It means what we feel now about you then:
How beautiful you were, and near, and young,
So vivid, you might still be there among
Those first few days, unfingermarked again.
So your old name shelters our faithfulness,
Instead of losing shape and meaning less
With your depreciating luggage laden.

Wires

The widest prairies have electric fences,
For though old cattle know they must not stray
Young steers are always scenting purer water
Not here but anywhere. Beyond the wires

Leads them to blunder up against the wires
Whose muscle-shredding violence gives no quarter.
Young steers become old cattle from that day,
Electric limits to their widest senses.

Church Going

Once I am sure there's nothing going on
I step inside, letting the door thud shut.
Another church: matting, seats, and stone,
And little books; sprawlings of flowers, cut
For Sunday, brownish now; some brass and stuff
Up at the holy end; the small neat organ;

And a tense, musty, unignorable silence,
Brewed God knows how long. Hatless, I take off
My cycle-clips in awkward reverence,

Move forward, run my hand around the font.
From where I stand, the roof looks almost new—
Cleaned, or restored? Someone would know: I don't.
Mounting the lectern, I peruse a few
Hectoring large-scale verses, and pronounce
'Here endeth' much more loudly than I'd meant.
The echoes snigger briefly. Back at the door
I sign the book, donate an Irish sixpence,
Reflect the place was not worth stopping for.

Yet stop I did: in fact I often do,
And always end much at a loss like this,
Wondering what to look for; wondering, too,
When churches fall completely out of use
What we shall turn them into, if we shall keep
A few cathedrals chronically on show,
Their parchment, plate and pyx in locked cases,
And let the rest rent-free to rain and sheep.
Shall we avoid them as unlucky places?

Or, after dark, will dubious women come
To make their children touch a particular stone;
Pick simples for a cancer; or on some
Advised night see walking a dead one?
Power of some sort or other will go on
In games, in riddles, seemingly at random;
But superstition, like belief, must die,
And what remains when disbelief has gone?
Grass, weedy pavement, brambles, buttress, sky,

A shape less recognisable each week,
A purpose more obscure. I wonder who
Will be the last, the very last, to seek
This place for what it was; one of the crew

285

That tap and jot and know what rood-lofts were?
Some ruin-bibber, randy for antique,
Or Christmas-addict, counting on a whiff
Of gown-and-bands and organ-pipes and myrrh?
Or will he be my representative,

Bored, uninformed, knowing the ghostly silt
Dispersed, yet tending to this cross of ground
Through suburb scrub because it held unspilt
So long and equably what since is found
Only in separation—marriage, and birth,
And death, and thoughts of these—for which was built
This special shell? For, though I've no idea
What this accoutred frowsty barn is worth,
It pleases me to stand in silence here;

A serious house on serious earth it is,
In whose blent air all our compulsions meet,
Are recognised, and robed as destinies.
And that much never can be obsolete,
Since someone will forever be surprising
A hunger in himself to be more serious,
And gravitating with it to this ground,
Which, he once heard, was proper to grow wise in,
If only that so many dead lie round.

Poetry of Departures

Sometimes you hear, fifth-hand,
As epitaph:
He chucked up everything
And just cleared off,
And always the voice will sound
Certain you approve
This audacious, purifying,
Elemental move.

And they are right, I think.
We all hate home
And having to be there:
I detest my room,
Its specially-chosen junk,
The good books, the good bed,
And my life, in perfect order:
So to hear it said

He walked out on the whole crowd
Leaves me flushed and stirred,
Like *Then she undid her dress*
Or *Take that you bastard;*
Surely I can, if he did?
And that helps me stay
Sober and industrious.
But I'd go today,

Yes, swagger the nut-strewn roads,
Crouch in the fo'c'sle
Stubbly with goodness, if
It weren't so artificial,
Such a deliberate step backwards
To create an object:
Books; china; a life
Reprehensibly perfect.

If, My Darling

If my darling were once to decide
Not to stop at my eyes,
But to jump, like Alice, with floating skirt into my head,

She would find no tables and chairs,
No mahogany claw-footed sideboards,
No undisturbed embers;

The tantalus would not be filled, nor the fender-seat cosy,
Nor the shelves stuffed with small-printed books for the Sabbath,
Nor the butler bibulous, the housemaids lazy:

She would find herself looped with the creep of varying light,
Monkey-brown, fish-grey, a string of infected circles
Loitering like bullies, about to coagulate;

Delusions that shrink to the size of a woman's glove
Then sicken inclusively outwards. She would also remark
The unwholesome floor, as it might be the skin of a grave,

From which ascends an adhesive sense of betrayal,
A Grecian statue kicked in the privates, money,
A swill-tub of finer feelings. But most of all

She'd be stopping her ears against the incessant recital
Intoned by reality, larded with technical terms,
Each one double-yolked with meaning and meaning's rebuttal:

For the skirl of that bulletin unpicks the world like a knot,
And to hear how the past is past and the future neuter
Might knock my darling off her unpriceable pivot.

JAMES DICKEY

(1923-)

The Heaven of Animals

Here they are. The soft eyes open.
If they have lived in a wood
It is a wood.
If they have lived on plains
It is grass rolling
Under their feet forever.

Having no souls, they have come,
Anyway, beyond their knowing.
Their instincts wholly bloom
And they rise.
The soft eyes open.

To match them, the landscape flowers,
Outdoing, desperately
Outdoing what is required:
The richest wood,
The deepest field.

For some of these,
It could not be the place
It is, without blood.
These hunt, as they have done,
But with claws and teeth grown perfect,

More deadly than they can believe.
They stalk more silently,
And crouch on the limbs of trees,
And their descent
Upon the bright backs of their prey

May take years
In a sovereign floating of joy.
And those that are hunted
Know this as their life,
Their reward: to walk

Under such trees in full knowledge
Of what is in glory above them,
And to feel no fear,
But acceptance, compliance.
Fulfilling themselves without pain

At the cycle's center,
They tremble, they walk
Under the tree,
They fall, they are torn,
They rise, they walk again.

In the Tree House at Night

And now the green household is dark.
The half-moon completely is shining
On the earth-lighted tops of the trees.
To be dead, a house must be still.
The floor and the walls wave me slowly;
I am deep in them over my head.
The needles and pine cones about me

Are full of small birds at their roundest,
Their fists without mercy gripping
Hard down through the tree to the roots
To sing back at light when they feel it.

We lie here like angels in bodies,
My brothers and I, one dead,
The other asleep from much living,

In mid-air huddled beside me.
Dark climbed to us here as we climbed
Up the nails I have hammered all day
Through the sprained, comic rungs of the ladder
Of broom handles, crate slats, and laths
Foot by foot up the trunk to the branches
Where we came out at last over lakes

Of leaves, of fields disencumbered of earth
That move with the moves of the spirit.
Each nail that sustains us I set here;
Each nail in the house is now steadied
By my dead brother's huge, freckled hand.
Through the years, he has pointed his hammer
Up into these limbs, and told us

That we must ascend, and all lie here.
Step after step he has brought me,
Embracing the trunk as his body,
Shaking its limbs with my heartbeat,
Till the pine cones danced without wind
And fell from the branches like apples.
In the arm-slender forks of our dwelling

I breathe my live brother's light hair.
The blanket around us becomes
As solid as stone, and it sways.
With all my heart, I close
The blue, timeless eye of my mind.
Wind springs, as my dead brother smiles
And touches the tree at the root;

A shudder of joy runs up
The trunk; the needles tingle;
One bird uncontrollably cries.

The wind changes round, and I stir
Within another's life. Whose life?
Who is dead? Whose presence is living?
When may I fall strangely to earth,

Who am nailed to this branch by a spirit?
Can two bodies make up a third?
To sing, must I feel the world's light?
My green, graceful bones fill the air
With sleeping birds. Alone, alone
And with them I move gently.
I move at the heart of the world.

In the Lupanar at Pompeii

There are tracks which belong to wheels
Long since turned to air and time.
Those are the powerful chariots
I follow down cobblestones,
Not being dragged, exactly,
But not of my own will, either,
Going past the flower sellers'
And the cindery produce market
And the rich man's home, and the house
Of the man who kept a dog
Set in mosaic.

As tourist, but mostly as lecher,
I seek out the dwelling of women
Who all expect me, still, because
They expect anybody who comes.
I am ready to pay, and I do,
And then go among them
Where on the dark walls of their home
They hold their eternal postures,
Doing badly drawn, exacting,
Too-willing, wide-eyed things
With dry-eyed art.

I sit down in one of the rooms
Where it happened again and again.
I could be in prison, or dead,
Cast down for my sins in a cell
Still filled with a terrible motion
Like the heaving and sighing of earth
To be free of the heat it restrains.
I feel in my heart how the heart
Of the mountain broke, and the women
Fled onto the damp of the walls
And shaped their embraces

To include whoever would come here
After the stone-cutting chariots.
I think of the marvel of lust
Which can always, at any moment,
Become more than it believed,
And almost always is less:
I think of its possible passing
Beyond, into tender awareness,
Into helplessness, weeping, and death:
It must be like the first
Soft floating of ash,

When, in the world's frankest hands,
Someone lay with his body shaken
Free of the self: that amazement—
For we who must try to explain
Ourselves in the house of this flesh
Never can tell the quick heat
Of our own from another's breathing,
Nor yet from the floating of feathers
That form in our lungs when the mountain
Settles like odd, warm snow against
Our willing limbs.

We never can really tell
Whether nature condemns us or loves us
As we lie here dying of breath

And the painted, unchanging women,
Believing the desperate dead
Where they stripped to the skin of the soul
And whispered to us, as to
Their panting, observing selves:
"Passion. Before we die
Let us hope for no longer
But truly know it."

The Dusk of Horses

Right under their noses, the green
Of the field is paling away
Because of something fallen from the sky.

They see this, and put down
Their long heads deeper in grass
That only just escapes reflecting them

As the dream of a millpond would.
The color green flees over the grass
Like an insect, following the red sun over

The next hill. The grass is white.
There is no cloud so dark and white at once;
There is no pool at dawn that deepens

Their faces and thirsts as this does.
Now they are feeding on solid
Cloud, and one by one,

With nails as silent as stars among the wood
Hewed down years ago and now rotten,
The stalls are put up around them.

Now if they lean, they come
On wood on any side. Not touching it, they sleep.
No beast ever lived who understood

What happened among the sun's fields,
Or cared why the color of grass
Fled over the hill while he stumbled,

Led by the halter to sleep
On his four taxed, worthy legs.
Each thinks he awakens where

The sun is black on the rooftop,
That the green is dancing in the next pasture,
And that the way to sleep

In a cloud, or in a risen lake,
Is to walk as though he were still
In the drained field standing, head down,

To pretend to sleep when led,
And thus to go under the ancient white
Of the meadow, as green goes

And whiteness comes up through his face
Holding stars and rotten rafters,
Quiet, fragrant, and relieved.

The Scarred Girl

All glass may yet be whole
She thinks, it may be put together
From the deep inner flashing of her face.
One moment the windshield held

The countryside, the green
Level fields and the animals,
And these must be restored
To what they were when her brow

Broke into them for nothing, and began
Its sparkling under the gauze.

Though the still, small war for her beauty
Is stitched out of sight and lost,

It is not this field that she thinks of.
It is that her face, buried
And held up inside the slow scars,
Knows how the bright, fractured world

Burns and pulls and weeps
To come together again.
The green meadow lying in fragments
Under the splintered sunlight,

The cattle broken in pieces
By her useless, painful intrusion
Know that her visage contains
The process and hurt of their healing,

The hidden wounds that can
Restore anything, bringing the glass
Of the world together once more,
All as it was when she struck,

All except her. The shattered field
Where they dragged the telescoped car
Off to be pounded to scrap
Waits for her to get up,

For her calm, unimagined face
To emerge from the yards of its wrapping,
Red, raw, mixed-looking but entire,
A new face, an old life,

To confront the pale glass it has dreamed
Made whole and backed with wise silver,
Held in other hands brittle with dread,
A doctor's, a lip-biting nurse's,

Who do not see what she sees
Behind her odd face in the mirror:
The pastures of earth and of heaven
Restored and undamaged, the cattle

Risen out of their jagged graves
To walk in the seamless sunlight
And a newborn countenance
Put upon everything,

Her beauty gone, but to hover
Near for the rest of her life,
And good no nearer, but plainly
In sight, and the only way.

The Poisoned Man

When the rattlesnake bit, I lay
In a dream of the country, and dreamed
Day after day of the river,

Where I sat with a jackknife and quickly
Opened my sole to the water.
Blood shed for the sake of one's life

Takes on the hid shape of the channel,
Disappearing under logs and through boulders.
The freezing river poured on

And as it took hold of my blood,
Leapt up round the rocks and boiled over.
I felt that my heart's blood could flow

Unendingly out of the mountain,
Splitting bedrock apart upon redness,
And the current of life at my instep

Give deathlessly as a spring.
Some leaves fell from trees and whirled under.
I saw my struck bloodstream assume,

Inside the cold path of the river,
The inmost routes of a serpent
Through grass, through branches and leaves.

When I rose, the live-oaks were ashen
And the wild grass was dead without flame.
Through the blasted corn field I hobbled,

My foot tied up in my shirt,
And met my old wife in the garden,
Where she reached for a withering apple.

I lay in the country and dreamed
Of the substance and course of the river
While the different colors of fever

Like quilt patches flickered upon me.
At last I arose, with the poison
Gone out of the seam of the scar,

And brought my wife eastward and weeping,
Through the copper fields springing alive
With the promise of harvest for no one.

DENISE LEVERTOV
(1923–)

The Gypsy's Window

It seems a stage
backed by imaginations of velvet,
cotton, satin, loops and stripes—

A lovely unconcern
scattered the trivial plates, the rosaries
and centered
a narrownecked dark vase,
unopened yellow and pink
paper roses, a luxury of open red
paper roses—

Watching the trucks go by, from stiff chairs
behind the window show, an old
bandanna'd brutal dignified
woman, a young beautiful woman
her mouth a huge contemptuous rose—

The courage
of natural rhetoric tosses to dusty
Hudson St. the chance of poetry, a chance
poetry gives passion to the roses,
the roses in the gypsy's window in a blue

vase, look real, as unreal
as real roses.

Laying the Dust

What a sweet smell rises
　　　when you lay the dust—
bucket after bucket of water thrown
on the yellow grass.
　　　　　　　The water
flashes
each time you
make it leap—
　　　arching its glittering back.
The sound of
　　　　　more water
pouring into the pail
almost quenches my thirst.
Surely when flowers
grow here, they'll not
smell sweeter than this
　　　wet ground, suddenly black.

Merritt Parkway

As if it were
forever that they move, that we
keep moving—

　　　Under a wan sky where
as the lights went on a star
　　　pierced the haze & now
follows steadily
　　　　　a constant
above our six lanes
the dreamlike continuum . . .

And the people—ourselves!
the humans from inside the
cars, apparent
only at gasoline stops
unsure,
eyeing each other

drink coffee hastily at the
slot machines & hurry
back to the cars
vanish
into them forever, to
keep moving—

Houses now & then beyond the
sealed road, the trees / trees, bushes
passing by, passing
the cars that
keep moving ahead of
us, past us, pressing behind us
and
over left, those that come
toward us shining too brightly
moving relentlessly

in six lanes, gliding
north & south, speeding with
a slurred sound—

Illustrious Ancestors

The Rav
of Northern White Russia declined,
in his youth, to learn the
language of birds, because
the extraneous did not interest him; nevertheless
when he grew old it was found
he understood them anyway, having

DENISE LEVERTOV

listened well, and as it is said, 'prayed
                    with the bench and the floor.' He used
what was at hand—as did
Angel Jones of Mold, whose meditations
were sewn into coats and britches.
                    Well, I would like to make,
thinking some line still taut between me and them,
poems direct as what the birds said,
hard as a floor, sound as a bench,
mysterious as the silence when the tailor
would pause with his needle in the air.

With Eyes at the Back of Our Heads

With eyes at the back of our heads
we see a mountain
not obstructed with woods but laced
here and there with feathery groves.

The doors before us in a facade
that perhaps has no house in back of it
are too narrow, and one is set high
with no doorsill. The architect sees

the imperfect proposition and
turns eagerly to the knitter.
Set it to rights!
The knitter begins to knit.

For we want
to enter the house, if there is a house,
to pass through the doors at least
into whatever lies beyond them,

we want to enter the arms
of the knitted garment. As one
is re-formed, so the other,
in proportion.

When the doors widen
when the sleeves admit us
the way to the mountain will clear,
the mountain we see with
eyes at the back of our heads, mountain
green, mountain
cut of limestone, echoing
with hidden rivers, mountain
of short grass and subtle shadows.

The Quarry Pool

Between town and the
old house, an inn—
the Half-Way House.
So far one could ride, I remember,

the rest was an uphill walk,
a mountain lane with
steep banks and sweet
hedges, half walls of

gray rock. Looking
again at this looking-glass face
unaccountably changed in a week,
three weeks, a month,

I think without thinking of
Half-Way House. Is it
the thought that this far
I've driven at ease, as in a bus,

a country bus where one could talk to the driver?
Now on foot towards the village;
the dust clears, silence
draws in around one. I hear
the rustle and hum of the fields: alone.

It must be the sense
of essential solitude that chills me
looking into my eyes.
I should remember

the old house at the walk's ending,
a square place with a courtyard,
granaries, netted strawberry-beds,
a garden that was many

gardens, each one
a world hidden from the
next by leaves, enlaced trees,
fern-hairy walls, gilly-flowers.

I should see, making
a strange face at myself,
nothing to fear in the thought of
Half-Way House—

the place one got down
to walk—. What is
this shudder, this
dry mouth?

Think, please, of the quarry pool,
the garden's furthest
garden, of your childhood's
joy in its solitude.

To the Snake

Green Snake, when I hung you round my neck
and stroked your cold, pulsing throat
        as you hissed to me, glinting
arrowy gold scales, and I felt
        the weight of you on my shoulders,

and the whispering silver of your dryness
   sounded close at my ears—

Green Snake—I swore to my companions that certainly
   you were harmless! But truly
I had no certainty, and no hope, only desiring
   to hold you, for that joy,
      which left
a long wake of pleasure, as the leaves moved
and you faded into the pattern
of grass and shadows, and I returned
smiling and haunted, to a dark morning.

A Map of the Western Part of the County of Essex in England

Something forgotten for twenty years: though my fathers
and mothers came from Cordova and Vitepsk and Caernarvon,
and though I am a citizen of the United States and less a
stranger here than anywhere else, perhaps,
I am Essex-born:
Cranbrook Wash called me into its dark tunnel,
the little streams of Valentines heard my resolves,
Roding held my head above water when I thought it was
drowning me; in Hainault only a haze of thin trees
stood between the red doubledecker buses and the boar-hunt,
the spirit of merciful Phillipa glimmered there.
Pergo Park knew me, and Clavering, and Havering-atte-Bower,
Stanford Rivers lost me in osier beds, Stapleford Abbots
sent me safe home on the dark road after Simeon-quiet evensong,
Wanstead draw me over and over into its basic poetry,
in its serpentine lake I saw bass-viols among the golden dead leaves,
through its trees the ghost of a great house. In
Ilford High Road I saw the multitudes passing pale under the
light of flaring sundown, seven kings
in somber starry robes gathered at Seven Kings
the place of law

where my birth and marriage are recorded
and the death of my father. Woodford Wells
where an old house was called The Naked Beauty (a white
statue forlorn in its garden)
saw the meeting and parting of two sisters,
(forgotten? and further away
the hill before Thaxted? where peace befell us? not once
but many times?).
All the Ivans dreaming of their villages
all the Marias dreaming of their walled cities,
picking up fragments of New World slowly,
not knowing how to put them together nor how to join
image with image, now I know how it was with you, an old map
made long before I was born shows ancient
rights of way where I walked when I was ten burning with desire
for the world's great splendors, a child who traced voyages
indelibly all over the atlas, who now in a far country
remembers the first river, the first
field, bricks and lumber dumped in it ready for building,
that new smell, and remembers
the walls of the garden, the first light.

Resting Figure

The head Byzantine or from
Fayyum, the shoulders naked,
a little of the
dark-haired breast visible
above the sheet,

from deep in the dark head
his smile glowing
outward into the
room's severe twilight,

he lies, a dark-shadowed
mellow gold against

the flattened white pillow,
a gentle man—

strength and despair
quiet there in the bed,
the line of his limbs
half-shown, as under stone
or bronze folds.

The Jacob's Ladder

The stairway is not
a thing of gleaming strands
a radiant evanescence
for angels' feet that only glance in their tread, and need not
touch the stone.

It is of stone.
A rosy stone that takes
a glowing tone of softness
only because behind it the sky is a doubtful, a doubting
night gray.

A stairway of sharp
angles, solidly built.
One sees that the angels must spring
down from one step to the next, giving a little
lift of the wings:

and a man climbing
must scrape his knees, and bring
the grip of his hands into play. The cut stone
consoles his groping feet. Wings brush past him.
The poem ascends.

Matins

I

The authentic! Shadows of it
sweep past in dreams, one could say imprecisely,
evoking the almost-silent
ripping apart of giant
sheets of cellophane. No.
It thrusts up close. Exactly in dreams
it has you off-guard, you
recognize it before you have time.
For a second before waking
the alarm bell is a red conical hat, it
takes form.

II

The authentic! I said
rising from the toilet seat.
The radiator in rhythmic knockings
spoke of the rising steam.
The authentic, I said
breaking the handle of my hairbrush as I
brushed my hair in
rhythmic strokes: That's it,
that's joy, it's always
a recognition, the known
appearing fully itself, and
more itself than one knew.

III

The new day rises
as heat rises,
knocking in the pipes
with rhythms it seizes for its own
to speak of its invention—
the real, the new-laid
egg whose speckled shell
the poet fondles and must break
if he will be nourished.

IV

A shadow painted where
yes, a shadow must fall.
The cow's breath
not forgotten in the mist, in the
words. Yes,
verisimilitude draws up
heat in us, zest
to follow through,
follow through,
follow
transformations of day
in its turning, in its becoming.

V

Stir the holy grains, set
the bowls on the table and
call the child to eat.

While we eat we think,
as we think an undercurrent
of dream runs through us
faster than thought
towards recognition.

Call the child to eat,
send him off, his mouth
tasting of toothpaste, to go down
into the ground, into a roaring train
and to school.

His cheeks are pink
his black eyes hold his dreams, he has left
forgetting his glasses.

Follow down the stairs at a clatter
to give them to him and save
his clear sight.

Cold air
comes in at the street door.

VI

The authentic! It rolls
just out of reach, beyond
running feet and
stretching fingers, down
the green slope and into
the black waves of the sea.
Speak to me, little horse, beloved,
tell me
how to follow the iron ball,
how to follow through to the country
beneath the waves
to the place where I must kill you and you step out
of your bones and flystrewn meat
tall, smiling, renewed,
formed in your own likeness.

VII

Marvelous Truth, confront us
at every turn,
in every guise, iron ball,
egg, dark horse, shadow,
cloud
of breath on the air,

dwell
in our crowded hearts
our steaming bathrooms, kitchens full of
things to be done, the
ordinary streets.

Thrust close your smile
that we know you, terrible joy.

VASSAR MILLER

(1924–)

The New Icarus

Slip off the husk of gravity to lie
Bedded with wind; float on a whimsy, lift
Upon a wish: your bow's own arrow, rift
Newton's decorum—only when you fly.
But naked. No false-feathered fool, you try
Dalliance with heights, nor, plumed with metal, shift
And shear the clouds, imperiling lark and swift
And all birds bridal-bowered in the sky.

Your wreck of bone, barred their delight's dominions,
Lacking their formula for flight, holds imaged
Those alps of air no eagle's wing can quell.
With arms flung crosswise, pinioned to wooden pinions,
You, in one motion plucked and crimson-plumaged,
Outsoar all Heaven, plummeting all Hell.

Adam's Footprint

Once as a child I loved to hop
On round plump bugs and make them stop
Before they crossed a certain crack.

My bantam brawn could turn them back,
My crooked step wrenched straight to kill
Live pods that then screwed tight and still.

Small sinner, stripping boughs of pears,
Shinnied past sweet and wholesome airs,
How could a tree be so unclean?
Nobody knows but Augustine.
He nuzzled pears for dam-sin's dugs—
And I scrunched roly-poly bugs.

No wolf's imprint or tiger's trace
Does Christ hunt down to catch with grace
In nets of love the devious preys
Whose feet go softly all their days:
The foot of Adam leaves the mark
Of some child scrabbling in the dark.

Bout with Burning

I have tossed hours upon the tides of fever,
Upon the billows of my blood have ridden,
Where fish of fancy teem as neither river
Nor ocean spawns from India to Sweden.
Here while my boat of body burnt has drifted
Along her sides crawled tentacles of crabs
Sliming her timbers; on the waves upwafted
Crept water rats to gnaw her ropes and ribs.
Crashing, she has dived, her portholes choking
With weed and ooze, the swirls of black and green
Gulping her inch by inch, the seagulls' shrieking
Sieved depth through depth to silence. Till blast-blown,
I in my wreck beyond storm's charge and churning
Have waked marooned upon the coasts of morning.

312

Fantasy on the Resurrection

Flaws cling to flesh as dews cling to a rose:
The cripples limp as though they would prolong,
Walking, a waltz; the deaf ears, opened, close
As if their convolutions hoard all song;
The blind eyes keep half shut as if to fold
A vision fast men never glimpse by staring;
Against their will the mute lips move that hold
A language which was never tongue's for sharing.
Shocked shag of earth and everything thereunder
Turned inside out—the nail-gnarled have caught Heaven
Like a bright ball. Not in their reknit wonder,
But in their wounds lies Christ's sprung grace engraven—
Not in the body lighter than word spoken,
But in the side still breached, the hands still broken.

The Final Hunger

Hurl down the nerve-gnarled body hurtling head-
Long into sworls of shade-hush. Plummeting, keep
The latch of eyelids shut to so outleap
Care's claws. Arms, legs, abandon grace and spread
Your spent sprawl—glutton ravening to be fed
With fats, creams, fruits, meats, spice that heavy-heap
The hands, that golden-gloss the flesh, of sleep,
Sleep, the sole lover that I take to bed.

But they couch crouching in the darkness, city
Of wakefulness uncaptured by assaulting—
Senses by sleep unravished and unwon.
Sun-sword night-sheathed, lie never between (have pity!)
Between me and my love, between me and the vaulting
Down the dense sweetness of oblivion.

No Return

Once over summer streams the ice-crusts harden,
No one can wade therein to wash his feet
Thence to go flying after nymphs that fleet
Naked and nimble through the woods. Time's warden
Has locked them all (or is it us?) past pardon.
Yet freed, we could not find the path that beat
Toward—call it any name—fauns, home, retreat;
For there is no returning to that garden.

No, not to Adam's. We must keep our own,
Remembering. In Eden's greenery
God walked. While in our garden rocks are brown
With His dried blood where He has crouched to groan.
Our apples rotted, only His crosstree
Bears crimson fruit. But no hand plucks it down.

Ballad of the Unmiraculous Miracle

Sit under a pine on Christmas Eve,
Heart bruised like a fallen nestling,
And the angels will sing you—no song save
The wind in the branches wrestling.

Peer down a mystical well and see
Far down in its waters mirrored—
The only sign there imaged for me,
My own face mournful and harrowed.

Seek out a stable known of old
And see the oxen kneel—
With me crouched here before the cold
And hunger sharp as steel.

Go wander through the winter snows
And spy the Christmas bud

314

Unfold itself—the only rose
The brambles bear, my blood.

Like wingless birds are wind and wood,
Well, oxen, flowering bush
Till Christmas Day when I see God
Plumaged in my plucked flesh.

Song for a Marriage

Housed in each other's arms,
Thatched with each other's grace,
Your bodies, flint on steel
Striking out fire to fend
The cold away awhile;
With sweat for mortar, brace
Your walls against the sleet
And the rib-riddling wind.

A house, you house yourselves,
Housed, you will house another,
Scaled to a subtler blueprint
Than architects can draw—
A triple function yours
In this world's winter weather,
Oh, breathing brick and stone,
I look on you with awe.

A fig for praise that calls
Flesh a bundle of sticks,
Kindling for flame that feels
Like swallowing the sun!
Yet luxury turned labor's
No old maid's rancid mix,
But how bone-masonry
Outweighs the skeleton.

The Whooping Crane

Observe the Whooping Crane
Who still enjoys the weather
Despite his wingdom's wane—
A bird of different feather.

Less amorous advance
Than art unparagoned,
His swirling, sweeping dance
Becomes a saraband,

To which he dedicates
Devotion so austere
His most attuned of mates
Lays but an egg a year.

He counts it bliss, not bother,
That less than half a dozen
Make free to call him father
Or even claim him cousin.

In Consolation

Do I love you? The question might be well
Rephrased, What do I love? Your face?
Suppose it twisted to a charred grimace.
Your mind? But if it turned hospital cell,
Though pity for its inmate might compel
Sick calls from time to time, I should embrace
A staring stranger whom I could not place.
So, cease demanding what I cannot tell

Till He who made you shows me where He keeps you,
And not some shadow of you I pursue
And, having found, have only flushed a wraith.
Nor am I Christ to cleave the dark that steeps you.

316

He loves you then, not I—Or if I do,
I love you only by an act of faith.

Return

From what I am, to be what I am not,
To be what once I was, from plan and plot
To learn to take no thought,
I go, my God, to Thee.

With act of faith whose throes and throbs convulse
My heart as if all other acts were else
Than dyings, prayer than pulse,
I go, my God, to Thee.

On feet thread through by seams of blood and fire,
Dancing the narrow pathway, strictest wire,
As butterflies a briar,
I go, my God, to Thee.

To balance like a bird with wings aflare,
Pinned to the cross as though I merely were
Stenciled by light on air,
I go, my God, to Thee.

My spirit, trim, uncorseted from stress,
Stripping to wind and sunlight, to the grace
Of Eden's nakedness
Will go, my God, to Thee.

For Instruction

Teach me some prayer
tender as you are tender when

one of my shadows mingles with one of yours and makes
an intricate weave we walk on for a moment,
gentle as you are gentle when
you humble yourself to take my kiss,
wordless as we are wordless when
a pause has fallen between us like a petal.

From an Old Maid

You come and say that it is restful here
to speak your pain into my silences,
wafting your words across them like the hair
of drowning sailors lost in churning seas.

And if I ever told you, you would laugh
to think I made your moment's reef of calm
by holding up your listless body, half
submerged in water, lightly on my palm.

Digging into my flesh with terror's claws
until the times you hope you hear the oar
of your salvation, do you never pause
to wonder when or where I drift to shore?

Protest

Where the air in this room warms by the fire like a cat,
where music no one can touch swaddles the ear in satin,
where one may hear words as though he were tasting them,
where wine curls over the tongue, sliding down like a lover's kiss,
where the merest shadow of love bears the odor of roses
in whose heart I am flayed as by fire,
here I lie naked, spitted upon my senses
like a plucked bird caught upon thorns.

Love's Eschatology

I touch you all over
as if every part were a petal
when now you are away.

Never has your body
before so budded to my senses
as to my empty fingers.

Love, may we in Heaven
view all for the first time forever
through the lens of the last.

JOHN WAIN
(1925–)

Reason for not Writing Orthodox Nature Poetry

The January sky is deep and calm.
The mountain sprawls in comfort, and the sea
Sleeps in the crook of that enormous arm.

And Nature from a simple recipe—
Rocks, water, mist, a sunlit winter's day—
Has brewed a cup whose strength has dizzied me.

So little beauty is enough to pay;
The heart so soon yields up its store of love,
And where you love you cannot break away.

So sages never found it hard to prove
Nor prophets to declare in metaphor
That God and Nature must be hand in glove.

And this became the basis of their lore.
Then later poets found it easy going
To give the public what they bargained for,

And like a spectacled curator showing
The wares of his museum to the crowd,
They yearly waxed more eloquent and knowing

More slick, more photographic, and more proud:
From Tennyson with notebook in his hand
(His truth to Nature fits him like a shroud)

To moderns who devoutly hymn the land.
So be it: each is welcome to his voice;
They are a gentle, if a useless, band.

But leave me free to make a sterner choice;
Content, without embellishment, to note
How little beauty bids the heart rejoice,

How little beauty catches at the throat,
Simply, I love this mountain and this bay
With love that I can never speak by rote,

And where you love you cannot break away.

This Above All Is Precious and Remarkable

This above all is precious and remarkable,
How we put ourselves in one another's care,
How in spite of everything we trust each other.

Fishermen at whatever point they are dipping and lifting
On the dark green swell they partly think of as home
Hear the gale warnings that fly to them like gulls.

The scientists study the weather for love of studying it,
And not specially for love of the fishermen,
And the wireless engineers do the transmission for love of
    wireless,

But how it adds up is that when the terrible white malice
Of the waves high as cliffs is let loose to seek a victim,
The fishermen are somewhere else and so not drowned.

And why should this chain of miracles be easier to believe
Than that my darling should come to me as naturally
As she trusts a restaurant not to poison her?

They are simply examples of well-known types of miracle,
The two of them,
That can happen at any time of the day or night.

Anniversary

These are my thoughts on realizing
That I am the same age as my father was
On the day I was born.

As a little scarlet howling mammal,
Crumpled and unformed, I depended entirely on someone
Not very different from what I am to-day.

When I think this over,
I feel more crumpled and unformed than ever:
I ask myself what I have done to compare with *that*.

It also makes me aware, inescapably,
Of having entered upon the high table-land,
The broad flat life of a mature man.

Where everything is seen from its actual distance,
E.g. childhood not so remote as to seem a boring myth,
Nor senility as something that awaits other people.

But deeper than that,
It is like entering a dark cone,
The shadow thrown across my life by the life it derives from.

And deeper than that still,
It is the knowledge that life is the one communicable thing.
It called. I heard it from where I slept in seed and liquid.

The patterns of seed and brine coalesced in a solemn dance,
Whence my life arose in the form of a crest,
And has carried itself blindly forward until now.

In ignorance of its uniqueness until now,
Until I stumbled over these thoughts solid as bricks,
And like bricks fearsome in their everyday squareness.

Apology for Understatement

Forgive me that I pitch your praise too low.
Such reticence my reverence demands,
For silence falls with laying on of hands.

Forgive me that my words come thin and slow.
This could not be a time for eloquence,
For silence falls with healing of the sense.

We only utter what we lightly know.
And it is rather that my love knows me.
It is that your perfection set me free.

Verse is dressed up that has nowhere to go.
You took away my glibness with my fear.
Forgive me that I stand in silence here.

It is not words could pay you what I owe.

Brooklyn Heights

This is the gay cliff of the nineteenth century,
Drenched in the hopeful ozone of a new day.

Erect and brown, like retired sea-captains,
The houses gaze vigorously at the ocean.

With the hospitable eyes of retired captains
They preside over the meeting of sea and river.

On Sunday mornings the citizens revisit their beginnings.
Whose families walk in the fresh air of the past.

Their children tricycle down the nineteenth century:
America comes smiling towards them like a neighbour.

While the past on three wheels unrolls beneath them,
They hammer in the blazing forge of the future.

Brooklyn Bridge flies through the air on feathers.
The children do not know the weight of its girders.

It is the citizens carry the bridge on their shoulders:
Its overhead lights crackle in their blood vessels.

But now it is Sunday morning, and a sky swept clean.
The citizens put down the bridge and stroll at ease.

They jingle the hopeful change in their pockets.
They forget the tripping dance of the profit motive.

The big ships glide in under the high statue,
The towers cluster like spear-grass on the famous island.

And the citizens dream themselves back in a sparkle of morning.
They ride with their children under a sky swept clean.

Dream on, citizens! Dream the true America, the healer,
Drawing the hot blood from throbbing Europe!

Dream the dark-eyed immigrants from the narrow cities:
Dream the iron steamers loaded with prayers and bundles:

Breathe the ozone older than the name of commerce:
Be the citizens of the true survival!

324

A Song about Major Eatherly

The book (Fernard Gigon's *Formula for Death—The Atom Bombs and After*) also describes how Major Claude R. Eatherly, pilot of the aircraft which carried the second bomb to Nagasaki, later started having nightmares. His wife is quoted as saying: 'He often jumps up in the middle of the night and screams out in an inhuman voice which makes me feel ill: "Release it, release it." '

Major Eatherly began to suffer brief periods of madness, says Gigon. The doctors diagnosed extreme nervous depression, and Eatherly was awarded a pension of 237 dollars a month.

This he appears to have regarded 'as a premium for murder, as a payment for what had been done to the two Japanese cities'. He never touched the money, and took to petty thievery, for which he was committed to Fort Worth prison.

Report in *The Observer*, August 1958.

I

Good news. It seems he loved them after all.
His orders were to fry their bones to ash.
He carried up the bomb and let it fall.
And then his orders were to take the cash,

A hero's pension. But he let it lie.
It was in vain to ask him for the cause.
Simply that if he touched it he would die.
He fought his own, and not his country's wars.

His orders told him he was not a man:
An instrument, fine-tempered, clear of stain,
All fears and passions closed up like a fan:
No more volition than his aeroplane.

But now he fought to win his manhood back.
Steep from the sunset of his pain he flew
Against the darkness in that last attack.
It was for love he fought, to make that true.

11

To take life is always to die a little: to stop
any feeling and moving contrivance, however ugly,
unnecesary, or hateful, is to reduce by so much the total
of life there is. And that is to die a little.

To take the life of an enemy is to help him,
a little, towards destroying your own. Indeed, that is why
we hate our enemies: because they force us to kill them.
A murderer hides the dead man in the ground:
but his crime rears up and topples on to the living,
for it is they who now must hunt the murderer,
murder him, and hide him in the ground: it is they
who now feel the touch of death cold in their bones.

Animals hate death. A trapped fox will gnaw
through his own leg: it is so important to live
that he forgives himself the agony,
consenting, for life's sake, to the desperate teeth
grating through bone and pulp, the gasping yelps.

That is the reason the trapper hates the fox.
You think the trapper doesn't hate the fox?
But he does, and the fox can tell how much.
It is not the fox's teeth that grind his bones,
It is the trapper's. It is the trapper, there,
Who keeps his head down, gnawing, hour after hour.

And the people the trapper works for, they are there too,
heads down beside the trap, gnawing away.
Why shouldn't they hate the fox? Their cheeks are smeared
with his rank blood, and on their tongues his bone
being splintered, feels uncomfortably sharp.

So once Major Eatherly hated the Japanese.

326

III

Hell is a furnace, so the wise men taught.
The punishment for sin is to be broiled.
A glowing coal for every sinful thought.

The heat of God's great furnace ate up sin,
Which whispered up in smoke or fell in ash:
So that each hour a new hour could begin.

So fire was holy, though it tortured souls,
The sinners' anguish never ceased, but still
Their sin was burnt from them by shining coals.

Hell fried the criminal but burnt the crime,
Purged where it punished, healed where it destroyed:
It was a stove that warmed the rooms of time.

No man begrudged the flames their appetite.
All were afraid of fire, yet none rebelled.
The wise men taught that hell was just and right.

'The soul desires its necessary dread:
Only among the thorns can patience weave
A bower where the mind can make its bed.'

Even the holy saints whose patient jaws
Chewed bitter rind and hands raised up the dead
Were chestnuts roasted at God's furnace doors.

The wise men passed. The clever men appeared.
They ruled that hell be called a pumpkin face.
They robbed the soul of what it justly feared.

Coal after coal the fires of hell went out.
Their heat no longer warmed the rooms of time,
Which glistened now with fluorescent doubt.

327

The chilly saints went striding up and down
To warm their blood with useful exercise.
They rolled like conkers through the draughty town.

Those emblematic flames sank down to rest,
But metaphysical fire can not go out:
Men ran from devils they had dispossessed,

And felt within their skulls the dancing heat
No longer stored in God's deep boiler-room.
Fire scorched their temples, frostbite chewed their feet.

That parasitic fire could race and climb
More swiftly than the stately flames of hell.
Its fuel gone, it licked the beams of time.

So time dried out and youngest hearts grew old.
The smoky minutes cracked and broke apart.
The world was roasting but the men were cold.

Now from this pain worse pain was brought to birth,
More hate, more anguish, till at last they cried,
'Release this fire to gnaw the crusty earth:

Make it a flame that's obvious to sight
And let us say we kindled it ourselves,
To split the skulls of men and let in light.

Since death is camped among us, wish him joy,
Invite him to our table and our games.
We cannot judge, but we can still destroy'.

And so the curtains of the mind were drawn.
Men conjured hell a first, a second time:
And Major Eatherly took off at dawn.

IV

Suppose a sea-bird,
its wings stuck down with oil, riding the waves
in no direction, under the storm-clouds, helpless,
lifted for an instant by each moving billow
to scan the meaningless horizon, helpless,
helpless, and the storms coming, and its wings dead,
its bird-nature dead:
                  Imagine this castaway,
loved, perhaps, by the Creator, and yet abandoned,
mocked by the flashing scales of the fish beneath it,
who leap, twist, dive, as free of the wide sea
as formerly the bird of the wide sky,
now helpless, starving, a prisoner of the surface,
unable to dive or rise:
              this is your emblem.
Take away the bird, let it be drowned
in the steep black waves of the storm, let it be broken
against rocks in the morning light, too faint to swim:
take away the bird, but keep the emblem.

It is the emblem of Major Eatherly,
who looked round quickly from the height of each wave,
but saw no land, only the rim of the sky
into which he was not free to rise, or the silver
gleam of the mocking scales of the fish diving
where he was not free to dive.

Men have clung always to emblems,
to tokens of absolution from their sins.
Once it was the scapegoat driven out, bearing
its load of guilt under the empty sky
until its shape was lost, merged in the scrub.

Now we are civilized, there is no wild heath.
Instead of the nimble scapegoat running out
to be lost under the wild and empty sky,

the load of guilt is packed into prison walls,
and men file inward through the heavy doors.

But now that image, too, is obsolete.
The Major entering prison is no scapegoat.
His penitence will not take away our guilt,
nor sort with any consoling ritual:
this is penitence for its own sake, beautiful,
uncomprehending, inconsolable, unforeseen.
He is not in prison for his penitence:
it is no outrage to our law that he wakes
with cries of pity on his parching lips.
We do not punish him for cries or nightmares.
We punish him for stealing things from stores.

O, give his pension to the storekeeper.
Tell him it is the price of all our souls.
But do not trouble to unlock the door
and bring the Major out into the sun.
Leave him: it is all one: perhaps his nightmares
grow cooler in the twilight of the prison.
Leave him; if he is sleeping, come away.
But lay a folded paper by his head,
nothing official or embossed, a page
torn from your notebook, and the words in pencil.
Say nothing of love, or thanks, or penitence:
say only 'Eatherly, we have your message.'

JOHN WAIN

from W I L D T R A C K [1]

Sestina for Khasan Israelov

The Chechen-Ingush, a mountain people in the northern Caucasus, resisted
domination by Catherine the Great of Russia, and were not finally subdued
till 1859; they revolted against the Czars in 1867, 1877 and 1905, and
after the Soviets came to power they continued to resist absorption and col-
lectivization. They rebelled in 1930, and were crushed. In 1941, the Chechen-
Ingush struck for their freedom one last time, under the leadership of a
young poet, Khasan Israelov. Stalin's answer was to obliterate the entire
nation by execution and mass deportation on February 23, 1944. Under the
direction of General Serov, the entire operation, whereby 500,000 people
were swept off to death or slavery, took just twenty-four hours.

1.

All those who knew you are dispersed or dead
five hundred thousand people wiped away
corpses or prisoners to the last one.
But listen, Khasan Israelov, where you lie.
I speak in a voice that wishes it were yours.
Listen, Khasan, with your mud-stopped ear.

2.

I saw your mountains once, not far away.
In the cold Caucasus I saw them lie
as the eagle sees them, high-shining, one by one.
They know you, Khasan, still, though you are dead.
The wind whose tunes put magic in your ear
whirls in the crannies where the wild goats lie.

3.

Eryri or Wicklow, half a world away
I tread on hill-paths that were never yours
and pluck the fragrant heather where I lie.

---

[1] *Wildtrack* is a book-length poem; "Sestina for Khasan Israelov" will be an
integral part of it when the longer work is completed. It is here included as an example of Mr. Wain's most recent work.—Ed.

Mountains are many, but their voice is one,
still crying freedom! into the world's ear,
though by each bluff stiffen the defiant dead.

4.
Climb with me, Khasan, till bitterness is dead.
I have not the strength to face an end like yours.
But take this homage, do not turn away.
I hear your mountain music, though my ear
is dulled with cowardice: you are the one
to guide me where the quiet heroes lie.

5.
Khasan, your written chronicle is a brief one.
Such sagas are banned from the captive ear.
Soldiers have killed, now bureaucrats must lie.
Five hundred thousand truths to sponge away.
If your name lives, the victory will be yours.
Your strength cannot be tamed now you are dead.

6.
The wild chamois is your symbol, if you need one:
Who, chased to the final edge where the hunt stops dead,
Leaps down, with a delicate madness much like yours.
May its gentle ghost be welcome where your bones lie,
Who thought rather to throw life steeply away
than make a story pleasant to the huntsman's ear!

Khasan, only courage like yours can burn hatred away.
Unstop your ear: pity me from where you lie:
Climb with me, turbulent one, till bitterness is dead!

ROBERT CREELEY
(1926–)

The Immoral Proposition

If you never do anything for anyone else
you are spared the tragedy of human relation-

ships. If quietly and like another time
there is the passage of an unexpected thing:

to look at it is more
than it was. God knows

nothing is competent nothing is
all there is. The unsure

egoist is not
good for himself.

The Operation

By Saturday I said you would be better on Sunday.
The insistence was a part of a reconciliation.

Your eyes bulged, the grey
light hung on you, you were hideous.

My involvement is just an old
habitual relationship.

Cruel, cruel to describe
what there is no reason to describe.

The Whip

I spent a night turning in bed,
my love was a feather, a flat

sleeping thing. She was
very white

and quiet, and above us on
the roof, there was another woman I

also loved, had
addressed myself to in

a fit she
returned. That

encompasses it. But now I was
lonely, I yelled,

but what is that? Ugh,
she said, beside me, she put

her hand on
my back, for which act

I think to say this
wrongly.

A Wicker Basket

Comes the time when it's later
and onto your table the headwaiter

puts the bill, and very soon after
rings out the sound of lively laughter—

Picking up change, hands like a walrus,
and a face like a barndoor's,
and a head without an apparent size,
nothing but two eyes—

So that's you, man,
or me. I make it as I can,
I pick up, I go
faster than they know—

Out the door, the street like a night,
any night, and no one in sight,
but then, well, there she is,
old friend Liz—

And she opens the door of her cadillac,
I step in back,
and we're gone.
She turns me on—

There are very huge stars, man, in the sky,
and from somewhere very far off someone hands me a slice of
    apple pie,
with a gob of white, white ice cream on top of it,
and I eat it—

Slowly. And while certainly
they are laughing at me, and all around me is racket
of these cats not making it, I make it

in my wicker basket.

She Went to Stay

Trying to chop mother down is like
hunting deer inside Russia
with phalangists for hat-pins.
I couldn't.

Ballad of the Despairing Husband

My wife and I lived all alone,
contention was our only bone.
I fought with her, she fought with me,
and things went on right merrily.

But now I live here by myself
with hardly a damn thing on the shelf,
and pass my days with little cheer
since I have parted from my dear.

Oh come home soon, I write to her.
Go screw yourself, is her answer.
Now what is that, for Christian word?
I hope she feeds on dried goose turd.

But still I love her, yes I do.
I love her and the children too.
I only think it fit that she
should quickly come right back to me.

Ah no, she says, and she is tough,
and smacks me down with her rebuff.
Ah no, she says, I will not come
after the bloody things you've done.

Oh wife, oh wife—I tell you true,
I never loved no one but you.

I never will, it cannot be
another woman is for me.

That may be right, she will say then,
but as for me, there's other men.
And I will tell you I propose
to catch them firmly by the nose.

And I will wear what dresses I choose!
And I will dance, and what's to lose!
I'm free of you, you little prick,
and I'm the one can make it stick.

Was this the darling I did love?
Was this that mercy from above
did open violets in the spring—
and made my own worn self to sing?

She was. I know. And she is still,
and if I love her? then so I will.
And I will tell her, and tell her right . . .

Oh lovely lady, morning or evening or afternoon.
Oh lovely lady, eating with or without a spoon.
Oh most lovely lady, whether dressed or undressed or partly.
Oh most lovely lady, getting up or going to bed or sitting only.

Oh loveliest of ladies, than whom none is more fair, more
    gracious, more beautiful.
Oh loveliest of ladies, whether you are just or unjust,
    merciful, indifferent, or cruel.
Oh most loveliest of ladies, doing whatever, seeing whatever,
    being whatever.
Oh most loveliest of ladies, in rain, in shine, in any weather.

Oh lady, grant me time,
please, to finish my rhyme.

The Door

for Robert Duncan

It is hard going to the door
cut so small in the wall where
the vision which echoes loneliness
brings a scent of wild flowers in a wood.

What I understood, I understand.
My mind is sometime torment,
sometimes good and filled with livelihood,
and feels the ground.

But I see the door,
and knew the wall, and wanted the wood,
and would get there if I could
with my feet and hands and mind.

Lady, do not banish me
for digressions. My nature
is a quagmire of unresolved
confessions. Lady, I follow.

I walked away from myself,
I left the room, I found the garden,
I knew the woman
in it, together we lay down.

Dead night remembers. In December
we change, not multiplied but dispersed,
sneaked out of childhood,
the ritual of dismemberment.

Mighty magic is a mother,
in her there is another issue
of fixture, repeated form, the race renewal,
the charge of the command.

338

The garden echoes across the room.
It is fixed in the wall like a mirror
that faces a window behind you
and reflects the shadows.

May I go now?
Am I allowed to bow myself down
in the ridiculous posture of renewal,
of the insistence of which I am the virtue?

Nothing for You is untoward.
Inside You would also be tall,
more tall, more beautiful.
Come toward me from the wall, I want to be with You.

So I screamed to You,
who hears as the wind, and changes
multiply, invariably,
changes in the mind.

Running to the door, I ran down
as a clock runs down. Walked backwards,
stumbled, sat down
hard on the floor near the wall.

Where were You.
How absurd, how vicious.
There is nothing to do but get up.
My knees were iron, I rusted in worship, of You.

For that one sings, one
writes the spring poem, one goes on walking.
The Lady has always moved to the next town
and you stumble on after Her.

The door in the wall leads to the garden
where in the sunlight sit

the Graces in long Victorian dresses,
of which my grandmother had spoken.

History sings in their faces.
They are young, they are obtainable,
and you follow after them also
in the service of God and Truth.

But the Lady is indefinable,
she will be the door in the wall
to the garden in sunlight.
I will go on talking forever.

I will never get there.
Oh Lady, remember me
who in Your service grows older
not wiser, no more than before.

How can I die alone.
Where will I be then who am now alone,
what groans so pathetically
in this room where I am alone?

I will go to the garden.
I will be a romantic. I will sell
myself in hell,
in heaven also I will be.

In my mind I see the door,
I see the sunlight before me across the floor
beckon to me, as the Lady's skirt
moves small beyond it.

Jack's Blues

       I'm going to roll up
       a monkey and smoke it, put

an elephant in the pot. I'm going out
and never come back.

What's better than that.
Lying on your back, flat
on your back with your
eyes to the view.

Oh the view is blue, I saw that
too, yesterday and you,
red eyes and blue,
funked.

I'm going to roll up
a rug and smoke it, put
the car in the garage and I'm
gone, like a sad old candle.

The Name

Be natural,
wise
as you can be,
my daughter,

let my name
be in you flesh
I gave you
in the act of

loving your mother,
all your days
her ways,
the woman in you

brought from
sensuality's measure,

no other,
there was no thought

of it but such
pleasure all women
must be in her,
as you. But not wiser,

not more of nature
than her hair,
the eyes
she gives you.

There will not be another
woman such as you
are. Remember
your mother,

the way you came,
the days of waiting.
Be natural,
daughter, wise

as you can be,
all my daughters,
be women
for men

when that time comes.
Let the rhetoric
stay with me
your father. Let

me talk about it,
saving you such
vicious self-
exposure, let you

                        pass it on
                        in you. I cannot
                        be more than the man
                        who watches.

The Rose

for Bobbie

                        Up and down
                        she walks, listless
                        form, a movement
                        quietly misled.

                        Now, speak to her.
                        "Did you want
                        to go, then why
                        don't you."

                        She went. There were
                        things she left
                        in the room
                        as a form of it.

                        He follows, walking.
                        Where do they walk now?
                        Do they talk now
                        where they are

                        in that other place
                        grown monstrous,
                        quiet quiet air
                        as breath.

                        And all about a rosy
                        mark discloses
                        her nature
                        to him, vague and unsure.

There roses, here roses,
flowers, a pose of
nature, her
nature has disclosed to him.

Yet breathing, crouched
in the dark,
he is there
also, recovers,

to bring her back
to herself, himself.
The room wavers,
wavers.

And as if,
as if a cloud had
broken at last
open

and all the rain
from that,
from that had fallen
on them,

on them there is a mark
of her nature, her flowers,
and his room, his nature,
to come home to.

The Wife

I know two women
    and the one
is tangible substance,
    flesh and bone.

The other in my mind
  occurs.
She keeps her strict
  proportion there.

But how should I
  propose to live
with two such creatures
  in my bed—

or how shall he
  who has a wife
yield two to one
  and watch the other die.

W. D. SNODGRASS

(1926–)

Orpheus

Stone lips to the unspoken cave;
Fingering the nervous strings, alone,
I crossed that gray sill, raised my head
To lift my song into the grave
Meanders of unfolding stone,
Following where the echo led
Down blind alleys of our dead.

Down the forbidden, backward street
To the lower town, condemned, asleep
In blank remembering mazes where
Smoke rose, the ashes hid my feet
And slow walls crumpled, settling deep
In rubble of the central square.
All ruin I could sound was there.

At the charred rail and windowsill,
Widows hunched in fusty shawls,
This only once the Furies wept;
The watchdog turned to hear me till
Head by head forgot its howls,
Loosed the torn images it kept,
Let sag its sore jaws and slept.

Then to my singing's radius
Seethed faces like a pauper's crowd
Or flies of an old injury.
The piteous dead who lived on us
Whined in my air, anarchic, loud
Till my soft voice that set them free,
Lost in this grievous enemy,

Rose up and laid them in low slumbers;
I meant to see in them what dark
Powers be, what eminent plotters.
Midmost those hushed, downcast numbers
Starved Tantalus stood upright, stark,
Waistdeep where the declining waters
Swelled their tides, where Danaus' daughters

Dropped in full surf their unfilled tub;
Now leaned against his rolling stone
Slept Sisyphus beneath the hill;
That screaming half-beast, strapped at the hub,
Whom Juno's animal mist had known,
Ixion's wheel creaked and was still.
I held all hell to hear my will.

"Powers of the Underworld, who rule
All higher powers by graft or debt,
Within whose mortgage all men live:
No spy, no shining power's fool,
I think in the unthought worlds to get
The light you only freely give
Who are all bright worlds' negative

You gave wink in an undue crime
To love—strong even here, they say.
I sing, as the blind beggars sing,
To ask of you this little time
—All lives foreclose in their due day—
That flowered bride cut down in Spring,
Struck by the snake, your underling."

In one long avenue she was
Wandering toward me, vague, uncertain,
Limping a little still, the hair
And garments tenuous as gauze
And drifting loose like a white curtain
Vacillating in black night air
That holds white lilacs, God knows where.

"Close your eyes," said the inner ear;
"As night lookouts learn not to see
Ahead but only off one side,
As the eye's sight is never clear
But blind, dead center, you must be
Content; look not upon your bride
Till day's light lifts her eyelids wide."

I turned my back to her, set out
My own way back and let her follow
Like some curious albino beast
That prowls in areas of drought,
Lured past the town's slack doors, the hollow
Walls, the stream-bed lost in mist,
That breathless long climb, with no least

Doubt she must track me close behind;
As the actual scent of flesh, she must
Trail my voice unquestioning where.
Yet where the dawn first edged my mind
In one white flashing of mistrust
I turned and she, she was not there.
My hands closed on the high, thin air.

It was the nature of the thing:
No moon outlives its leaving night,
No sun its day. And I went on
Rich in the loss of all I sing
To the threshold of waking light,
To larksong and the live, gray dawn.
So night by night, my life has gone.

The Marsh

Swampstrife and spatterdock
   lull in the heavy waters;
some thirty little frogs
   spring with each step you walk;
a fish's belly glitters
   tangled near rotting logs.

Over by the gray rocks
   muskrats dip and circle.
Out of his rim of ooze
   a silt-black pond snail walks
inverted on the surface
   toward what food he may choose.

You look up; while you walk
   the sun bobs and is snarled
in the enclosing weir
   of trees, in their dead stalks.
Stick in the mud, old heart,
   what are you doing here?

September in the Park

This pinched face of the moon
   all afternoon
spies through the hanging smoke
that glows where maples, turning,
   recall for one
more hour the tarnished sun
in rust of their last burning.

Still, those who are out walking
   will hear the laughter
of drab, blue-chevroned ducks;
the drunkard echo mocking

349

where they carouse
on minnow ponds still flowing.
Beyond the bare oak's
  reach of boughs,
as black as some charred rafter,
are slow and waiting flocks,
  but they are going.

  This world is going
to leave the furnitures
of its unsheltering house
  in snow's dustcovers.
This old moon on its rounds
of the estate and grounds
  can well make sure
that no trespasser stirs
the fireplace or uncovers
  the burned out bed
of ashes. The young lovers
will not be coming here
  to give the bear
the offer of their bread.
This watchful face of age
  set pale and stern
over the gray iron cage
where his old habits turn
  and pace again
must mind his days to turn
him back in single, deep,
  cold-blooded sleep.

The hurrying, gray squirrels
  gather together
their hoard of the rich acorns
to their tall, windblown nest.
  And I, dear girl,
remember I have gathered
my hand upon your breast.

The Operation

From stainless steel basins of water
They brought warm cloths and they washed me,
From spun aluminum bowls, cold Zephiran sponges, fuming;
Gripped in the dead yellow glove, a bright straight razor
Inched on my stomach, down my groin,
Paring the brown hair off. They left me
White as a child, not frightened. I was not
Ashamed. They clothed me, then,
In the thin, loose, light, white garments,
The delicate sandals of poor Pierrot,
A schoolgirl first offering her sacrament.

I was drifting, inexorably, on toward sleep.
In skullcaps, masked, in blue-green gowns, attendants
Towed my cart, afloat in its white cloths,
The body with its tributary poisons borne
Down corridors of the diseased, thronging:
The scrofulous faces, contagious grim boys,
The huddled families, weeping, a staring woman
Arched to her gnarled stick,—a child was somewhere
Screaming, screaming—then, blind silence, the elevator rising
To the arena, humming, vast with lights; blank hero,
Shackled and spellbound, to enact my deed.

Into flowers, into women, I have awakened.
Too weak to think of strength, I have thought all day,
Or dozed among standing friends. I lie in night, now,
A small mound under linen like the drifted snow.
Only by nurses visited, in radiance, saying, Rest.
Opposite, ranked office windows glare; headlamps, below,
Trace out our highways; their cargoes under dark
    tarpaulins,
Trucks climb, thundering, and sirens may
Wail for the fugitive. It is very still. In my brandy bowl
Of sweet peas at the window, the crystal world
Is inverted, slow and gay.

Home Town

I go out like a ghost,
nights, to walk the streets
I walked fifteen years younger—
seeking my old defeats,
devoured by the old hunger;
I had supposed

this longing and upheaval
had left me with my youth.
Fifteen years gone; once more,
the old lies are the truth:
I must prove I dare,
and the world, and love, is evil.

I have had loves, had such
honors as freely came;
it does not seem to matter.
Boys swagger just the same
along the curbs, or mutter
among themselves and watch.

They're out for the same prize.
And, as the evening grows,
the young girls take the street,
hard, in harlequin clothes,
with black shells on their feet
and challenge in their eyes.

Like a young bitch in her season
she walked the carnival
tonight, trailed by boys;
then, stopped at a penny stall
for me; by glittering toys
the pitchman called the reason

to come and take a chance,
try my hand, my skill.
I could not look; bereft
of breath, against my will,
I walked ahead and left
her there without one glance.

Pale soul, consumed by fear
of the living world you haunt,
have you learned what habits lead you
to hunt what you don't want;
learned who does not need you;
learned you are no one here?

The Campus on the Hill

Up the reputable walks of old established trees
They stalk, children of the *nouveaux riches*; chimes
Of the tall Clock Tower drench their heads in blessing:
"I don't wanna play at your house;
I don't like you any more."
My house stands opposite, on the other hill,
Among meadows, with the orchard fences down and falling;
Deer come almost to the door.
You cannot see it, even in this clearest morning.
White birds hang in the air between
Over the garbage landfill and those homes thereto adjacent,
Hovering slowly, turning, settling down
Like the flakes sifting imperceptibly onto the little town
In a waterball of glass.
And yet, this morning, beyond this quiet scene,
The floating birds, the backyards of the poor,
Beyond the shopping plaza, the dead canal, the hillside lying tilted
    in the air,
Tomorrow has broken out today:

Riot in Algeria, in Cyprus, in Alabama;
Aged in wrong, the empires are declining,
And China gathers, soundlessly, like evidence.
What shall I say to the young on such a morning?—
Mind is the one salvation?—also grammar?—
No; my little ones lean not toward revolt. They
Are the Whites, the vaguely furiously driven, who resist
Their souls with such passivity
As would make Quakers swear. All day, dear Lord, all day
They wear their godhead lightly.
They look out from their hill and say,
To themselves, "We have nowhere to go but down;
The great destination is to stay."
Surely the nations will be reasonable;
They look at the world—don't they?—the world's way?
The clock just now has nothing more to say.

These Trees Stand . . .

These trees stand very tall under the heavens.
While *they* stand, if I walk, all stars traverse
This steep celestial gulf their branches chart.
Though lovers stand at sixes and at sevens
While civilizations come down with the curse,
Snodgrass is walking through the universe.

I can't make any world go around *your* house.
But note this moon. Recall how the night nurse
Goes ward-rounds, by the mild, reflective art
Of focusing her flashlight on her blouse.
Your name's safe conduct into love or verse;
Snodgrass is walking through the universe.

Your name's absurd, miraculous as sperm
And as decisive. If you can't coerce
One thing outside yourself, why you're the poet!

354

What irrefrangible atoms whirl, affirm
Their destiny and form Lucinda's skirts!
She can't make up your mind. Soon as you know it,
Your firmament grows touchable and firm.
If all this world runs battlefield or worse,
Come, let us wipe our glasses on our shirts:
Snodgrass is walking through the universe.

BINK NOLL

(1927–)

The Picador Bit

Inside that figure rides opaque malice
who by drilling makes the great heart lift
its fountain and waste the lake of blood.
His lance strikes, holds. Longer, the don's full weight.

Men for this circumstance of sport have made
laws that order place, gear, conduct and four tries
but the bull learns rage instead. He erupts
through headlong pain and strikes wrath back again.

Today's malice, part horse saved by blindfold
and morphine from panic at horns, stands,
its legal right side out, and standing so
tempts this, the next enlargement of the hole

—and part brawny don, mechanic who finds
and fits his point to drain the immense will.
Again the spot. The centaur shocks sideward
till the hole is important, like a whale's spout.

The crowd feels the lance in its own ripe hole,
in its hump knows the monster with two heads,

the blackness of its law, this letting of force
and the pump emptying the tongue of red.

Blood foams down. The head is dropped forever now.
Justice is satisfied. Its constable trots
darkly off. Left to his killers, the bull—
danger's substance, lure, huge hate itself—

thrills every male groin while he swings there
and, helpless, spills the fire of his urine.

"All My Pretty Ones? Did You Say All?"

Sleep stands off to watch me brood the curse
That ripens even while hope—the star
That once adorned my eye—pales.
The hag Anguish keeps cave in my back.

These days in broad day harpies peck
While my three children swell into heirs
Of my disorder, plaiting garlands
From nettles and crazy buds and weeds

Bred in wild churchyards across Europe
And new forced from this other soil
Where moisture thrives the dead, gives them source,
Lifts their corollas to the flaming light.

As greenery threatens to parch and drop
The rich summer that fulfills all greens
So these heads I dream are beset
By like loveliness that prowls its parent.

Poised in Eden moments, they are ravished
With delight in mirrors, combing of hair.
Their songs will wake the morning doors
And float, still innocent, through this used air.

357

I their father wear the bethorned head,
The web knotted from every Noll's error,
The body wracked from every Noll's wife
And perfected in this adult fright.

For innocence takes its father for lens,
For very ear to garner up the mind.
I am the dream of their correctness.
The hero! The safety! I! The right!

I once thought to orphan them from this love,
Leave them to the wide world and change of names—
Thought to be of error and misery,
Imperfection and fever not the genitor

But last inheritor. As if a father
Might nip the booming miracle of his yeast!
Harpies warmed the egg of that disaster
But despair glared in the night of my mind:

A sour delicacy of stomach,
Congenital rage, shared tropisms, odd tics
And deeper intimacies of our blood
Had made their signs in each pretty one.

They are doomed beyond my bravery
To save them. The lesson tells of cause,
How the passion of the flesh for pain
Matures, how my seeds are cast and blasted

In the dread of time, how the law is waste
And glories, waste and glories, waste and glories.
The lesson instructs me to recall
A season of joy, an endless round noon

Of which I am the fat debris.
The noon is happening to virgins
While my thrilled nerves, having cast these seeds,
Die back into the dark humus.

358

Air Tunnel, Monticello

On Palladio's rural theme, a farmhouse
Flanked by sheds—because on that he'd improvise
A villa basic to his well-examined life

Mr. Jefferson contrived this tube—
Wheels, chain, pulley, mason's work, hooks, and crocks—
And had it buried to spirit out of view

The wilt, the waste, the metabolic slops,
An arch of stone hidden in the ground,
A modest device to purify the mansion.

Then on he planned, organizing light and space
Along the bellevues from his mountaintop,
Shaping the clean air with axioms.

The sun stopped to glare down on his marvel,
On dome, portico, skylights and marble,
On paths, plantings, lawns that prove still

The elegance of County Albemarle
And of the mind that crystallized it
Along these axes of his sane eye,

The mind that made it stand as simile
For the whole known world, felicitous and lucid.
What a lord's schedule this design meant!

Time planned, time valued, time husbanded,
Time kept fresh like fish in the brick pool,
The hours swimming brightly till his demand.

His tube required one field hand at the down end
To carry off and dump the smelly crocks,
One ignorant field hand lucky to get this near

The palazzo of his master's intellect,
Mr. Jefferson's order of elaborate balances—
The fulcrum for which is this discreet stone arch,

This nook of effluvium wedged
Where all planes of light intersect,
The orifice smoking in the county of hope.

Lunch on Omaha Beach

The killers are killed, their violent rinds
Conveyed, and the beach is back to summer.
I eat sausage with bread. Full of ease, the sea
Makes the sound of cows chewing through high grass.

They're deposited in government lawn
Set with nine thousand decencies of stone
To wet the eye, shake the heart, and lose
Each name in a catalog of graven names.

They are wasted in the blank of herohood.
They are dead to fondness and paradox.
They're all the same. In the field of lawn
Above the beach, they're put away the same.

They should be left exactly here below where
Death's great bronze mares shook earth and bloodied them,
Where violence of noise isolated each boy
In the body of his scream, and dropped him.

No worn Norman hill should be scarred and smoothed
To suit officials' tidy thoughts for graveyards
But the wreckage left, shrinking in rust and rags
And carrion to dust or tumuli.

To honor my thoughts against shrines, to find
The beast who naked wakes in us and walks

In flags, to watch the color of his day
I spill my last Bordeaux into the sand.

Watching, I wonder at the white quiet,
The fields of butter cows, my countrymen
Come to study battle maps, blue peasants
Still moving back and forth, the day's soft sea.

For Jane Kane, Whom We Knew in Our Young Marriages

Tall Jane is dark who was burnished bright,
Who walked her fine long bones through rooms
And fixed her striding in my eye's vigor.

Extravagance of cells broke the balance
Where Jane thrived and in her waste morality
Has made its blind ironic grave.

She is blind and night-eyed who drank our light,
Who thirsted back through the sleep of weeks.
News of her darkness darkens my bravery.

Among us the idea of her has been elevated.
She is the sign of our generation. She is sealed:
The first scattering from our number.

For her the filament of hunger has dried away.
Her mind's store is put in a cave.
Her movement is turned to salt. She is straight.

She is our edge, our pioneer and spy,
Our steeple at the curve where land stops.
For her we're paid back this warning of trumpets;

For tall Jane, lurking through the scrub of time,
Found for us the serpent stopped
Upon a slab of sunlight, letting out its long hiss.

Abraham's Madness

When Isaac watched his father strain back
the ram's head, its throat separate and bleed,
evisceration, and fat turn to smoke,

not *he* had heard any angel speak
but felt sharply where the rope still cut,
how his own neck cracked, his own flesh burned.

I likewise learned to distrust my sire
whose god in our house was powerful
as revenge shuddering through a plot.

Mornings, his story would begin,
"My dear boy, God will provide the lamb,"
when I knew I went the only lamb,

knew the god had repeated his demand
and violence on this man who adored
both of us past any hope of reason.

I was proving tall, bright, soft of voice.
Then he—his love wild to get me grown—
would change and cheat the law, then reach out

to slay some cheap and easy innocent,
then stop the silence raging in his ear
by reports of angels I never heard.

How we sons lay awake to ponder
the misery of such divided men
to whom patriarchal lies come true.

My son shall not watch me in a fury
of faith take fire to the altar where
I sacrifice nothing I cherish.

He may feel my hands grab like priest hands,
his eyes may die in the brightness
that I have meant obedience entire.

So much I walked with my mad Abraham.

Afternoon for a Small Boy

In that rest made green by window shades
Drawn two thirds against the open blaze
(The blinds slipping in the lilac breeze)
Christopher floats, bones gently askew
But wake as the eyes of a statue—
Floats inside the hushing of the bees
That sweetly sift the upstairs air.
The mower in the distance of his ear
Makes buzz; his sister whirs on tricycle
But he cribs a peace beyond words still
While down the sun flings parallelograms
Upon the rug and waits for him like games.

The Rented Garden

We Sunday strode—I in leather,
My kids in red—through pure October.
We smelled a country gone bright
From decay, but I went to delight
In such burning
                    until we stood
In our garden across Lyme Road,
A rectangle hired at minor cost
To grow our greens on. I saw: cornstalks
Rattled white against blue, the squash vine
Had sprawled down in softness, and slime
Cracked from bleached tomato skins. Just thus
Our richness went, by three quick frosts.
The youngsters sang along the packed earth.
I listened. As if for some birth

363

The fool crickets whirred for this cloudless
Relic of summer. Deaf and dauntless,
My girl ran to a bonfire the wind
Had readied gaily, at the end
Of the garden. My boy followed; he
Ran right through the blighted broccoli.

Song in a Winter Night

Blanche is
And navy the tree full of holes
Blanche is the snowmountain over the sea

The militant everblues under the jingle road
Jingle the winter its bedquilt is
Blanche is but songblues is icelocked the sea
Is the sea holed in the land its snow
So still, is empty is behind itself the sky
Above
        or is it mountains
                is how low

Lullaby lies softer blue than jewels
Cotton as giants under the forests
  (and the rabbits asleep)
Trees are navy the shape of caves
But fled the summerbird and now a wind
Caskets itself transparent in the North
Aeoli o jingle men frostfoot on the road to—
Hush

Under the mountain lies lullaby blue
Is blanche for this stillness in tree peaks
Blanche is blue is under the crystal is bells
Is in the sea
        is blanche
            is stillness as white
Is settled on the land

ANNE SEXTON

(1928–)

Some Foreign Letters

I knew you forever and you were always old,
soft white lady of my heart. Surely you would scold
me for sitting up late, reading your letters,
as if these foreign postmarks were meant for me.
You posted them first in London, wearing furs
and a new dress in the winter of eighteen-ninety.
I read how London is dull on Lord Mayor's Day,
where you guided past groups of robbers, the sad holes
of Whitechapel, clutching your pocketbook, on the way
to Jack the Ripper dissecting his famous bones.
This Wednesday in Berlin, you say, you will
go to a bazaar at Bismarck's house. And I
see you as a young girl in a good world still,
writing three generations before mine. I try
to reach into your page and breathe it back . . .
but life is a trick, life is a kitten in a sack.

This is the sack of time your death vacates.
How distant you are on your nickel-plated skates
in the skating park in Berlin, gliding past
me with your Count, while a military band
plays a Strauss waltz. I loved you last,
a pleated old lady with a crooked hand.

Once you read *Lohengrin* and every goose
hung high while you practiced castle life
in Hanover. Tonight your letters reduce
history to a guess. The Count had a wife.
You were the old maid aunt who lived with us.
Tonight I read how the winter howled around
the towers of Schloss Schwöbber, how the tedious
language grew in your jaw, how you loved the sound
of the music of the rats tapping on the stone
floors. When you were mine you wore an earphone.

This is Wednesday, May 9th, near Lucerne,
Switzerland, sixty-nine years ago. I learn
your first climb up Mount San Salvatore;
this is the rocky path, the hole in your shoes,
the yankee girl, the iron interior
of her sweet body. You let the Count choose
your next climb. You went together, armed
with alpine stocks, with ham sandwiches
and *seltzer wasser*. You were not alarmed
by the thick woods of briars and bushes,
nor the rugged cliff, nor the first vertigo
up over Lake Lucerne. The Count sweated
with his coat off as you waded through top snow.
He held your hand and kissed you. You rattled
down on the train to catch a steamboat for home;
or other postmarks: Paris, Verona, Rome.

This is Italy. You learn its mother tongue.
I read how you walked on the Palatine among
the ruins of the palaces of the Caesars;
alone in the Roman autumn, alone since July.
When you were mine they wrapped you out of here
with your best hat over your face. I cried
because I was seventeen. I am older now.
I read how your student ticket admitted you
into the private chapel of the Vatican and how
you cheered with the others, as we used to do

on the Fourth of July. One Wednesday in November
you watched a balloon, painted like a silver ball,
float up over the Forum, up over the lost emperors,
to shiver its little modern cage in an occasional
breeze. You worked your New England conscience out
beside artisans, chestnut vendors and the devout.

Tonight I will learn to love you twice;
learn your first days, your mid-Victorian face.
Tonight I will speak up and interrupt
your letters, warning you that wars are coming,
that the Count will die, that you will accept
your America back to live like a prim thing
on the farm in Maine. I tell you, you will come
here, to the suburbs of Boston, to see the blue-nose
world go drunk each night, to see the handsome
children jitterbug, to feel your left ear close
one Friday at Symphony. And I tell you,
you will tip your boot feet out of that hall,
rocking from its sour sound, out onto
the crowded street, letting your spectacles fall
and your hair net tangle as you stop passers-by
to mumble your guilty love while your ears die.

Her Kind

I have gone out, a possessed witch,
haunting the black air, braver at night;
dreaming evil, I have done my hitch
over the plain houses, light by light:
lonely thing, twelve-fingered, out of mind.
A woman like that is not a woman, quite.
I have been her kind.

I have found the warm caves in the woods,
filled them with skillets, carvings, shelves,
closets, silks, innumerable goods;

367

fixed the suppers for the worms and the elves:
whining, rearranging the disaligned.
A woman like that is misunderstood.
I have been her kind.

I have ridden in your cart, driver,
waved my nude arms at villages going by,
learning the last bright routes, survivor
where your flames still bite my thigh
and my ribs crack where your wheels wind.
A woman like that is not ashamed to die.
I have been her kind.

The Truth the Dead Know

*For my mother, born March 1902, died March 1959
and my father, born February 1900, died June 1959*

Gone, I say and walk from church,
refusing the stiff procession to the grave,
letting the dead ride alone in the hearse.
It is June. I am tired of being brave.

We drive to the Cape. I cultivate
myself where the sun gutters from the sky,
where the sea swings in like an iron gate
and we touch. In another country people die.

My darling, the wind falls in like stones
from the whitehearted water and when we touch
we enter touch entirely. No one's alone.
Men kill for this, or for as much.

And what of the dead? They lie without shoes
in their stone boats. They are more like stone
than the sea would be if it stopped. They refuse
to be blessed, throat, eye and knucklebone.

ANNE SEXTON

The Starry Night

That does not keep me from having a terrible need of—shall I say the word
—religion. Then I go out at night to paint the stars.

VINCENT VAN GOGH in a letter to his brother

The town does not exist
except where one black-haired tree slips
up like a drowned woman into the hot sky.
The town is silent. The night boils with eleven stars.
Oh starry starry night! This is how
I want to die.

It moves. They are all alive.
Even the moon bulges in its orange irons
to push children, like a god, from its eye.
The old unseen serpent swallows up the stars.
Oh starry starry night! This is how
I want to die:

into that rushing beast of the night,
sucked up by that great dragon, to split
from my life with no flag,
no belly,
no cry.

In the Deep Museum

My God, my God, what queer corner am I in?
Didn't I die, blood running down the post,
lungs gagging for air, die there for the sin
of anyone, my sour mouth giving up the ghost?
Surely my body is done? Surely I died?
And yet, I know, I'm here. What place is this?
Cold and queer, I sting with life. I lied.
Yes, I lied. Or else in some damned cowardice
my body would not give me up. I touch

369

fine cloth with my hands and my cheeks are cold.
If this is hell, then hell could not be much,
neither as special nor as ugly as I was told.

What's that I hear, snuffling and pawing its way
toward me? Its tongue knocks a pebble out of place
as it slides in, a sovereign. How can I pray?
It is panting; it is an odor with a face
like the skin of a donkey. It laps my sores.
It is hurt, I think, as I touch its little head.
It bleeds. I have forgiven murderers and whores
and now I must wait like old Jonah, not dead
nor alive, stroking a clumsy animal. A rat.
His teeth test me; he waits like a good cook,
knowing his own ground. I forgive him that,
as I forgave my Judas the money he took.

Now I hold his soft red sore to my lips
as his brothers crowd in, hairy angels who take
my gift. My ankles are a flute. I lose hips
and wrists. For three days, for love's sake,
I bless this other death. Oh, not in air—
in dirt. Under the rotting veins of its roots,
under the markets, under the sheep bed where
the hill is food, under the slippery fruits
of the vineyard, I go. Unto the bellies and jaws
of rats I commit my prophecy and fear.
Far below The Cross, I correct its flaws.
We have kept the miracle. I will not be here.

The Fortress

while taking a nap with Linda

> Under the pink quilted covers
> I hold the pulse that counts your blood.
> I think the woods outdoors
> are half asleep,

left over from summer
like a stack of books after a flood,
left over like those promises I never keep.
On the right, the scrub pine tree
waits like a fruit store
holding up bunches of tufted broccoli.

We watch the wind from our square bed.
I press down my index finger—
half in jest, half in dread—
on the brown mole
under your left eye, inherited
from my right cheek: a spot of danger
where a bewitched worm ate its way through our soul
in search of beauty. My child, since July
the leaves have been fed
secretly from a pool of beet-red dye.

And sometimes they are battle green
with trunks as wet as hunters' boots,
smacked hard by the wind, clean
as oilskins. No,
the wind's not off the ocean.
Yes, it cried in your room like a wolf
and your pony tail hurt you. That was a long time ago.
The wind rolled the tide like a dying
woman. She wouldn't sleep,
she rolled there all night, grunting and sighing.

Darling, life is not in my hands;
life with its terrible changes
will take you, bombs or glands,
your own child at
your breast, your own house on your own land.
Outside the bittersweet turns orange.
Before she died, my mother and I picked those fat
branches, finding orange nipples
on the gray wire strands.
We weeded the forest, curing trees like cripples.

Your feet thump-thump against my back
and you whisper to yourself. Child,
what are you wishing? What pact
are you making?
What mouse runs between your eyes? What ark
can I fill for you when the world goes wild?
The woods are underwater, their weeds are shaking
in the tide; birches like zebra fish
flash by in a pack.
Child, I cannot promise that you will get your wish.

I cannot promise very much.
I give you the images I know.
Lie still with me and watch.
A pheasant moves
by like a seal, pulled through the mulch
by his thick white collar. He's on show
like a clown. He drags a beige feather that he removed,
one time, from on old lady's hat.
We laugh and we touch.
I promise you love. Time will not take away that.

THOM GUNN

(1929–)

The Beach Head

Now that a letter gives me ground at last
For starting from, I see my enterprise
Is more than application by a blast
Upon a trumpet slung beside a gate,
Security a fraud, and how unwise
Was disembarking on your Welfare State.

What should they see in you but what I see,
These friends you mention whom I do not know?
—You unsuspecting that a refugee
Might want the land complete, write in a tone
Too matter-of-fact, of small affairs below
Some minister's seduction of the Crown.

And even if they could be innocent,
They still applaud you, keep you satisfied
And occupy your time, which I resent.
Their werewolf lust and cunning are afraid
Of night-exposure in the hair, so hide
Distant as possible from my palisade.

I have my ground. A brain-sick enemy
Pacing the beach head he so plotted for

373

Which now seems trivial to his jealousy
And ignorance of the great important part,
I almost wish I had no narrow shore.
I seek a pathway to the country's heart.

Shall I be John a Gaunt and with my band
Of mad bloods pass in one spectacular dash,
Fighting before and after, through your land,
To issue out unharmed the farther side,
With little object other than panache
And showing what great odds may be defied?

That way achievement would at once be history:
Living inside, I would not know, the danger:
Hurry is blind and so does not brave mystery;
I should be led to underrate, by haste,
Your natural beauties: while I, hare-brained stranger,
Would not be much distinguished from the rest.

Or shall I wait and calculate my chances,
Consolidating this my inch-square base,
Picking off rival spies that tread your glances:
Then plan when you have least supplies or clothing
A pincer-move to end in an embrace,
And risk that your mild liking turn to loathing?

On the Move

'Man, you gotta Go.'

The blue jay scuffling in the bushes follows
Some hidden purpose, and the gust of birds
That spurts across the field, the wheeling swallows,
Have nested in the trees and undergrowth.
Seeking their instinct, or their poise, or both,
One moves with an uncertain violence
Under the dust thrown by a baffled sense
Or the dull thunder of approximate words.

374

On motorcycles, up the road, they come:
Small, black, as flies hanging in heat, the Boys,
Until the distance throws them forth, their hum
Bulges to thunder held by calf and thigh.
In goggles, donned impersonality,
In gleaming jackets trophied with the dust,
They strap in doubt—by hiding it, robust—
And almost hear a meaning in their noise.

Exact conclusion of their hardiness
Has no shape yet, but from known whereabouts
They ride, direction where the tires press.
They scare a flight of birds across the field:
Much that is natural, to the will must yield.
Men manufacture both machine and soul,
And use what they imperfectly control
To dare a future from the taken routes.

It is a part solution, after all.
One is not necessarily discord
On earth; or damned because, half animal,
One lacks direct instinct, because one wakes
Afloat on movement that divides and breaks.
One joins the movement in a valueless world,
Choosing it, till, both hurler and the hurled,
One moves as well, always toward, toward.

A minute holds them, who have come to go:
The self-defined, astride the created will
They burst away; the towns they travel through
Are home for neither bird nor holiness,
For birds and saints complete their purposes.
At worst, one is in motion; and at best,
Reaching no absolute, in which to rest,
One is always nearer by not keeping still.

California

The Silver Age

Do not enquire from the centurion nodding
At the corner, with his head gentle over
The swelling breastplate, where true Rome is found.
Even of Livy there are volumes lost.
All he can do is guide you through the moonlight.

When he moves, mark how his eager striding,
To which we know the darkness is a river
Sullen with mud, is easy as on ground.
We know it is a river never crossed
By any but some few who hate the moonlight.

And when he speaks, mark how his ancient wording
Is hard with indignation of a lover.
'I do not think our new Emperor likes the sound
Of turning squadrons or the last post.
Consorts with Christians, I think he lives in moonlight.'

Hurrying to show you his companions guarding,
He grips your arm like a cold strap of leather,
Then halts, earthpale, as he stares round and round.
What made this one fragment of a sunken coast
Remain, far out, to be beaten by the moonlight?

The Inherited Estate

To Mike Kitay, an American in Europe

A mansion, string of cottages, a farm,
Before you reach the last black-timbered barn
And set your foot upon the path that leads
Up to the hill where Follies and façades
—Typical products of intelligence
That lacks brute purpose—split, disintegrate,
    And, falling with their own rich weight,
Litter the slopes, a record of expense.

So generations of the reckless dead
Put up the ruins you inherited,
And generations of ganged village boys
Have used as fort and ammunition those
Droppings of fashion you explore today.
   What country boys and gentlemen have left
     Now smells of green, the fat dark drift
Where the weed's impulse couples with decay.

Is comfort so impermanently built,
A summer house with blurring fungus spilt
At random on the leaning walls? is time
Only a carved head that you fish from slime,
That winks with muddied eyeball? does the crash
Of failing stonework sound for all desires?
   For, once the dilettante tires,
The ornaments he raises fall in trash.

A calm discrimination marks your hate:
Once you inherited the wide estate
The Follies like the land and farm were yours.
Distance has flattered them, for from the moors
The fronts resembled solid palaces:
And though you are not so trusting to believe
   That all is sound which others leave,
You come not crediting half your bailiff says.

He told you all, an honest labourer.
But had not noticed this, that in the year
When you were born a twist of feckless wind
Brought one small seed and left it on the ground
Between the chance and choice to live or die.
It drew the means of living undeterred,
   Uncurling in the shell it stirred,
To rise, and sway upon your property.

Its art is merely holding to the earth—
But see how confidently, from its birth,
Its branches, lifting above failures, keep

Vigour within the discipline of shape.
Come here, friend, yearly, till you've carved the bark
With all the old virtues, young in fibre, names
   That swell with time and tree, no dreams,
No ornaments, but tallies for your work.

The Corridor

A separate place between the thought and felt
The empty hotel corridor was dark.
But here the keyhole shone, a meaning spark.
What fires were latent in it! So he knelt.

Now, at the corridor's much lighter end,
A pierglass hung upon the wall and showed,
As by an easily deciphered code,
Dark, door, and man, hooped by a single band.

He squinted through the keyhole, and within
Surveyed an act of love that frank as air
He was too ugly for, or could not dare,
Or at a crucial moment thought a sin.

Pleasure was simple thus: he mastered it.
If once he acted as participant
He would be mastered, the inhabitant
Of someone else's world, mere shred to fit.

He moved himself to get a better look
And then it was he noticed in the glass
Two strange eyes in a fascinated face
That watched him like a picture in a book.

The instant drove simplicity away—
The scene was altered, it depended on
His kneeling, when he rose they were clean gone
The couple in the keyhole; this would stay.

For if the watcher of the watcher shown
There in the distant glass, should be watched too,
Who can be master, free of others; who
Can look around and say he is alone?

Moreover, who can know that what he sees
Is not distorted, that he is not seen
Distorted by a pierglass, curved and lean?
Those curious eyes, through him, were linked to these—

These lovers altered in the cornea's bend.
What could he do but leave the keyhole, rise,
Holding those eyes as equal in his eyes,
And go, one hand held out, to meet a friend?

Innocence

for Tony White

He ran the course and as he ran he grew,
And smelt his fragrance in the field. Already,
Running he knew the most he ever knew,
The egotism of a healthy body.

Ran into manhood, ignorant of the past:
Culture of guilt and guilt's vague heritage,
Self-pity and the soul; what he possessed
Was rich, potential, like the bud's tipped rage.

The Corps developed, it was plain to see,
Courage, endurance, loyalty and skill
To a morale firm as morality,
Hardening him to an instrument, until

The finitude of virtues that were there
Bodied within the swarthy uniform
A compact innocence, child-like and clear,
No doubt could penetrate, no act could harm.

When he stood near the Russian partisan
Being burned alive, he therefore could behold
The ribs wear gently through the darkening skin
And sicken only at the Northern cold,

Could watch the fat burn with a violet flame
And feel disgusted only at the smell,
And judge that all pain finishes the same
As melting quietly by his boots it fell.

Flying Above California

Spread beneath me it lies—lean upland
sinewed and tawny in the sun, and

valley cool with mustard, or sweet with
loquat. I repeat under my breath

names of places I have not been to:
Crescent City, San Bernardino

—Mediterranean and Northern names.
Such richness can make you drunk. Sometimes

on fogless days by the Pacific,
there is a cold hard light without break

that reveals merely what is—no more
and no less. That limiting candor,

that accuracy of the beaches,
is part of the ultimate richness.

My Sad Captains

One by one they appear in
the darkness: a few friends, and

a few with historical
names. How late they start to shine!
but before they fade they stand
perfectly embodied, all

the past lapping them like a
cloak of chaos. They were men
who, I thought, lived only to
renew the wasteful force they
spent with each hot convulsion.
They remind me, distant now.

True, they are not at rest yet,
but now that they are indeed
apart, winnowed from failures,
they withdraw to an orbit
and turn with disinterested
hard energy, like the stars.

The Goddess

When eyeless fish meet her on
her way upward, they gently
turn together in the dark
brooks. But naked and searching
as a wind, she will allow
no hindrance, none, and bursts up

through potholes and narrow flues
seeking an outlet. Unslowed
by fire, rock, water or clay,
she after a time reaches
the soft abundant soil, which
still does not dissipate her

force—for look! sinewy thyme
reeking in the sunlight; rats

breeding, breeding, in their nests;
and the soldier by a park
bench with his greatcoat collar
up, waiting all evening for

a woman, any woman
whose dress is tight across her
ass as bark in moonlight.
Proserpina! it is we,
vulnerable, quivering,
who stay you to abundance.

TED HUGHES

(1930–)

The Hawk in the Rain

I drown in the drumming ploughland, I drag up
Heel after heel from the swallowing of the earth's mouth,
From clay that clutches my each step to the ankle
With the habit of the dogged grave, but the hawk

Effortlessly at height hangs his still eye.
His wings hold all creation in a weightless quiet,
Steady as a hallucination in the streaming air.
While banging wind kills these stubborn hedges,

Thumbs my eyes, throws my breath, tackles my heart,
And rain hacks my head to the bone, the hawk hangs
The diamond point of will that polestars
The sea drowner's endurance: and I,

Bloodily grabbed dazed last-moment-counting
Morsel in the earth's mouth, strain towards the master-
Fulcrum of violence where the hawk hangs still.
That maybe in his own time meets the weather

Coming the wrong way, suffers the air, hurled upside down,
Fall from his eye, the ponderous shires crash on him,
The horizon trap him; the round angelic eye
Smashed, mix his heart's blood with the mire of the land.

Secretary

If I should touch her she would shriek and weeping
Crawl off to nurse the terrible wound: all
Day like a starling under the bellies of bulls
She hurries among men, ducking, peeping,

Off in a whirl at the first move of a horn.
At dusk she scuttles down the gauntlet of lust
Like a clockwork mouse. Safe home at last
She mends socks with holes, shirts that are torn

For father and brother, and a delicate supper cooks:
Goes to bed early, shuts out with the light
Her thirty years, and lies with buttocks tight,
Hiding her lovely eyes until day break.

The Jaguar

The apes yawn and adore their fleas in the sun.
The parrots shriek as if they were on fire, or strut
Like cheap tarts to attract the stroller with the nut.
Fatigued with indolence, tiger and lion

Lie still as the sun. The boa-constrictor's coil
Is a fossil. Cage after cage seems empty, or
Stinks of sleepers from the breathing straw.
It might be painted on a nursery wall.

But who runs like the rest past these arrives
At a cage where the crowd stands, stares, mesmerized,
As a child at a dream, at a jaguar hurrying enraged
Through prison darkness after the drills of his eyes

On a short fierce fuse. Not in boredom—
The eye satisfied to be blind in fire,

By the bang of blood in the brain deaf the ear—
He spins from the bars, but there's no cage to him

More than to the visionary his cell:
His stride is wildernesses of freedom:
The world rolls under the long thrust of his heel.
Over the cage floor the horizons come.

Childbirth

When, on the bearing mother, death's
Door opened its furious inch,
Instant of struggling and blood,
The commonplace became so strange

There was not looking at table or chair:
Miracle struck out the brain
Of order and ordinary: bare
Onto the heart the earth dropped then

With whirling quarters, the axle cracked,
Through that miracle-breached bed
All the dead could have got back;
With shriek and heave and spout of blood

The huge-eyed looming horde from
Under the floor of the heart, that run
To the madman's eye-corner came
Deafening towards light, whereon

A child whimpered upon the bed,
Frowning ten-toed ten-fingered birth
Put the skull back about the head
Righted the stagger of the earth.

Law in the Country of the Cats

When two men meet for the first time in all
Eternity and outright hate each other,
Not as a beggar-man and a rich man,
Not as cuckold-maker and cuckold,
Not as bully and delicate boy, but
As dog and wolf because their blood before
They are aware has bristled into their hackles,
Because one has clubbed the other to death
With the bottle first broached to toast their transaction
And swears to God he went helpless black-out
While they were mixing smiles, facts have sacked
The oath of the pious witness who judged all men
As a one humble brotherhood of man.

When two men at first meeting hate each other
Even in passing, without words, in the street,
They are not likely to halt as if remembering
They once met somewhere, where in fact they met,
And discuss "universal brotherhood,"
"Love of humanity and each fellow-man,"
Or "the growing likelihood of perpetual peace,"
But if, by chance, they do meet, so mistaking,
There will be that moment's horrible pause
As each looks into the gulf in the eye of the other,
Then a flash of violent incredible action,
Then one man letting his brains gently to the gutter,
And one man bursting into the police station
Crying: "Let Justice be done. I did it. I."

Mayday on Holderness

This evening, motherly summer moves in the pond.
I look down into the decomposition of leaves—
The furnace door whirling with larvae.

From Hull's sunset smudge
Humber is melting eastward, my south skyline:
A loaded single vein, it drains
The effort of the inert North—Sheffield's ores,
Bog pools, dregs of toadstools, tributary
Graves, dunghills, kitchens, hospitals.
The unkillable North Sea swallows it all.
Insects, drunken, drop out of the air.

Birth-soils,
The sea-salts, scoured me, cortex and intestine,
To receive these remains.
As the incinerator, as the sun,
As the spider, I had a whole world in my hands.
Flowerlike, I loved nothing.
Dead and unborn are in God comfortable.
What a length of gut is growing and breathing—
This mute eater, biting through the mind's
Nursery floor, with eel and hyena and vulture,
With creepy-crawly and the root,
With the sea-worm, entering its birthright.

The stars make pietas. The owl announces its sanity.

The crow sleeps glutted and the stoat begins.
There are eye-guarded eggs in the hedgerows,
Hot haynests under the roots in burrows.
Couples at their pursuits are laughing in the lanes.

The North Sea lies soundless. Beneath it
Smoulder the wars: to heart-beats, bomb, bayonet.
"Mother, Mother!" cries the pierced helmet.
Cordite oozings of Gallipoli,

Curded to beastings, broached my palate,
The expressionless gaze of the leopard,
The coils of the sleeping anaconda,
The nightlong frenzy of shrews.

387

Dick Straightup

Past eighty, but never in eighty years—
Eighty winters on the windy ridge
Of England—has he buttoned his shirt or his jacket.
He sits in the bar-room seat he has been
Polishing with his backside sixty-odd years
Where nobody else sits. White is his head,
But his cheek high, hale as when he emptied
Every Saturday the twelve-pint tankard at a tilt,
Swallowed the whole serving of thirty eggs,
And banged the big bass drum for Heptonstall—
With a hundred other great works, still talked of.
Age has stiffened him, but not dazed or bent,
The blue eye has come clear of time:
At a single pint, now, his memory sips slowly,
His belly strong as a tree bole.

He survives among hills, nourished by stone and height.
The dust of Achilles and Cuchulain
Itches in the palms of scholars; thin clerks exercise
In their bed-sitters at midnight, and the meat salesman can
Loft fully four hundred pounds. But this one,
With no more application than sitting,
And drinking, and singing, fell in the sleet, late,
Dammed the pouring gutter; and slept there; and, throughout
A night searched by shouts and lamps, froze,
Grew to the road with welts of ice. He was chipped out at dawn
Warm as a pie and snoring.

The gossip of men younger by forty years—
Loud in his company since he no longer says much—
Empties, refills and empties their glasses.
Or their strenuous silence places the dominoes
(That are old as the house) into patterns
Gone with the game; the darts that glint to the dartboard
Pin no remarkable instant. The young men sitting

Taste their beer as by imitation,
Borrow their words as by impertinence
Because he sits there so full of legend and life
Quiet as a man alone.

He lives with sixty and seventy years ago,
And of everything he knows three quarters is in the grave,
Or tumbled down, or vanished. To be understood
His words must tug up the bottom-most stones of this village,
This clutter of blackstone gulleys, peeping curtains,
And a graveyard bigger and deeper than the village
That sways in the tide of wind and rain some fifty
Miles off the Irish sea.
            The lamp above the pub-door
Wept yellow when he went out and the street
Of spinning darkness roared like a machine
As the wind applied itself. His upright walk,
His strong back, I commemorate now,
And his white blown head going out between a sky and an
   earth
That were bundled into placeless blackness, the one
Company of his mind.

Obit.

Now, you are strong as the earth you have entered.

This is a birthplace picture. Green into blue
The hills run deep and limpid. The weasel's
Berry-eyed red lock-head, gripping the dream
That holds good, goes lost in the heaved calm

Of the earth you have entered.

Lupercalia

1

The dog loved its churlish life,
Scraps, thefts. Its declined blood

An anarchy of mindless pride.
Nobody's pet, but good enough

To double with a bitch as poor.
It had bitten ears and little stone eyes,
A mouth like an incinerator.
It held man's reasonable ways

Between its teeth. Received death
Closed eyes and grinning mouth.

2

This woman's as from death's touch: a surviving
Barrenness: she abides; perfect,
But flung from the wheel of the living,
The past killed in her, the future plucked out.

The dead are indifferent underground.
Little the live may learn from them—
A sort of hair and bone wisdom,
A worn witchcraft accoutrement

Of proverbs. Now the brute's quick
Be tinder: old spark of the blood-heat
And not death's touch engross her bed,
Though that has stripped her stark indeed.

3

Goats, black, not angels, but
Bellies round as filled wine-skins
Slung under carcase bones.
Yet that's no brute light

And no merely mountain light—
Their eyes' golden element.
Rustle of their dry hooves, dry patter,
Wind in the oak-leaves; and their bent

Horns, stamp, sudden reared stare
Startle women. Spirit of the ivy,
Stink of goat, of a rank thriving,
O mountain listener.

4

Over sand that the sun's burned out
Thudding feet of the powerful,
Their oiled bodies brass-bright
In a drift of dust. The earth's crammed full,

Its baked red bellying to the sky's
Electric blue. Their attitudes—
A theorem of flung effort, blades:
Nothing mortal falters their poise

Though wet with blood: the dog has blessed
Their fury. Fresh thongs of goat-skin
In their hands they go bounding past,
And deliberate welts have snatched her in

To the figure of racers. Maker of the world,
Hurrying the lit ghost of man
Age to age while the body hold,
Touch this frozen one.

Dark Women

My neighbour moves less and less, attempts less.
If his right hand still moves, it is a farewell
Already days posthumous.

But the left hand seems to freeze,
And the left leg with its crude plumbing,
And the left half jaw and the left eyelid and the words,
  all the huge cries

Frozen in his brain his tongue cannot unfreeze—
While somewhere through a dark heaven
The dark bloodclot moves in.

I watch it approaching, but I cannot fear it.
The punctual evening star,
Worse, the warm hawthorn blossoms, their foam,

Their palls of deathly perfume,
Worst of all the beanflower
Badged with jet like the ear of the tiger

Unmake and remake me. That star
And that flower and that flower
And living mouth and living mouth all

One flaring annihilation
Of old brains, old bowels, old bodies
In the scarves of dew, the wet hair of nightfall.

New Moon in January

A splinter, flicked
Into the wide eyeball,
Severs its warnings.

The head, severed while staring,
Felt nothing, only
Tilted slightly.

O lone
Eyelash on the darkening
Stripe of blood, O sail of death!

Frozen
In ether
Unearthly

Shelley's faint-shriek
Trying to thaw while zero
Itself loses consciousness.

Encounter

A cool small evening shrunk to a dog bark and the clank of a bucket—

And you listening.
A spider's web, tense for the dew's touch,
A pail lifted still and brimming—mirror
To tempt a first star to a tremor.

Cows are going home in the lane there, looping the hedges with
    their warm wreaths of breath—
A dark river of blood, many boulders,
Balancing unspilled milk.

Moon, you cry suddenly, Moon! Moon!

The moon has stepped back like an artist gazing amazed at a work

That points at him amazed.

The cows submerge.
The moon has opened you wide and bright like a pond.

The moon lifts you off the grass—
A cat's cradle of spider's web, where the stars are trembling
    into place.

The brimming moon looks through you and you cannot move.

Any minute
A bat will fly out of a cat's ear.

Wodwo

What am I? nosing here, turning leaves over
following a faint stain on the air to the river's edge
I enter water. What am I to split
the glassy grain of water looking upward I see the bed
of the river above me upside down very clear
what am I doing here in mid-air? Why do I find
this frog so interesting as I inspect its most secret
interior and make it my own? Do these weeds
know me and name me to each other have they
seen me before, do I fit in their world? I seem
separate from the ground and not rooted but dropped
out of nothing casually I've no threads
fastening me to anything I can go anywhere
I seem to have been given the freedom
of this place what am I then? And picking
bits of bark off this rotten stump gives me
no pleasure and it's no use so why do I do it
me and doing that have coincided very queerly
But what shall I be called am I the first
have I an owner what shape am I what
shape am I am I huge if I go
to the end on this way past these trees and past these trees
till I get tired that's touching one wall of me
for the moment if I sit still how everything
stops to watch me I suppose I am the exact centre
but there's all this what is it roots
roots roots roots and here's the water
again very queer but I'll go on looking

DEREK WALCOTT

(1930–)

A *Far Cry from Africa*

A wind is ruffling the tawny pelt
Of Africa. Kikuyu, quick as flies
Batten upon the bloodstreams of the veldt.
Corpses are scattered through a paradise.
But still the worm, colonel of carrion, cries:
'Waste no compassion on these separate dead'
Statistics justify and scholars seize
The salients of colonial policy.
What is that to the white child hacked in bed?
To savages, expendable as Jews?

Threshed out by beaters, the long rushes break
In a white dust of ibises whose cries
Have wheeled since civilization's dawn
From the parched river or beast-teeming plain;
The violence of beast on beast is read
As natural law, but upright man
Seeks his divinity with inflicting pain.
Delirious as these worried beasts, his wars
Dance to the tightened carcass of a drum,
While he calls courage still, that native dread
Of the white peace contracted by the dead.

Again brutish necessity wipes its hands
Upon the napkin of a dirty cause, again
A waste of our compassion, as with Spain.
The gorilla wrestles with the superman.

I who am poisoned with the blood of both,
Where shall I turn, divided to the vein?
I who have cursed
The drunken officer of British rule, how choose
Between this Africa and the English tongue I love?
Betray them both, or give back what they give?
How can I face such slaughter and be cool?
How can I turn from Africa and live?

Ruins of a Great House

> though our longest sun sets at right declensions and makes but winter
> arches, it cannot be long before we lie down in darkness, and have our light
> in ashes . . .
>
> BROWNE: *Urn Burial*

Stones only, the *disjecta membra* of this Great House,
Whose moth-like girls are mixed with candledust,
Remain to file the lizard's dragonish claws;
The mouths of those gate cherubs streaked with stain.
Axle and coachwheel silted under the muck
Of cattle droppings.

               Three crows flap for the trees,
And settle, creaking the eucalyptus boughs.
A smell of dead limes quickens in the nose
The leprosy of Empire.

             'Farewell, green fields'
             'Farewell, ye happy groves!'

Marble as Greece, like Faulkner's south in stone,
Deciduous beauty prospered and is gone;

But where the lawn breaks in a rash of trees
A spade below dead leaves will ring the bone
Of some dead animal or human thing
Fallen from evil days, from evil times.

It seems that the original crops were limes
Grown in that silt that clogs the river's skirt;
The imperious rakes are gone, their bright girls gone,
The river flows, obliterating hurt.

I climbed a wall with the grill ironwork
Of exiled craftsmen, protecting that great house
From guilt, perhaps, but not from the worm's rent,
Nor from the padded cavalry of the mouse.
And when a wind shook in the limes I heard
What Kipling heard; the death of a great empire, the abuse
Of ignorance by Bible and by sword.

A green lawn, broken by low walls of stone
Dipped to the rivulet, and pacing, I thought next
Of men like Hawkins, Walter Raleigh, Drake,
Ancestral murderers and poets, more perplexed
In memory now by every ulcerous crime.
The world's green age then was a rotting lime
Whose stench became the charnel galleon's text.
The rot remains with us, the men are gone.
But, as dead ash is lifted in a wind,
That fans the blackening ember of the mind,
My eyes burned from the ashen prose of Donne.

Ablaze with rage, I thought
Some slave is rotting in this manorial lake,
And still the coal of my compassion fought:
That Albion too, was once
A colony like ours, 'Part of the continent, piece of the main'
Nook-shotten, rook o'er blown, deranged
By foaming channels, and the vain expense
Of bitter faction.

> All in compassion ends
> So differently from what the heart arranged:
> 'as well as if a manor of thy friend's . . .'

Parang

. . . the second cuatroman sings.

Man, I suck me tooth when I hear
How dem croptime fiddlers lie,
And de wailing, kiss-me-arse flutes
That bring water to me eye!
O, when I t'ink how from young
I wasted time at de fêtes,
I could bawl in a red-eyed rage
For desire turned to regret,
Not knowing the truth that I sang
At parang and la comette.
Boy, every damned tune them tune
Of love that will last forever
Is the wax and the wane of the moon
Since Adam catch body-fever.

I old, so the young crop won't
Have these claws to reap their waist,
But I know 'do more' from 'don't'
Since the grave cry out 'Make haste!'
This banjo world have one string
And all man does dance to that tune:
That love is a place in the bush
With music grieving from far,
As you look past her shoulder and see
Like her one tear afterwards
The falling of a fixed star.
Young men does bring love to disgrace
With remorseful, regretful words,
When flesh upon flesh was the tune

Since the first cloud raise up to disclose
The breast of the naked moon.

A *Letter from Brooklyn*

An old lady writes me in a spidery style,
Each character trembling, and I see a veined hand
Pellucid as paper, travelling on a skein
Of such frail thoughts its thread is often broken;
Or else the filament from which a phrase is hung
Dims to my sense, but caught, it shines like steel,
As touch a line, and the whole web will feel.
She describes my father, yet I forget her face
More easily than my father's yearly dying;
Of her I remember small, buttoned boots and the place
She kept in our wooden church on those Sundays
Whenever her strength allowed;
Grey haired, thin voiced, perpetually bowed.

'I am Mable Rawlins,' she writes, 'and know both your parents;'
He is dead, Miss Rawlins, but God bless your tense:
'Your father was a dutiful, honest,
Faithful and useful person.'
For such plain praise what fame is recompense?
'A horn-painter, he painted delicately on horn,
He used to sit around the table and paint pictures.'
The peace of God needs nothing to adorn
It, nor glory nor ambition.
'He is twenty-eight years buried,' she writes, 'he was called home,
And is, I am sure, doing greater work.'

The strength of one frail hand in a dim room
Somewhere in Brooklyn, patient and assured,
Restores my sacred duty to the Word.
'Home, home,' she can write, with such short time to live,
Alone as she spins the blessings of her years;
Not withered of beauty if she can bring such tears,
Nor withdrawn from the world that breaks its lovers so;

Heaven is to her the place where painters go,
All who bring beauty on frail shell or horn,
There was all made, thence their lux-mundi drawn,
Drawn, drawn, till the thread is resilient steel,
Lost though it seems in darkening periods,
And there they return to do work that is God's.

So this old lady writes, and again I believe,
I believe it all, and for no man's death I grieve.

The Polish Rider

The grey horse, Death, in profile bears the young Titus
To dark woods by the dying coal of day;
The father, with worn vision portrays the son
Like Dürer's knight astride a Rozinante;
The horse disturbs more than the youth delights us.
The warrior turns his sure gaze for a second,
Assurance looks its father in the eye,
The inherited, bony hack heads accurately
Towards the symbolical forests that have beckoned
Such knights, squired by the scyther, where to lie.
But skill dispassionately praises the rider,
Despair details the grey, cadaverous steed,
The immortal image holds its murderer
In a clear gaze for the next age to read.

Bronze

Hammered to the serenity of copper,
Her drowsing mask with slitted eyes,
Cupped in a palm and quiet as a plaque,
By tears unrunnelled, guiltless of surprise,
Bathes in dawn's wind, the wild night hair blown back.

Those mottled marbles I admired,
Bone-coloured in their pagan calm,

Sea-flowering Aphrodite borne on shells,
That blunt, androgynous Venus with one arm,
Male-thighed Dianas in their hunting dells,
And Ledas lost in blizzards of the swan,
Not one of those in such fierce sex was fired
Or holds its cunning secret as this one
Of lasting bronze, art of a savage race,
Marble, bronze, ebonwood, white, creole, black.

The elongated eyes look Arawak,
Arawak or Carib, but nakedness unsurprised
By armoured men dividing jungle leaves,
The sun ablaze on helmet, breastplate, greaves;
They close in groaning irony at their rape,
For that earth-colored flesh buries all men
In immolations mocked by the wild ape,
At that brute cry all civilizations crack.

The high-boned ridges of the drowsing cheek
Are Amerindian by West African,
And is there any Egypt in that head?

Though, by the books, it seems impossible;
Still, those flinched nostrils have smelt the dead
And in my book that's sibylline; our sibyl
Has seen worse death in our Egyptian past
Than ritualistic slaughter to a faith;
That metal peace was hammered in a blast
Of burning heaps of pyramidical dead. Those veins
Are coloured rivers of the violent slain,
Cooled by dawn's wind, like sea-wind over canes
Which the East Indian heaps with burning back.

The hair is night, its skeins are the night's winds,
Out of such savage, tangled roots was born
This monolithic, unforgiving face
Wrought in a furious kiln, in which each race
Expects its hundredth dawn.

ROBERT MEZEY

(1935–)

In Defense of Felons

Winter will not let go of earth. The lust
Of a listless sun finds April difficult,
Weakly astonished that frost fights so hard.
The black earth still is tough in my back yard,
The brittle stubble has not begun to melt,
And in the shed, my frozen spade turns rust.

Possibly Winter is afraid of what
The softening soil might turn up to the sight—
Perhaps my spade would scrape against a bone,
Perhaps some half-starved animal would moan,
Having endured the long, relentless night—
Possibly Winter is ashamed of that.

How many stiff-furred bodies has she buried,
How many coverts converted into graves
About my house? All that I want to know
Is underground or underneath of snow.
But circumstantial icicles plunge from the eaves.
I know that Winter is at large, and worried.

Well, late or soon, the sun will have his day
And drive her into hiding, in the north.

And when that trouble's over, there will come
Swallows venturing back to their summer home,
And many citizen flowers will step forth
In the green wake of Winter's getaway.

And what of this felon who is doomed to be
The hack and executioner of Time?
Her cruel hands are sweet, and death is worth
The green and giant labor of the earth—
I call her conscience clear, her breath sublime,
Striving with heat for balance, harmony.

Sometime, not now, in bloody boot and glove,
Stirred by compulsive memories, she will turn
Back to these fields, again and again, until
The earth be driven against heaven's will
To its old asylum, where the sun would burn
Winter and earth to ashes with its love.

Street Scene

Afternoon.
Teacher and nun, bleak refugee, a stone
Splinters with the cold, and the vacant streets
Await you.
Tattered, and driven by the wind,
A sheet of newspaper borne in a swarm of snow
Scrapes on the curb and pavement.

The parish children,
Home from school and church, escaped and safe,
Stand at the windows. With expressionless eyes
They scan
Lonely slope and parapet,
A purity of contour in the gulleys,
A terrain bare of soldiers.

403

Hour after hour
The strange light persists. Snow dawdles down.
It is a violet haze in which the snow
Seems grey,
And a solitary nun becomes
A slim black hill possessing empty lands.
Her hood is peaked with snow.

The first crystals
Blazed in constellations on her gown,
And then that somber gown relaxed its bald
Silhouette,
And merged with the densely pointed air.
It must be grave compliance that lets her move
Without seeming to move.

Teacher and nun,
You are the heiress of warm, refused embraces,
Who now in the sisterless twilight mutely tread
In drifts
Through the buried paper, the splintered stone;
In whose infinite midnight hover the small flakes
Inseparable from stars.

Carmina

for Carol

Wherever she is moving now, an air
Of her subtle breath or bodily emanation
Moves on the wind. Most flowers being dead
Or odorless these many months, I know
The fragrance to be hers, that comes to me
Where I stand the friendly day and do not dream
That earth and sky are anything but kind.
I bid them meet and part as she and I do—
And suddenly, I think of her as theirs.

As I write, I know that what she is
Eludes me when I cast my finest net;
Only the elements, that have no delight
In their own fortune, hold her without end.
And she is proud of it, is like the earth,
That blooms at times, arousing boundless love,
Only to keep her distance with a smile.
Darkness has come. I darken at its touch,
Envying the ground, hating the senseless air.

2

Although the bed, by hollow shadowing
And a slight sag, shows where she slept last night,
A simpler thing, a chair, or the very room
Recalls her presence in her absent hours,
Deeper impressions than her body made.
Alone, I feel the soft wave of her spirit,
That touches every thing she sees and touches;
These bare things move, a trick of the late sunlight,
And I move also, her light hands on me.

But more than this, simplicities become
Themselves her landscape and her room of sleep—
Homely, familiar forms, uncluttered space,
In which love spurs the motions of the mind.
Soft lights and deeper darknesses of sleep
Fall from its hard ascent and shape for me
The forests and bare uplands of her body,
As I, a stranger in a strange terrain,
Ride with my hands the length of naked lines.

3

Now with winter returning, what will you say?
Love was sometimes the word. You said you felt
My heavier substance churning in your blood,
And my inmost life enacted silently,
Intimately, in the dark ducts of your body,
And something soft, a petal or moth's wing,
Brushing your lips. This birth, this effleurage—

It was like Nature, who, in the guise of fluid,
Rises on spring days in the trunks of trees.

I think of likenesses, it gives me hope.
It lets me flourish in your deepest soil,
In the fleshy vessel where I chose to thrive.
And you, are you the seasons of my year,
Convolving with my moods and with my weathers?
Or will you change, is it true you wait upon
Some solstice when you leave my heavens bare
And me despairing in a starless night,
Thinking of what you were, what you were like?

You Could Say

Yesterday rain fell in torrents,
stripping the branches of leaves and
deepening the arroyo. Now,
although the sun glances like flint
at the edges of cars, houses,
antennas, the water remains.
It lies in the hollows of rocks
and in lakes by the roads. Last night
it signalled a great change; today
winter breathes at my window, and
a few last flies, stunned by cold
into fearlessness, nestle close
to my skin. Summer is burnt out.
Why does this season, with its joy
in killing and its hard iron breath,
always find me alone? You could say
but you won't, and I am slowly
drifting away, I am growing
oblique like the sun, striking out
feebly at what is gone.

My love,
it was my nature to want you,

lascivious, aloof, a body
fresh as new-fallen snow, and as
cold. Like other men in my
desire, I asked for it and now
I have it—the wind, the black trees,
scum of ice on the roadside pools—
all that the rain promised, and more.

After Hours

Not yet five, and the light
is going fast. Milky and veined
a thin frost covers the flooded
ruts of the driveway, the grass
bends to the winter night. Her face
is before me now; I see it

in the misted glass, the same
impenetrable smile and I can feel
again on my bare shoulder
the dew of her breath. We made
a life in two years, a sky
and the very trees, lost in thought.

I know what it is, to be
alone, to have asked for everything
and to do without, to search
the mind for a face already dim,
to wait, and what it exacts.
I don't fear it, I say,

but I do, and this night
the wind against my window
and the top branches thrashing about
enter my life and I see
the coming time loose and dark
above me, with new strength

No Country You Remember

But for the steady wash of rain,
The house is quiet now. Outside,
Occasional cars move past the lawn
And leave the stillness purified.

I find myself in a dark chair
Idly picking a banjo, lost
In reveries of another time,
Thinking at what heavy cost

I came to this particular place,
This house in which I let my life
Play out its subterranean plot,
My Christian and enduring wife.

What if I paid for what I got?
Nothing can so exhaust the heart
As boredom and self-loathing do,
Which are the poisons of my art.

All day I resurrect the past.
This instrument I love so ill
Hammers and rings and, when I wish,
Lies in its coffin and is still.

I think of winter mornings when
Between bare woods and a wrecked shack
I came down deep, encrusted slopes,
A bag of dead birds at my back;

Then let my mind go blank and smile
At what small game the mind demands,
As dead time flickers in the blind
Articulation of my hands.

I know you must despise me, you
Who judge and measure everything
And live by little absolutes—
What would you like to hear me sing?

A strophe on the wasted life?
Some verses dealing with my fall?
Or would you care to contemplate
My contemplation of the wall?

I write from down here, where I live.
In the cold light of a dying day,
The covered page looks cold and dead.
And then, what more is there to say

Except, you read this in a dream.
I wrote nothing. I sat and ate
Some frozen dinner while I watched
The Late Show, and the Late Late.

NOTES ON THE POETS

The following brief notes provide basic information about each poet. In many cases, only the more important or recent books are mentioned. Occasionally there is reference to commentaries discussing the poet's work.

Certain of the poets have been, or shortly will be, treated in individual volumes of the Twayne Authors series. Four books that are particularly helpful in the study of modern poetry are: John Press, *Rule and Energy: Trends in British Poetry Since the Second World War* (Oxford University Press, London, New York, Toronto, 1963), M. L. Rosenthal, *The Modern Poets: A Critical Introduction* (Oxford University Press, New York, 1960), Donald M. Allen, ed., *The New American Poetry: 1945–1960* (Grove Press, New York, 1960), and Stephen Spender and Donald Hall, eds., *The Concise Encyclopedia of English and American Poets and Poetry* (Hawthorn Books, New York, 1963).

The brief comments on the work of individual poets are not intended as formal, critical judgments; they merely serve to point out certain qualities that make the poetry interesting and worth reading.

Brother Antoninus

"Probably the most profoundly moving and durable of the poets of the San Francisco Renaissance," the *Evergreen Review* terms Brother Antoninus, who—as William Everson—was born in 1912 in Sacramento, Calif., and grew up in Selma. Earning his living as a laborer and farmer, he married—a marriage that did not survive World War II—and under the influence of Robinson Jeffers began writing the poems that later were to put him in the front rank of the Beat wing, and indeed of contemporary poetry in general.

Drafted as a conscientious objector during the War, the poet later settled in the San Francisco area and was active in the anarcho-pacifist group that gathered around Kenneth Rexroth. He had previously published some books of poetry privately; in 1948 he became nationally known when New Directions brought out *The Residual Years*, leading to a Guggenheim fellowship. Entering the church in 1949, he was drawn to the Catholic Worker movement, but in 1951 he became a lay brother of the Dominican Order (Saint Albert's College, Oakland). When the San Francisco Renaissance burst upon public attention in 1957, he was one of its most prominent figures, and soon found himself doing poetry readings all over the country. Two further books of his poetry have appeared: *The Crooked Lines of God* (1959) and *The Hazards of Holiness* (1962). He has recorded his poetry for Harvard, the Library of Congress, Fenn College, and the Poetry Center of YMHA-YWHA (New York). Stylistically, his work often shows the influence of Jeffers' long cadenced line, but Brother Antoninus has baptized the line and made it the vehicle for exploring the dark night of the soul and proclaiming the unbearable glory of God.

George Barker

When George Barker's *Collected Poems: 1930–1955* appeared in 1957, a curious note was printed at the front: "One long poem, *The True Confession of George Barker*, which Mr. Barker wished to include in this volume, has been omitted at the publishers' request." *The True Confession* had earlier been broadcast in the Home Service of the BBC, and its plain, often downright crude treatment of sex had outraged so many listeners that the Director-General of the BBC had been obliged to make an official apology.

Critical opinion is divided down the middle on Barker. Some see him as a poet with impressive force and vision; others find him chaotic, uneven, and frequently tasteless. In an England still largely dominated by the well-behaved "Movement," his poetry seems brash and strident.

Barker was born in 1913, educated at Marlborough Road London County Council School, Chelsea. In 1939 he was professor of English literature at Imperial Tohoku University, Japan. He visited the United States in 1943. Despite the anti-privilege tone of his poems, he is a fellow of the Society for the Preservation of Ancient Monuments, and in "Stanzas on a Visit to Longleat House in Wiltshire, October 1953" he shows himself as hostile to the complacent proletariat as he has always been to the merely rich.

Thirty Preliminary Poems appeared in 1933, and was followed by a long succession of poetry books, culminating in the *Collected Poems* and *The View from a Blind I* (1962).

Carl Bode

One of the most distinguished scholars in the field of American literature, Carl Bode is also a highly gifted poet, though so far better known in England—where he was cultural attaché 1957–59 and was elected to the Royal Society of Literature—than in America. In his three published volumes of verse—*The Sacred Seasons* (1953), *The Calendar of Love* (1959), and *The Man Behind You* (1959) he reveals an easy mastery of traditional forms, the sonnet in particular, which he uses to celebrate both the sacred and secular moments of life. Underlying his poetry is the tension between his candid sensuousness and his preoccupation with God.

He has been professor of English at the University of Maryland since 1947. He received a Guggenheim fellowship, 1954–55. His numerous scholarly works include an edition of Thoreau's *Collected Poems* (1943), *The American Lyceum: Town Meeting of the Mind* (1956), and *The Anatomy of American Popular Culture, 1840–1861* (1959). He is now writing a life of H. L. Mencken. He was married in 1938 to Margaret Emilie Lutze and they have three children.

Bode was born in 1911 in Milwaukee, and received his undergraduate degree at the University of Chicago and his graduate degrees at Northwestern.

John Ciardi

John Ciardi was born in 1916 in Boston of Italian parents, Carmin and Concetta di Benedictus Ciardi. It is easy to speculate that something of that heritage is revealed in his poetry, which has a direct, sensuous richness rare today—a wide-eyed openness to the delights of the world without any excessive illusions about its reliability.

Ciardi was educated at Bates College and Tufts (magna cum laude, 1938). In 1939 he went to the University of Michigan and studied for his M.A. under the famous teacher of writing, Professor Cowden, who in his long career launched many poets on a successful career. Winning the Hopwood Award in poetry, Ciardi went on to a succession of teaching positions—University of Kansas City, Harvard, Rutgers—with a Salzburg Seminar along the way in 1951. Since 1955 he has been director of the Bread Loaf Writers Conference, and since 1956 he has served as poetry editor of the *Saturday Review*, where his witty and sometimes mordant articles on contemporary poets have provoked countless letters to the editor. In 1961 he resigned from Rutgers to free lance.

A member of the air force during the war, Ciardi married in 1946 the Judith who figures in many of his poems. They have three children and live in Metuchen, N.J.

Ciardi's first book, *Homeward to America* (1940) was followed by frequent others, including *As If: Poems New and Selected* (1955), and the most recent, *In Fact* (1963). He is the author of a college textbook, *How Does a Poem Mean?* (1959), a joint author of another, *Poetry: A Closer Look* (1963), several books of poetry for children, and the best poetic translation of Dante's *Inferno* (1954) and *Purgatorio* (1961). He is currently working on the *Paradiso*.

Robert Creeley

Robert Creeley has expressed his views on poetry in the appendix to *The New American Poetry: 1945–1960* (ed. Donald M. Allen, 1960) and *The Sullen Art* (interviews by David Ossman, 1963), but his poetry speaks best for itself. Usually short, curiously artless at first glance, it has at its best a suddenly luminous quality. He is one of the most individual poets now writing in America.

Born in 1926 in Arlington, Mass., Creeley attended Harvard, but took his B.A. at Black Mountain College, an experimental North Carolina college now defunct. His master's degree was at the University of New Mexico. During the last days of Black Mountain he taught there and was editor of the *Black Mountain Review*. Much of his life—before and after he finished his B.A.—has been spent in distant places, including India and Burma where he was with the American Field Service. During 1963 Creeley, together with Denise Levertov, Charles Olson, Robert Duncan, Allen Ginsberg, and Margaret Avison, conducted a writers' workshop at the University of British Columbia in Vancouver. He is now a lecturer in English at the University of New Mexico.

Creeley's first book of verse, *Le Fou*, was published in 1952; it was followed by a rapid succession, mostly issued by small presses. *For Love: Poems 1950–1960*, published in 1962, revealed the growing scope of his work. He has also published short stories and a novel, *The Island* (1963). He is married and the father of three daughters. At present, in addition to writing more poems, he is completing a book-length study of Charles Olson and a novel about his experiences in Guatamala where (after his M.A.) he taught for a time on a coffee *finca*.

James Dickey

"I am trying to find a way to make poetry (or my poetry, anyway) the kind of thing that means something to people in their life-situations, and get away from the notion of the poem as a sort of display of literary virtues," James Dickey writes. His poetry, coming out of a deep Southern background (he was born in Atlanta, 1923; on Ground Hog Day, he is careful to point out), reveals a deep sense of ordinary experience, but goes beyond the mere chronicling of happenings. His first appearance in book form, *Into the Stone and Other Poems* (published in *Poets of Today*, VII, 1960) displayed a highly individual talent which has matured in his successive volumes, *Drowning with Others* (1962) and *Helmets* (1964). A prolific author of literary criticism, he confesses that he keeps getting poison-pen letters about articles he cannot recall having written. A collection of his essays, *The Suspect in Poetry*, was published in 1963, and he is now working on further poems and a short novel. He has recorded his poetry for the Library of Congress and it is available in the Spoken Arts series.

Dickey attended Clemson College, graduated from Vanderbilt University with Phi Beta Kappa, magna cum laude, and the distinction of winning the Cotton Carnival High Hurdles at Memphis. He also took a master's degree at Vanderbilt. He is passionately devoted to hunting and archery ("I am an absolute nut, spending all my money on arrows") and plays the guitar in the style of "three-finger picking." His numerous honors have included a Guggenheim fellowship, a *Sewanee Review* Creative Writing fellowship, and several prizes awarded by *Poetry*. He has taught at Rice University, the University of Florida, and Reed College. He is married and the father of two sons.

Lawrence Durrell

Of Irish ancestry, Lawrence Durrell's life has taken in a large part of the far-flung British Commonwealth and its interests. He was born in Jullunder in the Himalayas in 1912, educated first in the College of St. Joseph, Darjiling, and then in St. Edmund's School, Canterbury. At one time or another he was Foreign Service press officer in Athens and Cairo, press attaché in Alexandria, and director of the British Council institutes of Kalamata, Greece, and Cordoba (Argentina). More recently he was director of public relations for the Government of Cyprus. Meanwhile, he had been a fantastically productive writer, famous most of all for the four novels constituting the "Alexandria quartet." His poetry, though he began to publish it in the 1930's, is still to be appreciated at its full worth. More than half a dozen volumes of verse have appeared in recent years, including the *Selected Poems* (1956) and *Collected Poems* (1960).

Married and the father of two daughters, Durrell is a poet who stands apart from most of the fashionable movements and trends. A deeply experienced observer of the human scene, elegant and meditative, he captures the moments and impressions of a life spent far away from the British Isles. His work is discussed in *The World of Lawrence Durrell*, ed. Harry T. Moore.

Richard Eberhart

Richard Eberhart, the oldest poet in this anthology, was born in 1904 in Austin, Minn., studied at the University of Minnesota, received his A.B. from Dartmouth, and went to Cambridge University (St. John's College) where he received his B.A. and M.A. degrees. He studied also at the Harvard Graduate School. Dartmouth conferred on him its Honorary Litt. D. in 1954, and in 1956 he returned to Dartmouth where he is Professor of English and Poet in Residence. He is married to Helen Elizabeth Butcher and they have a son and a daughter.

Eberhart's career has included a period as tutor to the son of King Prajadhipok of Siam, teaching in private schools, and professorships at the University of Washington, the University of Connecticut, Wheaton College (Norton, Mass.), and Princeton (Christian Gauss lectures). He was also an executive in a Boston manufacturing concern. During 1959–61 he was Consultant in Poetry at the Library of Congress, and he has been appointed Honorary Consultant in American Letters by the Library of Congress for 1963–66. Among his awards are the Shelley Memorial Prize, the Harriet Monroe Memorial Award, and in 1962 he was co-winner of the Bollingen Prize. He is a member of the National Institute of Arts and Letters.

A Bravery of Earth (1930) was the first of a long series of poetry books, brought together in *Collected Poems 1930–1960: Including 51 New Poems* (1960). More recently he has published *Collected Verse Plays* (1962) and a new book of his poetry, *The Quarry*, appeared in 1964.

Eberhart is gradually being recognized as one of the major living poets in America. His work, versatile in subject matter and technique, has been frequently analyzed, notably in a recent essay by Richard Mills, Jr., in the *Chicago Review* (Fall 1962: Vol. 15, number 4). He has recorded his poetry on Carillon 314.

William Empson

William Empson is the author of a uniquely influential work in poetics, *Seven Types of Ambiguity* (1930), and his own highly intellectual and complex poetry illustrates all of them. A poet's poet and critic's poet, he has had an influence out of proportion to the small amount of verse he has committed to print. ("There will be a hell of a flow of poetry after I retire in 1971," he promises.) His earlier works were gathered together in *Collected Poems* (latest version, 1955). His most recent book is a work of literary criticism, *Milton's God* (1961) which has provoked violent controversy among scholars.

Born in 1906 at Yokefleet Hall, near Howden (Yorkshire), Empson was educated at Winchester and at Magdalene College, Cambridge. For a time he held the chair in English literature at Bunrika Daigaku, Tokyo. During 1937–39 he was professor of English literature at Peking National University, followed by several years as the BBC Chinese editor. He returned to Peking National University in 1947. Since 1953 he has been professor of English Literature at Sheffield University.

In an article entitled "Rhythm and Imagery in English Poetry" (*British Journal of Aesthetics*, January, 1962) Empson discusses certain aspects of his poetic theory. Numbers 6 and 7 of *The Review* (Oxford) are a combined Empson number containing a recorded dialogue and "insults and nasty thoughts galore," as the poet expresses it.

Married in 1941 to Hester Henrietta Crouse, Empson is the father of two sons.

Lawrence Ferlinghetti

Publisher of many Beat poets and some not Beat, and an outstanding San Francisco poet himself, Lawrence Ferlinghetti is known for three books of poetry: *Pictures of the Gone World* (1955), *A Coney Island of the Mind* (1958), and *Starting from San Francisco* (1961). He is particularly interested in the oral aspects of poetry, and frequently goes on the poetry-reading circuit; he is a favorite of college audiences, which unfailingly identify with him and his poetry. Some of his readings are also available on Fantasy LP recordings 7004 and 7010. In addition to poetry, Ferlinghetti has published a novel, *Her* (1960), and *Unfair Arguments with Existence: Seven Plays for a New Theatre* (1963).

Ferlinghetti was born in Yonkers, New York, in 1919. He received an A.B. from the University of North Carolina, M.A. from Columbia, and

Doctorat de l'Université from the Sorbonne. Returning to the United States, he and Peter D. Martin founded the first all-paperbound bookstore in the country, City Lights, which soon became a publishing house, and issued, among many other notable books, Allen Ginsberg's *Howl*. The flat-footed attempt of the San Francisco authorities to suppress the book as obscene greatly redounded to the fame and prestige of the poet and the publisher.

Insisting that the poet must be *engagé*, Ferlinghetti breaks ranks with some of the Beats: "The wiggy nihilism of the Beat hipster, if carried to its natural conclusion actually means the death of the creative artist himself" (from *The New American Poetry*, ed. Donald M. Allen, 1960). He is convinced that poets spend too much time concentrating on sheer technique, and that a social concern, akin to that of the 1930's, must inspire the next movement in poetry.

Roy Fuller

"Only Roy Fuller has carried over into the nineteen-fifties and early nineteen-sixties the kind of concern with social values, the blend of Marxist historicism and Freudian analysis, which lent the verse of Auden and his coevals so pungent and curious a flavour," the British critic, John Press, writes in *Rule and Energy* (1963).

Born in 1912 in Failsworth, Roy Fuller was educated at private schools and qualified as a solicitor, 1933. He served in the Royal Navy, 1941–46, an experience reflected in many of his poems. He is now solicitor to the Woolwich Equitable Building Society, and among his publications is *The Building Societies Acts, 1874–1960, with Extracts from Associated Legislation*, which he edited. He is married to Kathleen Smith and they have one son, John, who published a first book of poetry a year after graduating from Oxford.

Fuller's *Poems* appeared in 1939, followed by half a dozen other books of verse, the last being *Collected Poems 1936–61* (1962). He has published a novel for children, *Savage Gold* (1946), and a great deal of adult fiction, the latest being *The Perfect Fool* (1963). Tapes of his poetry are at Harvard and the Library of Congress, and he has done records for the British Council.

Though often compared to the early Auden, Fuller has gone his own way, deeply concerned about mankind and its public and private fate, but too wary of easy answers to give himself completely to any ideology.

417

Thom Gunn

American universities have been importing young English poets on an increasing scale; one of the most notable is Thom Gunn, who appears in the "Movement" anthology, *New Lines,* but has since developed in a distinctly individual direction. His American experience, which began when he came to the United States on a Fulbright award, has included time at Stanford and San Antonio State College; since 1958 he has been a member of the English Department at the University of California.

Gunn was born in 1929, is unmarried. He was educated at University College School, Hampstead, and Trinity College, Cambridge. He served in the British Army, 1948–50, and lived in Paris for a large part of 1950, and Rome during 1953–54, before coming to the United States.

An early bloomer, while still at Cambridge Gunn wrote the poems included in his first book, *Fighting Terms* (1954), a work he has several times subsequently revised. He first came to general attention on John Lehmann's BBC program, "New Soundings." His later books are *The Sense of Movement* (1957) and *My Sad Captains and Other Poems* (1961).

In his earlier poetry there is a tough-minded celebration of black-jacketed motorcycle boys; Gunn himself wrecked his motorcycle while in San Antonio. The emphasis on ruthlessness and will is less evident in his later and more varied work. He writes of himself: "I don't deliberately belong to any school, but I suppose I am part of the National Service generation and have a few of its characteristics: i.e. lack of concern with religion, lack of class, a rather undirected impatience." He lists "reading, drinking, going to films" as his preferred activities.

Ted Hughes

A poet, like a prophet, frequently is first honored in another country. Robert Frost's first book was published and acclaimed in England. Ted Hughes—born in 1930 in Mytholmroyd (Yorkshire)—came to public attention during a long stay in America, when his book, *The Hawk in the Rain* (1957), won the first publication award of the Poetry Center of the New York City YM–YWHA. This was followed by *Lupercal* (1960), *Meet My Folks* (verse for children, 1961), and *Selected Poems* (with Thom Gunn, 1962). He quickly became recognized in both countries as one of the most interesting poets since the "Movement." His violence of imagery and preoccupation with animal symbols has stirred up a lively critical discussion and controversy.

A ground wireless mechanic in the Royal Air Force after the War, Hughes subsequently studied at Cambridge, where he met and married the distinguished American poetess, Sylvia Plath, who was on a Fulbright fellowship. She died in 1963.

Among the honors Hughes has received are first place in the Guinness Poetry Awards, 1958, a Guggenheim fellowship, 1959–60, and the Hawthornden Prize, 1961.

Philip Larkin

In many ways the most representative of the "Movement" poets is Philip Larkin, who was born in 1922 in Coventry (Warwickshire). Educated at King Henry VIII School, Coventry, and St. John's College, Oxford, he earns his living as librarian of the University of Hull, and lists "listening to jazz" as his favorite recreation. He has published two novels, *Jill* (1946), and *A Girl in Winter* (1947). The two slender volumes of verse on which his reputation mainly rests are *The North Ship* (1945) and *The Less Deceived* (1955).

His poetry has little in common with the jazz that he listens to. The American poetic appetite, accustomed to the bloody meat offered by the Beats and the exotically spiced dishes of the more academic poets, may at first find Larkin's verse flat, unexciting. He writes about ordinary events and experiences and emotions in a world of suburbs and unheroic days. It is, however, a poetry with great accuracy of observation and an almost unfailing sense for the low-keyed but completely right word and phrase. If he scales no Dantean or Miltonic heights, he is the laureate of the flat plain on which most of life is lived.

Laurie Lee

A lyric poet with an exquisitely accurate sense of language is Laurie Lee, who was born in 1914 in the Cotswolds, one of a family of eight. At the age of nineteen he ran away to London and from there went to Spain, playing the fiddle in the streets and taverns, and sleeping where he could. The Spanish Civil War began; he was hustled out of the country but later smuggled himself back in and began broadcasting from Madrid. Subsequently he traveled in Italy, Greece, and Cyprus.

With the onset of World War II he was back in London, where he began to publish poetry. He made documentary films, continuing with this work some time after the end of the war, and visiting Cyprus and India. He was caption writer-in-chief for the Festival of Britain, 1950–51, and was decorated by the Queen. During this time he married Catherine Francesca Polge, the daughter of a French fisherman.

His varied background is reflected in several of his prose books: *We Made a Film in Cyprus* (with Ralph Keene, 1947), *The Voyage of Magellan: A Dramatic Chronicle for Radio* (1948), and *Epstein: A Camera Study of the Sculptor at Work* (1957). He is also the author of *A Rose for Winter: Travels in Andalusia* (1955) and an autobiography, *Cider with Rosie* (1959), published as *The Edge of Day* in the United States.

It is, however, his poetry on which Lee's literary reputation is most firmly based. His first book of verse was *The Sun My Monument* (1944), followed by *The Bloom of Candles* (1947), and *My Many-Coated Man* (1955). A selection from these three volumes is available in the Pocket Poets series (Vista Books, London, 1960).

Denise Levertov

Metaphorically speaking, Denise Levertov is the meeting of the poetic east and the poetic west. She is the only poet who appears both in the predominantly conservative *New Poets of England and America: Second Selection* (ed. Donald Hall and Robert Pack, 1962) and the more experimental *The New American Poetry 1945–1960* (ed. Donald M. Allen, 1960). In still other ways, she is a bridge between differing worlds. Her father was related to a famous Hasid philosopher, Schneour Zalman, and, after leaving Russia, eventually became an Anglican priest in England. Her mother was a descendant of the Welsh tailor and mystic, Angel Jones of Mold. Denise Levertov was born in England, educated at home except for ballet school. She met her future husband, the American novelist, Mitchell Goodman, in 1947 at Geneva, and since 1948 has been mainly in America. She has become an American citizen. They have one son, Nikolai.

Denise Levertov is the author of *The Double Image* (1946), *Here and Now* (1957), *Overland to the Islands* (1958), *With Eyes at the Back of Our Heads* (1959), and *The Jacob's Ladder* (1961). Her recorded poetry is on permanent file at Harvard. A book-length study of her work is due to appear in the Twayne American Authors series.

Robert Lowell

By ancestry, Robert Traill Spence Lowell, born in 1917 in Boston, is a Brahmin of the Brahmins—related to James Russell Lowell, Amy Lowell, and President Lowell of Harvard. The stubborn and rebellious New England conscience is part of his heritage. In 1943 he tried twice to enlist but was rejected. Then when he was drafted he refused to serve, maintaining that America was now out of danger and that the mass air raids against enemy civilians could not be defended. He spent five months in federal prison, an experience reflected in some of his poems. Meanwhile he became for a time a Roman Catholic, and his early poetry mirrors a Catholic sensibility superimposed over the Puritan heritage.

Lowell's education was first at Harvard, then at Kenyon (summa cum laude, 1940), where he studied with John Crowe Ransom. He has since been an occasional teacher at various colleges and universities. He was married in 1940 to Jean Stafford. After their divorce in 1948, he married Elizabeth Hardwick. They have one daughter and live in New York City.

Land of Unlikeness, Lowell's first book of poetry, appeared in 1944 with an introduction by Allen Tate. It was followed by *Lord Weary's Castle* (1946), which won the Pulitzer Prize, and the poet was awarded a Guggenheim fellowship, 1947–48. *The Mills of the Kavanaughs and Other Poems* appeared in 1951. The most recent collection of poems, *Life Studies* (1959), is marked by a growing relaxation of poetic form and a heavier concentration on personal and psychological themes, as compared with the predominantly religious emphasis of the earlier books. Lowell has also done outstanding work as a translator and adaptor, including a version of Racine's *Phaedra* and a collection of poems from many languages, *Imitations* (1961). H. B. Staples has written a book-length study, *Robert Lowell* (1962). From early in his career, Lowell has been recognized as the major figure among the American poets in his age group. He has recorded certain of his poems (Carillon 301).

Robert Mezey

Robert Mezey is one of the most interesting of the many gifted poets who have attended the University of Iowa. His first book of poems, *The Lovemaker* (1961), won the highly coveted Lamont Award.

Born in 1935 in Philadelphia, Mezey worked at various times in factories and mental hospitals, served in the U.S. Army as an infantryman and a "psychology technician." He has taught at Iowa, Fresno State College, Memphis State University, and Western Reserve University. He is married to Ollie Simpson, and has one child by a previous marriage.

Mezey has recorded his poetry for the library of Congress. At the moment, in addition to writing more poetry, he is preparing a book-length study of Thomas Hardy's poetry, and continuing a long-term project, verse translations of Catullus.

In the poetry of Robert Mezey one discerns several tendencies characteristic of many of the younger poets—in particular, increasing attention to exact technique, and a turning toward frankly personal themes—but Mezey's poetry has a particular bitter-sweet flavor that makes it unmistakably his.

Vassar Miller

Louis Untermeyer quotes Vassar Miller as saying: "Poetry, like all art, has a trinitarian function: creative, redemptive, and sanctifying. It is creative because it takes the raw materials of fact and feeling and makes them into that which is neither fact nor feeling. It is redemptive because it can transform the pain and ugliness of life into joy and beauty. It is sanctifying because it thus gives the transitory at least a relative form and meaning. Hence poetry, whether avowedly so or not, is always religious; it is akin to prayer, an act of love."

In Vassar Miller's first two books of poetry there is the marriage of strict forms strictly written—the sonnet has been a favorite of hers—with a religious intensity seldom encountered since Gerard Manley Hopkins. Her more recent work has represented a movement toward freer forms and a greater variety of subject matter, though the religious themes are still central.

Born in 1924 in Houston, Texas, Vassar Miller received her B.S. and M.A. at the University of Houston and lives in Houston. Afflicted with cerebral palsy from birth, she has dedicated herself singlemindedly to poetry and has demonstrated—if demonstration were needed—that craftsmanship, religious fervor, and personal joy and agony can produce major poetry. Her books: *Adam's Footprint* (1956), *Wage War on Silence* (1960), *My Bones Being Wiser* (1963).

Howard Nemerov

Howard Nemerov, born in 1920 in New York City, published his first book of poetry, *The Image and the Law*, in 1947. This has been followed by five other books of verse, the latest being *New and Selected Poems* (1960) and *The Next Room of the Dream* (1962). He is also the author of three novels, a book of short fiction—*A Commodity of Dreams and Other Stories* (1959)—and *Poetry and Fiction* (1963), a collection of critical essays.

A Harvard graduate, Nemerov served as a pilot with the RCAF and

USAAF during the War. He taught at Hamilton College 1946–48, and since then has been a member of the Faculty in Literature, Bennington College. He has been invited to many other institutions: visiting lecturer at the University of Minnesota, 1958–59, lecturer at the Salzburg Seminar in American Studies, Winter 1962, writer in residence at Hollins College, 1962–63, Consultant in Poetry at the Library of Congress, 1963–64. Among the honors he has received are the Kenyon Review Fellowship in Fiction, 1955, and a citation and award from Brandeis University, 1963. He is married to Margaret Russell, an Englishwoman, and they have two sons, David and Alexander.

Nemerov's poetic career has been one of steadily widening and deepening talent, so that now he unquestionably ranks as one of the most solidly established poets of his generation. He is here represented by several short poems as well as the fifteen-part "Runes," which illustrates his command of the architecture of long poems.

Bink Noll

Bink Noll (born 1927) grew up in South Orange, N.J. He received his A.B. at Princeton, M.A. in writing at Johns Hopkins, and Ph.D. in English at the University of Colorado. A member of the English Department at Dartmouth for a number of years, he went to Beloit College in 1961 and is associate professor of English. He has three children—Lynne, Christopher, and Sarah. His wife, June, is a talented amateur actress as well as a full-time teacher of third grade; Noll is much interested in libretto writing as well as poetry. During 1960–61 the entire family was in Zaragoza, Spain, where Noll was Fulbright lecturer in American literature.

The Center of the Circle (1962) is the traditional "slender first volume" but reveals a highly developed and unusual talent. The author proposed at first to call it "Elegies and Other Pieces," and the elegiac tone—half wry, half resigned—is strong throughout the book. Many of the poems grow from intensely personal experiences of family or friendship, but the experience becomes the starting point for poems more than merely personal. These extremely civilized poems show an extraordinary sense of language and the formal aspects of poetry, and beneath their urbane surface lurks a savage intensity. Noll's work has sometimes been compared to that of W. D. Snodgrass (*q.v.*) because of its frankly personal inspiration, but whereas Snodgrass gives the impression of telling all, there is a reticence in all that Noll writes, implying much that is not explicitly said.

423

Gil Orlovitz

Gil Orlovitz has never before been included in a widely distributed anthology; his work is known only to a handful of poetry lovers who read the verse magazines and purchase slender books issued by publishing houses with names like Inferno Press and Hearse Press. He is nonetheless one of the finest—the most versatile—poets now writing in English.

Long before the San Francisco Renaissance exploded with public and police clamor and articles in *Time*, Orlovitz was writing with a Dionysian frenzy combined with perfect control of language that has been equaled by few, if any, of the Beats. At the same time, he is one of the few contemporary masters of the sonnet and the short lyric. He also has the rare distinction of carrying on a lover's quarrel with society without falling into cheap contempt for individual classes of humanity.

Born in 1918 in Philadelphia of Russian Jewish background, Orlovitz describes his higher education as "capricious." He has held a variety of jobs from staff screenwriter (Columbia Pictures) to his present position as associate editor with a New York publishing house specializing in paperback fiction. He is married and the father of two sons and a daughter.

Orlovitz's first book of poetry, *Concerning Man*, was published in 1947. Among his other works are *Selected Poems* (1960) and *Art of the Sonnet* (1961). He has written numerous short stories and had several plays produced. The Spoken Word has issued a disk (120) of his poetry under the title, "The Rooster," and he has prepared a tape for the Library of Congress. Detailed discussions of his poetry have been published by George Dillon (*Poetry*, August, 1955), David Ignatow (*Poetry*, January, 1962), and Guy Daniels (*Nation*, August 2, 1958).

Kenneth Patchen

"Patchen seems to me more like Blake than any other contemporary poet," Frederick Eckman wrote in *Poetry* (September, 1958—Vol. 92, number 6). "There is the same sense of deep isolation, partly self-willed, from the mass of humanity; of choking rage at shoddy secularity, orthodoxy, and materialism; of a tender, child-like wonder for the beautiful, pure, and innocent; of a desire for joy and freedom that leads at last into mystic contemplation."

The son of a steelmill worker, Patchen was born in 1911 in Niles, Ohio. At seventeen he went to work in the steelmill. For a year he studied at Alexander Meiklejohn's Experimental College, then functioning at the University of Wisconsin. Several years of drifting about the country followed. He was married in 1934 to Miriam Oikemus. He received a Guggenheim fellowship in 1936, the same year in which his first book of poetry, *Before the Brave*, was published. He has since written several dozen books, mostly poetry or combinations of poetry and prose or poetry and drawings, and despite a severe spinal injury which has long limited his activities, he has been one of the most productive and provocative American poets. A representative sampling of his highly varied poetry is available in *Selected Poems* (enlarged edition, 1958).

A pioneer in reading poetry with jazz, Patchen (like Blake) is notably successful in combining poetry with the visual arts. Many of his more recent books, such as *Because It Is* (1960), *The Moment* (1962), and *But Even So* (1963) illustrate this marriage of the arts. The "Painted Edition Patchen Books" are volumes created individually by the author.

Discussed in detail by Amos N. Wilder in *Spiritual Aspects of the New Poetry* (1940), Patchen's poetry is out of all conventional modern poetic grooves, and is full of both violent and tender surprises for the perceptive reader.

Theodore Roethke

A poet so versatile in technique and subject matter that the critics find in him not a single "voice" but a whole choir of singers is Theodore Roethke. Born in 1908 in Saginaw, Michigan, he studied at the University of Michigan and Harvard. After teaching at Lafayette College, Pennsylvania State University, and Bennington College, he went to the University of Washington in 1947 and was professor of English until his death in 1963. His widow is the former Beatrice Heath O'Connell, whom he married in 1953.

Roethke's first book appeared in 1941, *Open House and Other Poems*. It was followed by several others, which were later included in *The Waking: Poems 1933–1953*, published in 1953 and winner of the Pulitzer Prize. More recent works are *Words for the Wind* (1958), *I am! Says the Lamb* (verse for children, 1961), and *The Far Field*, published posthumously.

A succession of poetic honors came to Roethke—among others, two Guggenheim fellowships, and the Bollingen Prize for poetry (1958). During 1955 he was a Fulbright lecturer in American literature, in Italy.

Moving easily from meditations in a greenhouse to tender lovesongs and vast portraits of wild countryside, Roethke is a poet of singularly varied moods and poetic forms. In his most recent poetry the mystic came more to the fore. He never boxed himself in by premature success. His poetry continued to grow and evolve to the end of his life.

Howard Sergeant

Howard Sergeant for more than a decade has been active in all phases of British poetic life, and is himself an interesting and important poet, resistant to certain, though not all, tendencies of the "Movement." He was born at Hull (Yorkshire) in 1914. His father was killed in World War I, and Sergeant's early life was a difficult struggle. He was educated at grammar school, college of commerce, and then by correspondence colleges over a number of years, and, though never acquiring the standard British passport to status, a university degree, Sergeant has four professional qualifications. In 1963 he was appointed lecturer in Accountancy, Law, Economics, and English Literature at Norwood Technical College. He and his wife, Jean, have two children, and he has a daughter by a previous marriage.

Sergeant's poetry is contained in *The Leavening Air* (1946) and *The Headlands* (1953) and appears frequently in magazines. He has published several volumes of literary criticism, including *Tradition in the Making of Modern Poetry* (1952). With Dannie Abse he edited *Mavericks* (1957), an anthology issued as a counteraction to the Movement's *New Lines*. Recently he has been editing an anthology of "hospital poems," *The Whole Earth*, and another of poems by the "Dulwich Group" of poets, which meets periodically in a pub, under Sergeant's chairmanship. He is founder and editor of *Outposts* (1944), the oldest independent poetry magazine in the British Isles; is the sole reader and adviser for the Gregory Awards (trustees—T. S. Eliot, Professor Bonamy Dobrée, Sir Herbert Read, Henry Moore); serves on the Management Board of Universities' Poetry; and contributes the annual report on British poetry to the *British Encyclopaedia Book of the Year*. He also serves as British representative on the editorial Board of Borestone Mountain Poetry Awards which produces an annual anthology of the best poems in English-language periodicals.

Anne Sexton

Anne Sexton—*née* Harvey—has lived a thoroughly New England life. She was born in 1928 in Newton, Mass., grew up in Wellesley, and lives now in Newton Lower Falls, frequently summering in Gloucester, on Cape Ann and in Maine. She is the mother of two daughters who often figure in her intensely personal and frequently stark poetry. While in high school she wrote poetry but lost interest until later, when she resumed under the stimulation of Robert Lowell at Boston University. Along the way

426

she was a fashion model and a librarian. Her first book, *To Bedlam and Part Way Back* (1960) revealed a classical severity of technique combined with a probing examination of the author's mental breakdown and recovery. The second book, *All My Pretty Ones* (1962) continues the same autobiographical strain, but with greater breadth and freedom of style.

Anne Sexton has received a series of awards. She was Robert Frost Fellow at Bread Loaf, and was one of the first persons selected for the recently created Radcliffe New Institute for Independent Study. When the American Academy of Arts and Letters came to a parting of the ways with the American Academy in Rome and abolished its *prix de Rome* award, she was chosen to receive the first traveling Literary Fellowship established to take the place of the former *prix*.

In the poetry of Anne Sexton one finds combined an exquisite and precise sense of technique and the agonizing compulsion to explore psychological experiences to their roots, without pity for the poet or the reader. The themes of death and love weave in and out of her poetry, and the reality of the present moment is constantly seen against the backdrop of extinction. She has recorded tapes of her poetry for Harvard and the Library of Congress, and is represented in an album, *Treasury of Modern American Poetry*, issued by Spoken Arts.

Karl Shapiro

Karl Shapiro was born in 1913 in Baltimore, educated at the University of Virginia and at Johns Hopkins. Drafted into the Army in March, 1941, he served in the South Pacific until 1945, when he returned home and married Evalyn Katz, who had been his literary representative in America meanwhile. They have two daughters and a son.

During 1946–47 Shapiro was Consultant in Poetry at the Library of Congress. He taught at Johns Hopkins 1947–50 and was editor of *Poetry* magazine 1950–56. Since then he has been professor of English at the University of Nebraska.

Shapiro's first book, *Poems*, appeared—privately printed—in 1935. His reputation dates from *Person, Place and Thing* (1942). In this and in several other wartime books, notably *V-Letter and Other Poems* (1944), the War generation seemed to find its voice, despite the poet's insistence that he was not a "war poet." These early poems of Shapiro's are disillusioned, in the sense that they offer no ready-made ideologies and solutions, but there is in them a feeling and sometimes a real tenderness beneath the realistic and hard-bitten surface. In 1953 his previous poetry was brought together in *Poems, 1940–1953*, followed in 1958 by *Poems of a Jew* and in 1964 by *The Bourgeois Poet*. For the student wishing to trace Shapiro's development, there is *Karl Shapiro: A Bibliography* (ed. William White, 1960).

Twice Shapiro has been awarded a Guggenheim fellowship. He won the Pulitzer Prize in 1945. In his critical thinking, he has been moving away from the "school of Eliot" and has become a defender of the contemporary wild men of poetry—see his *Beyond Criticism* (1953) and *In Defense of Ignorance* (1960). Shapiro's own poetry has evolved toward a greater awareness of his Jewishness, and at the moment seems mutating into wilder and freer forms, quite different from the tightly disciplined verse of his earlier periods.

W. D. Snodgrass

That remarkable training ground for young writers, the University of Iowa, could claim another success in 1960 when William DeWitt Snodgrass' *Heart's Needle* (1959) won the Pulitzer Prize and was written up in *The Saturday Evening Post*.

Snodgrass was born in 1926 in Wilkinsburg, Pa. He attended Geneva College one year, then joined the Navy. Upon his discharge he returned to Geneva College for a year, subsequently transferred to the State University of Iowa for his B.A., M.A., and Master of Fine Arts degrees. After teaching at various universities, he went to Wayne State University in 1959, where he is associate professor of English.

Married in 1946 and the father of a daughter, Snodgrass was divorced in 1953, remarried in 1954. He has two children by this marriage. The details of his family life, together with his experiences under psychoanalysis, are highly relevant to his poetry, some of which is extremely personal. The title poem of his book is a ten-part sequence, built around the pathos of his relationship with his little daughter at the time of the divorce. Few modern poets have laid their hearts as directly bare, and few have done it with a surer touch or greater technical skill.

For a detailed and human-interest discussion of Snodgrass and his work, see *Current Biography*.

Dylan Thomas

A legend long before his death (1953) at the age of thirty-nine, Thomas captured the imagination of the general public which alternatively clucked disapprovingly and chuckled with delight as it read of his buffooneries on his lecture tours in America and his undisputed ability to outdrink any of his poetic companions.

Thomas may have drunk himself to an early grave; he did not drink when he wrote. Despite what at first seems a barbaric splendor of chaos in his poems, they show a highly disciplined poetic intelligence back of the kaleidoscopic surface. Few poets have been as conscious of sheer technique or worked at it more unrelentingly.

Born in 1914 in Swansea (Wales) and sketchily educated at the local school, Thomas published his first volume at the age of twenty, *18 Poems* (1934), a work utterly out of key with the dominant Auden-Spender school of socially-conscious poetry. It was followed by a steady stream of books—stories, autobiography, plays, and verse. *Collected Poems* came out the year before his death, and was followed by various post-humous works, including the wholly delightful radio play, *Under Milk Wood* (1954). Many of his poems are available on disks.

A vast amount of scholarship has already been devoted to Thomas, including John Malcolm Brinnin, *Dylan Thomas in America: An Intimate Journal* (1955), Elder Olson, *Poetry of Dylan Thomas* (1954), William York Tindall, *A Reader's Guide to Dylan Thomas* (1962), and Henry Treece's revised *Dylan Thomas: Dog Among the Fairies* (1958). Thomas' wife, Caitlin Thomas, has told her side of their relationship in *Leftover Life to Kill* (1957).

R. S. *Thomas*

A long line of country parsons—Herbert, Herrick, Crabbe, Andrew Young, to mention a few—has enriched British verse with accurate and frequently hard-bitten observations of rural life. The latest is the Welsh-man, R. S. Thomas (no relation to Dylan Thomas) who emerged in 1955 when his privately published volumes, plus some new poems, appeared in *Song at the Year's Turning*, with a long, laudatory introduction by John Betjeman. This won the Heinemann Award of the Royal Society of Literature. It was followed by three other books of verse, *Poetry for Supper* (1958), *Tares* (1961), and *The Bread of Truth* (1963).

Born in 1913 at Cardiff, Thomas studied at the University of Wales and St. Michael's College (Llandaff). Ordained deacon in 1936 and priest in 1937, he has served a number of country churches, teaching himself Welsh meanwhile. His poetry contains no easy piety and consolation. He is said to be a dour and taciturn man; certainly his poetry has something of the angular and harsh quality of Thomas Hardy, as he pictures the stark life of the small Welsh farmers. At times he broadens out to consider the condition of twentieth century mankind as a whole, and occasionally he deals with an explicitly religious theme. Living in Wales, he has been shielded from the literary coteries that flourish in London, and has developed his own style. Within his somewhat limited scope of subject matter he is one of the most gifted poets now writing in Great Britain, though practically unknown in America.

John Wain

One of the most interesting and promising of the "Movement" poets, John Wain has evolved from the deliberate understatement and *terza rima* fixation of his first book, *A Word Carved on a Sill* (1956) toward a freer use of form, an outspoken social conscience, and more willingness to pull out all the stops when appropriate as in *Weep Before God* (1961) which contains one of the few successful poems about the atomic bomb, "A Song about Major Eatherly." His book-length poem, *Wildtrack*, on which he is now working (part of it is included in this anthology) reveals a still further departure from the tidy doctrines of the Movement, and demonstrates that Wain is now completely following his own strong and individual poetic impulses.

John Wain was born in 1925 at Stoke-on-Trent, and received his degree from St. John's College, Oxford. He is married and has two sons. During 1947–55 he was lecturer in English literature at the University of Reading, a position he resigned to become a free-lance author and critic. Supporting himself by lecturing "on three continents," film and dramatic criticism, radio and TV work, etc., he has found time to write half a dozen novels in addition to the poetry, and is the author of several works of literary criticism, including the recent *Essays on Literature and Ideas* (1963). His poetry is available on the "Poets Reading" series of Jupiter Recordings and also has been issued by Sound News Productions. *Sprightly Running* (1962) is his autobiography.

Derek Walcott

The most interesting poetic voice to come from the West Indies in recent years is Derek Walcott, who is still almost completely unknown in the United States. Born in 1930 in Castries, Saint Lucia, he was educated at St. Mary's College, and the University of the West Indies. Twice married, he has one son, Peter, by his first marriage. A teacher and journalist at various times in the past, he is now art critic for the *Sunday Guardian* (Trinidad).

In 1957 Walcott was awarded a fellowship by the Rockefeller Foundation to study the American theater. This took him to New York. In England several of his plays have been produced on the BBC and once at the Royal Court Theatre. A Guinness Prize for poetry was awarded to him in 1961.

Walcott's first book of poetry, *In a Green Night: Poems 1948–1960* (1962) revealed an impressively rich command of the magic of language, and a point of view rarely represented in English poetry. Many of the poems reflect the poet's double heritage: awareness of his African background, tempered by his equal familiarity with English civilization and culture. From the dialogue between these two elements of his background some of his most moving poems arise. He is at present preparing a second volume of verse for publication, and writing two full-length plays. Of the poets in this anthology he is one of the hardest to classify; he falls into no conventional "school," and has created for himself an individual subject matter and poetic style. He may well become a major poet. His work received American publication in 1964, *Selected Poems.*

Richard Wilbur

Endowed with a superb command of poetic technique and an observant eye, Richard Wilbur (born in 1921 in New York City) established himself with his first book of poetry, *The Beautiful Changes* (1947), followed by *Ceremony and Other Poems* (1950), *Things of This World* (1956), *Advice to a Prophet* (1961), and *The Poems of Richard Wilbur* (paperback, 1963). His versatility is revealed by other books: *A Bestiary* which he edited (1955), translations of Molière's *Misanthrope* (1955) and *Tartuffe* (1963), and his edition of Poe's poems (1959).

Among the honors he has received are two Guggenheim awards, the Prix de Rome, 1954 (where he wrote "A Baroque Wall-Fountain in the Villa Sciarra," included in this anthology), the Pulitzer Prize, 1957, and an extended trip to Russia in 1961 as State Department cultural representative, under the cultural exchange program. His work is discussed in detail by L. D. Lerner in *Listen* (England, Vol. 2, number 3), and Donald Hall, *Poetry* (September, 1956).

Wilbur received his A.B. and an honorary A.M. at Amherst, an A.M. at Harvard, and an honorary L.H.D. at Lawrence College. He is married to Mary Charlotte Hayes Ward, and they have a daughter and three sons. He has taught at Harvard and Wellesley, and is now professor of English at Wesleyan University.

It is often remarked that the universities and foundations have replaced the traditional patrons of the arts. Wilbur is one of the most gifted of the poets who demonstrate that the new system of "patronage" can sometimes discern and encourage a first-rate talent when it first becomes evident. He has recorded his poetry for Spoken Arts (747), Caedmon, and the Library of Congress.

INDEX

INDEX

of Authors, Titles, and First Lines

Names of authors are in CAPITALS. The first page reference after each name refers to the poems, the second to the biographical note.

Titles are in *italics*, first lines in roman type. When the title is the same as the first line (or the beginning of it), the poem is usually listed only under the title. The initial words *a*, *an*, and *the* are disregarded in the alphabetical arrangement of titles and first lines.